To order, please write:
P. O. Box 2087
Gig Harbor, WA 98335

Cover Detail

Ribbons from left: Philippine Liberation, one campaign (star).
Purple Heart with two oak leaf clusters (three total); Pacific
Theater, two campaign stars, and one beachhead arrow.

The two Ancient Trees are Douglas firs 500-600 years old with
red alder in the understory, Washington state.

Infantry photo: June 1944 Warkworth, New Zealand, 3rd Platoon, L Company. 103rd Infantry Regiment, 43rd Division.
Taken just before embarking for Aitape, New Guinea.

Back Cover: The Combat Infantry Badge was created during
World War II. It is worn with pride and earned with pain.

Copyright © 1997 Jay Gruenfeld
All rights reserved. No part of this publication may be reproduced without express written permission of the publisher, except in the case of brief quotations embodied in critical articles or reviews. The words "Jap" and "Nip" were socially acceptable names while at war with the Japanese. The author recognizes these are no longer acceptable terms.

ISBN 0-89716-667-1
LOC 96-071685
01.0057

Cover creation: David Marty
Cover design & Editing: Susan Givens
Cover Photography: Jeff Schroeder
Production: Elizabeth Lake

First printing May 1997
10 9 8 7 6 5 4 3 2 1

PB Publishing
226 2nd Avenue West • Seattle, WA 98119
(206) 281-5965 • FAX (206) 281-5969
Portland, OR (503) 222-5527 • Denver, CO (303) 322-0065
Vancouver, B.C. (604) 688-0320 • Scottsdale, AZ (602) 947-3575
e mail: pnutpub@aol.com
WWW home page: http://www.pbpublishing.com

Printed in the United States of America

This book is dedicated to my wife Jan,
the best thing that has happened to me
in a full and largely happy life.

Jan and Buddy on our deck.

Contents

Appendix

Photos are on: Dedication page, 36-38, 47-49, 55-56, 66-67, 91, 103-107, 131-133, 144, 156-158, 186-187, 201, 231-232, 240, 249, 260-261, 271-272, 283, 299.

Acknowledgements

In the Philippines: Thanks to those civilian thousands who during World War II often risked their lives to provide information that reduced our casualties; and to the Filipino guerrilla troops who did good work, including perhaps barely beating the 103rd Infantry, 43rd Division to the Ipo Dam objective in my last engagement. More recently, thanks to those who were especially helpful in 1995 when I returned to Luzon for the 50th Anniversary of the beachhead and to rewalk some of our battle sites; Dean and Mrs. Virgilio Fernandez, head of the Forestry School, University of the Philippines; Eugelio Perez, Pozorrubio; Romeo Bauzon, Manila; who now owns part of Hill 600, near Pozorrubio, a bloody bit of 43rd Division history.

Special thanks to my army friends and their relatives who answered my questions about the war and since, and were also totally helpful and encouraging in other ways. The following list is bound to be incomplete: From C Company, 103rd Infantry, 43rd Division: Harry Horne, Bill Mitchell, Ed Barker, Ed Hoe, Hollis Morang, Chuck Wakeley, Jim Renton, Verl Shufelt, Danny Rice Delberts's nephew, and Mrs. Francis Hitt. From L. Company: Loren McAllister, Chalmus Brammer, Frank Fecser Jr., relatives of Louis Magrames; Bud Shaw of B company, Mrs. Marsh, sister of Buck Rogers, ex-CO G Company.

Thanks to all the foresters who have helped make my life happy and forests sustainably productive; and to a family that brought me mostly happiness.

Appreciation to Susan Givens whose gentle editing enabled the book and its occasional off-the-wall grammar and syntax to remain mine; and to publisher Elliott Wolf and Elizabeth Lake, production, real pro's; and to Kathleen Isaac, publicist, for future help. Wife Jan was her usual, patient, kind, witty, encouraging self as she helped produce what to her finally became the damnbook.

Finally, many thanks to four-star General David A. Bramlett, U.S. Army who did the Foreword because of our instant-friendship when we met in Lingayen, Philippines at the January 1995 celebration and reenactment of the 1945 beachhead.

Foreword

I met Jay Gruenfeld at Lingayen Gulf January 8, 1995. Jay had arrived there on a spur of the moment decision to complete a journey begun some 50 years earlier when he and his buddies had come ashore with the 43rd Infantry Division to liberate Luzon. My trip was more contemporary and more deliberate. I was there to represent the United States in commemorating the landing at Luzon and the extraordinary service of those US, Philippine, and Allied veterans who participated.

Jay quickly joined the small group of US veterans and their families who had made the arduous trip through the assistance of a travel agency. I was honored to be included, to listen, to ask, and to be reminded again of how very much we owe these men and their generation. Jay's energy, interest, and infectious enthusiasm made us family and our Filipino hosts welcome in-laws. Fifty years had not dampened the spontaneous affection these veterans feel for each other and for their Filipino comrades.

We talked throughout the two days together, about experiences, wounds, losses, memories, and lives changed forever. Within our group was Jay, wounded five times with three Purple Hearts; another who was totally blinded a few days into the landing, whose last sights were Lingayen Gulf, January, 1945; and others with different experiences, but linked to events 50 years ago that defined their subsequent life in ways beyond explanation to most.

Jay Gruenfeld's pilgrimage to Lingayen served as a catalyst for him to complete his reflections on a life defined by the horrors of war and fulfilled by events that were to follow. After receiving a copy of the final draft of *Purple Hearts and Ancient Trees*, I asked how could he remember the full names of so many so long ago, he remembers them and other incidents as if they happened yesterday. This is a remarkable story of courage, fear, frustration, and agony as seen by a soldier fighting in a brutally horrific theater of war. There is an everyman quality here, but it is finally Jay Gruenfeld's war.

Jay came out of the war to become a prominent and productive citizen. His success in industry, both as entrepreneur and spokesman, reflects many of the same qualities that distinguished him as a soldier. Tough, principled, and dedicated, he has never wavered in beliefs and convictions. He is a man of strong opinions, strongly held. You need not agree with all of them, but you will admire his candor, his commitment, and his strength of character. And, you will recognize his generation in these qualities.

I had hoped Jay could come to Honolulu for the nation's commemoration of the 50thAnniversary of the End of the World War II. Jay couldn't be there to hear the tributes of praise, of gratitude, and of admiration for those who served and for those who waited and supported. We cannot thank Jay Gruenfeld and his generation enough or in too many ways. Jay's book is yet another offering to those who follow and hope to fulfill the promise of their legacy, left for us. It's a great read.

Thanks again, Jay, for who you are, what you have done, and for all you represent.

David A. Bramlett
General, United States Army
18 March 1997

Preface

When World War II ended, I had enough infantry combat experience to provide the framework for a book on "my war." After all, I had been in two Pacific campaigns and was awarded a Battlefield Commission to Second Lieutenant. I had led a rifle squad and rifle platoon in combat, was wounded five times (three purple hearts) and killed many enemy. But when the war ended, I was only twenty, a non-drinking virgin, and had a year-and-a-half of college. Had I written this book then, it would have been rather one dimensional—I didn't want to write one anyway. Now, I'm 72 with seven grandchildren and I want to tell them and others about "my" war.

In addition, and with some humor, I want to relate some experiences and give opinions about the management of our public and private forest lands, the functioning of our business system and make some philosophical comments. Tennis, hunting and fishing have been a big part of my life. These are matched only by my love of wilderness areas where I have spent over 300 days. As a sportsman, and one who revels in the great outdoors, I have included a few highlights of my adventures.

As a professional forester for over 45 years, I've managed two large private forests in the Pacific Northwest, done some logging, been a Vice President and Director of a couple of major corporations and been rather deeply involved in the politics of forestry. Since 1979, I've had my own forest resource consulting business. From 1982 until July 1994, we published the 16-page monthly *Pacific Rim Wood Market Report.* Currently, Russia is a major area of interest, and my work

13

has taken me there and to Japan, Korea, Taiwan, Fiji, New Zealand, Chili and Europe. I am still working.

Naturally, this autobiography will be different than others because it is *my* life. But I think you will find it interesting because of the unique combination of my life experiences. These include the impact of combat, my study of politics and philosophy at the University of Oxford as a Fulbright Scholar, over 45 years in the business system, my love of wilderness recreation, and helping to raise six children from two marriages—a big part of my learning process. Incidentally, I now enjoy a drink.

Introduction

On November 24, 1924, the temperature ranged between 28° and 30° degrees in Chicago, Illinois. The barometer was at 30.2 and Chicago had snow. That was the day I was born. I grew up in Chicago and in McHenry, Illinois. McHenry was a small town near the Wisconsin border and 50 miles northwest of Chicago.

My sister, Barbara Jean was born a year later, but died when I was five. Grief almost killed my mother, and that grief affected my childhood. I was given an unusual amount of freedom and I wandered around the woods, rivers, creeks and swamps of the McHenry countryside. This, I suspect, is where I developed an insatiable love for the out-of-doors which finally led me into forestry. I've hiked, hunted and fished virtually my entire life. Although my children all like to be outside, there isn't a hunter among them — and only a couple of casual fisherpersons. However, I'm working on the grandchildren.

Dad wasn't a hunter, but he was an avid fisherman. He made me a fishing pole out of a willow switch when I was four — I actually caught fish with it. One of the dumbest but most satisfying things he ever did was to give me a .22 rifle when I was eight. Luckily, nothing serious happened.

Dad was a strict follower of the Catholic faith, with the exception of allowing his son to be raised Lutheran. Dad was born in Chicago and had Bavarian-German ancestry. He was a hard-working, good citizen and a strong-minded guy. However, he married a hard-working woman of pure Norwegian ancestry Beulah Johnson, (Grandpa Anton Johnson came over from Christiania, now Oslo, in 1872). So, before my parents were married, Mom said, "Julius, I love you and will marry you, but it must be understood the children will be raised Lutheran." Dad agreed and as far as I know there were never any hard feelings over religion.

My folks were great parents. Dad had a two-year mechanical engineering degree from Illinois Institute of Technology. Mom had one year at Milwaukee Downer College and always regretted not getting a two-year degree in home economics.

We didn't have much money, but I didn't notice it. For a couple of years during the depression, Dad was unemployed. Nevertheless, every day at 7:30 a.m. he left the house all dressed up and returned about 5:30 p.m. each night.

He would spend the day keeping up his contacts. I didn't know this until I went to the University of Illinois in September 1941, two months before I turned 17. Relatives helped us financially; Mom made a few dollars selling lingerie, and we lived modestly. I had some sort of job every summer. When I was eight, I sold magazines (the *Saturday Evening Post*, *Colliers* and the *Ladies Home Journal*) door-to-door. At age 10, I started caddying at the McHenry Country Club. Grandpa and Grandma Johnson lived in McHenry, and we spent all summer and many weekends there. After World War II, the folks moved there permanently. Mother's parents were long gone by then.

Dad died in Idaho in 1978 at the age of 91 He worked until he was 72. His last job was with Simpson Engineering Co. in Chicago. In 1976, Mom died in McHenry when she was 87— great people. Values are best taught by example and my parents were fine examples of kindness, generosity and honesty. They exemplified the importance of strong family values and hard work. Dad served overseas in World War I in the Pioneer Infantry as a corporal. He was quite a character. My wife Jan loved Dad and helped make his last years happy.

Education

I went to Carl Schurz High School in Chicago, northwest side, and graduated in June, 1941. I was just an okay student — about a B minus average, but a voracious reader as I still am. However, I was mostly interested in competitive swimming, mainly the backstroke. I was the high school swimming team captain, and after the war was the captain and assistant coach at Colorado A&M — now Colorado State.

I withdrew from competitive swimming after college, and started to log for Weyerhauser Co. at Longview, Washington in April 1949. But after getting a Fulbright scholarship, I swam and played water polo on the Oxford University team. In the 1950 Oxford-Cambridge match, I won the 100-yard backstroke, in a lousy time, but it was good enough for a new meet record in that longtime rivalry. Oxford swimming has improved since then.

Girls were a big part of high school, but I was pretty shy. Went to the proms, but never really had a steady girl until Ruth Oksendahl. That was just before I went into the service in April 1943, from the University of Illinois where I was studying pre-forestry.

In high school, I had four years of ROTC (Reserve Officers Training Corps). At the University of Illinois, I was in Advanced ROTC and could have received a commission right after my second year. But I was thinking of being a paratrooper, and didn't want to start as an officer. So I voluntarily left school, entered the army in April 1943 and went to Camp Croft, Spartanburg, South Carolina for infantry basic training, and went overseas in December from Camp Shanks, New York. It took our lone troop ship, the U.S.S. Santa Cruz, a converted Grace Lines tramp steamer, 43 days to get to New Caledonia.

If it hadn't been for the war, I would have graduated from a western university at 20 with a so-so academic record. Instead, I went into the Army in April of 1943 at 18 and served for three years. That matured me in many ways. After the war, in three-and-a-half years of university, before going to Oxford, the lowest grade I got was a B. Most were A's. For a good student, I must have been in the top two percent in total sleep time. Regardless of the test schedule, I slept eight hours every night almost without exception. The war had taught me to value "sack time."

My Bachelor of Science degree was heavy in science, but I took as many liberal arts courses as possible, e.g. Great Books, philosophy, and psychology. I received a Bachelors Degree in March 1948 and a Masters in Forest Management in March 1949. Then in April 1949, I left with my wife, Barbara (Hunsucker) for a logging job (setting chokers) with Weyerhaeuser in Longview, Washington ($1.61 per hour).

In early 1949, I was one of two Rhodes Scholar finalists from Colorado. Neither of us got a Rhodes (there were four given from a 6 state area including California). But both of us were given Fulbrights to Oxford. (I didn't use any marijuana in the year and a term there and did receive a diploma — President Clinton please note.) Despite taking all my tutorials in politics and philosophy I still got a Diploma in Forestry, since my thesis was in international forest products trade and I took the forestry field trips to Europe and around the UK, plus some seminars. The seminars were mostly refresher courses for returning colonial foresters and were fascinating. More about Oxford later.

Two Marriages

Barbara Ann Hunsucker and I were married, too young, (21 and 23) in June 1948. I rate the first eight years of our marriage as very good, the second eight as average and falling and the last eight as awful. Our one-lawyer divorce was in Bend, Oregon in 1972. We raised three fine girls — twins Kimberly and Wendy, now 46 (born in Oxford), and Barbara now 41. Barbi is legally separated from her husband and has four nice kids; Sarah 16, Luke 15, Paul 12 and Daniel 8. Luke and Paul like rifles, shotguns, fishing and hunting. The twins have no children and three divorces between them — ah, America, America.

About two months after our divorce, on December 17, 1972, at the urging of a good friend Bob Cother, I called Janet Clark Evans, a counselor at Bend High School. She was recently divorced. We had a dinner date on the 18th that lasted from 4 p.m. to 2 a.m. I went home, didn't sleep all night — since I knew I was going to marry this superb gal — and was in for some busy times. I was between jobs and buying some land. Guess it was egotistical to think that we would become

18

husband and wife, but I felt that this marriage would be a real winner and it has been. Jan is easily the best thing that has ever happened to this lucky guy.

We were married on June 9, 1973, the month I started with Potlatch Corporation in Lewiston, Idaho as corporate Vice President of Lands and Forestry. Later that year I adopted Jan's children Deni (Denise) 21, Lisa 15 and Christopher 13. The two youngest weren't so sure that a name change from Evans to Gruenfeld was such a good deal. But Deni leaned on them, as she can, and it has worked beautifully. Deni and husband Steve have Grant, who at four just received his first fish pole — it was from me. Lisa and husband Chris have two children, Erin 12 and Janna 9 who love to fish, but will probably never shoot anything. Son Chris, now 36, is an Enterprise (WA Mutual) Vice President in Seattle, Washington. He's a good guy and is usually tolerant of our advice on how to improve his wife-hunting skills.

Forest Career Overview

In the final chapters of this book, I'll make some pointed suggestions about managing the federal forest lands of the United States and other subjects. Until then, the narrative is written partly to develop my credibility as someone who has had unusually broad and enriching experiences. Of course I also want it to be interesting and useful to you and provide a few laughs. Here is a brief overview of my business experience.

Forestry was my choice of a profession and I have spent over 45 years in forest-related work. I've planted and protected trees, logged and managed two large (60,000 and 200,000 acre) private forests. Both forests included old-growth timber, and the harvest was mostly of trees over 150-years old. In recent years, in the Pacific Northwest, these trees are now called Ancient Trees and there is strong movement to preserve them "forever," that is, until they die naturally. Some people, (including as of April 1996, Sierra Club voters) would like to stop all tree cutting on federal land regardless of the cost to society which would be massive.

Most foresters and other people would regard this as the waste of a renewable resource. But the "no-cutters," many of whom seem to worship nature rather than having Judeo-Christian values, are politically powerful.

The positions I've held dealt primarily with the management of private forests as a business. The forests of the Pacific Northwest, in Washington, Oregon and Idaho are where I gained most of my professional experience. In addition, I've have done work in nearly every major forest area of the United States, and in Russia, Japan, Taiwan, Korea, Fiji, New Zealand, Canada, Chile and in several European countries. I've never wanted to be anything but a forester.

Forest-related private business dominated my later career, but I did have some government service in addition to the army time. During my university work at the University of Illinois, prior to going into the Army in April 1943, and Colorado State University (then Colorado A&M), I worked two summers for the US Forest Service in the West (Idaho and California), and one summer for a small private logging and saw milling company in Lyons, Colorado (near Boulder).

My 18-years-plus with the forest giant, Weyerhaeuser Company, saw me in jobs that ranged from looping short, self-tightening cables around logs on cable logging operations (setting chokers) to tree farm manager, logging superintendent, (the trees harvested were mostly old-growth, Ancient Trees), assistant land supervisor, director of business development for the Timberland Division, and manager of timber and log sales. I was primarily responsible for developing and leading Weyerhaeuser Company's first log export business.

At Brooks-Scanlon, Inc. (lumber company) in Bend, Oregon, February 1969-1972, my title was Raw Materials Manager, and I was responsible for all forestry and logging on a 200,000-acre forest in addition to buying and selling logs and timber. From 1973-79 with Potlatch Corporation in Lewiston, Idaho, I was corporate Vice President of Lands and Forestry. Potlatch then had 1.5 million acres of forest in Idaho, Arkansas and Minnesota.

Since 1979 to the present, my wife and I have operated a forest resource consulting business (Jay Gruenfeld Associates Inc.), originally based in Seattle, but now in Gig Harbor, Washington. In 1994, we sold the monthly 16-page *Pacific Rim Wood Market Report* to Linda Keller Barr, Wood Note

Publishing. In addition to doing a wide variety of consulting, we give conferences on the general subject — Marketing Forest Products of the Pacific Rim. Beginning in 1983, we have given 31 conferences, including three in Chili (latest in May of 1996), and one in England (1993) at the University of Oxford. Most of the others have been in Seattle.

The consulting has been fun while providing a good living. I like variety and you get it in the type of consulting we do. Clients have ranged in size from giants like Weyerhaeuser Company to small loggers and individuals. Most projects relate to wood supply, wood marketing or both. The marketing subjects have ranged from chopsticks to old-growth timber. The geography covered includes the Russian Far East, much of the Orient, New Zealand, the United Kingdom, Chili, most of the United States and British Columbia.

My experience in log exporting began in 1960 and I continue to have work related to this unusually profitable business. Japan is the world's biggest importer of wood. I now have many Japanese friends — what a change since World War II. One of my best Japanese friends, Ichiro Ito, was trained as a kamikaze pilot — but Ichiro-san was lucky. He never got his plane.

Comment

This diversity of business experience plus the war and rather broad academic training gives the foundation for opinions on forest management and other subjects which has a relatively balanced perspective. After reading the book, you can decide for yourself about the balance.

Now for a narrative on some life highlights. Some soap operas "are" life, so you can probably guess that this life includes some happenings that are hard to believe — Hollywood stuff. However, everything in this book actually happened the way it is told, subject only to memory failures. The names given are real except when I say otherwise.

This has been fun to write. I hope it is enjoyable to read.

The Stage

"All the world's a stage,
And all the men and women merely players:"
Shakespeare — *As You Like It*

Shakespeare was right about life being like a stage. This is the reason that soap operas are often so lifelike. It is also why we sometimes choose a certain role and play it to the best of our ability. Then, sometimes it is no longer just a "role." It's us. In wars, many boys are asked to play "the man," and in the playing they become men.

War, forests, family and business are the major factors that shaped my experience. This book contains what I think was most significant or interesting in nearly 72 years of living. Hopefully, for many readers, parts of this book will not only be interesting and useful, but will be fun. It is all truthful. Even the war stories are exactly as my war buddies and I remember them. Therefore, though they may not be totally accurate, they are the truth as we remember it. My memory is superior in some ways. I can recall the serial numbers of my two rifles used in the army and details of battles, including names and unit designations, but almost never remember to take out the garbage on Thursday night.

Imprinting

Renewing World War II friendships with combat buddies helped make writing *Purple Hearts and Ancient Trees* a pleasant experience. I was deeply affected by World War II. Wounded five times, the war imprinted itself on my body and mind. I earned three Purple Hearts and a battlefield commission to Second Lieutenant, infantry. So it isn't too surprising that infantry combat experience has strongly influenced my life and that some memories of combat remain vivid. In a person's life, years 18 to 21 are especially important. Like so many young men, I spent most of those three years in the Army infantry. Twenty months were overseas in the Pacific Theater in the Northern New Guinea (Aitape) campaign, and the beachhead and later operations in the liberation of the island of Luzon, Philippines.

Two war episodes will quickly illustrate why the war had such a great impact on me and other combatants. This is followed by an introductory comment on why trees have been so important in my life. Thereafter, the sequence is roughly as it happened within the subject areas of war, forestry, business and politics, wilderness, tennis, hunting and fishing. The final section is a summary of forest management suggestions to the forest industry, the politicians and the public.

How I Gained An Undeserved Super-Shot Rep
And Finally Lost It

After some combat in New Guinea and six weeks of intense combat on the island of Luzon, Philippines, on February 15, 1945 I was given a battlefield commission and assigned to lead a rifle platoon in another battalion. Before I joined the new platoon, the men knew, via the grapevine, that I was a good shot and had killed quite a few enemy. The super-shot reputation came soon after meeting the men I was going to lead, but I wasn't a super-shot.

True, I was an above average shot. I should have been. My Dad gave me a .22 rifle when I was eight years old and taught me how to shoot it. Usually Dad was sane. By the time I went into the Army, I had put several thousand rounds through .22s. (In firearm language .22 is the caliber of the rifle, meaning, the diameter of the bore is .22 inches or 5.6 millimeters.) At age 12 (1936), I bought a new .410 single shot shotgun (Eastern Arms) with my own hard earned $6.95. Later I shot hundreds of rounds through a borrowed 12 gauge shotgun (Winchester Model 12 pump). Then the Army trained me. My eyesight was excellent, 20/15 in each eye without glasses, and I didn't flinch when I fired. One day a friend and I were on the rifle range and he noticed that usually I wouldn't blink even when I fired. So, it wasn't too surprising when I qualified as

Expert (the top rating) with the M1 (Garand) rifle, BAR (Browning Automatic Rifle) and the light machine gun. The super-shot rep came mostly from the following two happenings.

Building The Crackshot Rep

Due to their fear of the Japanese, the Filipinos had abandoned their small farms, but semi-wild chickens stayed on. A couple of weeks after joining the 2nd platoon as its leader, about 10 of us went on a chicken hunt — the only one for me. A brightly colored rooster flew across a little creek and lit in a tree about 50 yards away. I told the guys I would take it. Since we were shooting high powered .30 caliber bullets, you had to be careful where you hit or you ended up with mostly feathers and skin. So, I put on my rifle sling and sat down to shoot.

My rifle was zeroed almost perfectly and I had memorized its ballistics, so knew where it should hit at any range if I shot right. To save meat I held very high on the rooster's shoulder, maybe an inch and a half below its head since he was crouched a little. At my shot, he fell straight down, beating his wings rapidly. The men said, "Great shot, Jay." Then they were dumbfounded when they saw my bullet had neatly cut the bird's head off. For some reason I didn't tell them I had shot a little high.

Soon after that, a hen ran across the creek and up a little hill. The men fired eight to ten shots, but it kept going. For the men it was a pretty tough shot since the bird was crossing in front of them at a dead run. The chicken was about 10 yards from me, and it was a fairly easy shot as the bird was running straight away from me, almost like it was standing still. I squeezed off a careful shot, offhand (standing) and made a nice clean kill that saved practically all the meat. My shooting rep was established.

A couple of weeks later while on patrol — my chicken feat still fresh in everyone's mind — three enemy ran out of a cave. We got them all. I fired twice, but there were at least 10 other shots. It was impossible to tell who had scored. When we got back to the perimeter I heard one of the replacements say, "Yeah, Jay got two and we got the third one." So it goes.

How I Lost The Rep

The day before my final woundings was a full one. Early that day, we relieved a platoon dug-in on the reverse slope of a prominent ridge just below the crest. We had been warned that the enemy kept the ridge under constant surveillance and fired frequently at anyone showing on the ridge top. This didn't keep the men in the 2nd Platoon from — without any urging from me — crawling carefully to the ridge top and starting to take an occasional shot at visible Nips. This went on for a few minutes and then I got involved.

What I'm about to recount, even though there were extenuating circumstances, is a little embarrassing. So, I'd like to make sure you get the full picture.

I crawled up to a place on the ridge top, where I was just to the left of a rock ledge that gave good protection. I used my binoculars to observe the enemy positions. About 600 yards away to the right-front was a large caliber Nip machine gun. It was clearly visible on the crest of a ridge and was classed as an antiaircraft gun. However, it was being used against our infantry. The caliber was maybe 20 millimeter. Shells were loaded from the top in a curved magazine about 18 inches long. At first, the gun was shooting at 90 degrees from my position. But after I fired a couple of shots at them, they turned and started to fire at me. As soon as the gun pointed toward me, I would duck my head back behind the rock ledge. The velocity of their bullets was relatively slow and there was a definite lag between the time you saw the smoke at the muzzle and when the bullets cracked by. I was going to make use of this lag-time. (Note: If the velocity of the bullet was 2,200 feet per second it would take the bullet about 8 tenths of a second to go 600 yards. A fast runner can go 8 yards in that time.)

This rather sticky situation became even tighter when one of the men said, "Jay, there is a Nip off to your left." And there was, downhill and to the left. He was in range and was sitting outside of a cave eating. I said, "Get him."

The soldier said, "I can't shoot at him without exposing myself to that big machine gun, but I can see him with my telescope and still be under cover. I'll spot for you." Things were now complicated.

In order to shoot at the cave-Nip, I had to rise up to a kneeling position with my weight on both knees. In that position the machine gunner could see me against the skyline. Also, it was an unsteady shooting position. Nevertheless, I was in a role that required me to do it. So, I did.

When the machine gun was firing off to my right, I could see the big magazine on the top of the gun. So I would make sure that the machine gun wasn't pointing at me, then rise to the kneeling position and take a crack at the Nip. One time I pulled off a quick shot even though the gun turned toward me. I knew I had almost a second after he fired to drop into a covered position.

After every shot, I expected the hungry Nip to either slump over from a hit, or to at least take cover. He did neither. Sure, I was wobbling some, but every shot was close to him. He was only about 125 yards away. Finally, I had fired eight shots and my rifle was empty. I can still hear my spotter say in a disgusted voice, "Eight rounds and the son-of-a-bitch is still eating his lunch. And you were supposed to be such a great shot." Later, I told everyone the Nip was either starving or eating dope. Oh well, it turned out I only had to endure the kidding for one day since I was wounded twice the next day.

Am kind of glad I missed him. Not because of compassion, but because I've enjoyed telling this true story so much. (Our 81mm mortars eliminated the machine gun position later that day.)

Trees

A fool sees not the same tree a wise man sees.
William Blake 1757-1827 *Milton*, Preface

My earliest recollection of trees occurred when I was about five — trees were pretty and I wanted to climb them. My mother might have had a heart attack if she had seen some of my tree-climbing stunts. Tarzan was my hero and I wanted to prepare myself in case he ever wanted a helper. I knew he was just a cartoon character but that didn't stop my fantasizing.

Gradually I learned the names of all the common trees and birds. The native trees were mostly oaks and hickories. My favorite tree-climbing place when I was about eight was on a hillside by the river (Fox). There I could climb way up (maybe 15 feet) in a chokecherry, reach out and barely catch the end of a hickory branch (I knew they were strong) and swing a couple of feet to where I could straddle a flexible water birch limb. I would ride it down until it caught in the forked top of another water birch where I would slide down the smooth trunk to the ground and repeat this scary process.

With most trees that I chose to climb, the challenge was to get high enough so that the tree and I swayed in the breeze. I never had a bad fall, but created a few sewing jobs for Mom. Usually this wasn't much of a problem because the tree climbing was usually during the hot Illinois summer days and all I wore for play was a pair of jeans and occasionally a shirt and sneakers. There were a few of my friends who enjoyed this sort of thing, but much of the time I was alone.

By the time I was ten I would take day-long hikes (probably never getting over two miles from home) with only dog

28

Patch (who was mostly Sheltie). The high adventure on these hikes through the local farm hardwood wood lots around Lake Defiance usually involved Patch being chased by cows. At first I cried, but then learned that he was quicker than they were and there was little to fear. I was very wary of bulls.

It was on these solo hikes in hardwood forests that I first had those mystical feelings of comfort and awe that eventually helped lead me into forestry.

Note: When I took our twins (Kimberly and Wendy) on these same hikes 25 years later I was amazed to see deer tracks. When I was a child, the nearest deer were about 100 miles north in Wisconsin. Now there is a large deer herd. The woods had changed very little otherwise. Today, some of this of this area is in a county park. Another wildlife change is the increase in the pheasant population.

Around 1929, ring-necked pheasants were rare and my mother would stop the car (a second hand Whippet) so my sister and I could see them. My sister died that year and I began to hike frequently after that.

Some of my earliest memories of my grandfather Anton Johnson involved trees. When he was 86, he pulled some muscles around his heart while chopping down a two-foot diameter red oak and died soon after.

He and I, sometimes with my Mother, would gather hickory nuts every fall. Grandpa would carefully crack them using a vice and pry out the meat with a nut picker. His Christmas gift to many was a one-pound candy box filled with nothing but hickory nut halves. We ate the smaller pieces or they were used in baking. To me, hickory nuts are even better than walnuts for baking. So early on I learned that trees were things of beauty that provided what people need.

I felled my first big tree, a 16-inch diameter Lombardy poplar when I was 14. It was overtopping some shrubs of a neighbor. Dad had shown me at an early age how to make the undercut to determine the direction the tree would fall.

Note: Like millions of children, I learned how to use an ax by helping split firewood. I liked to chop because I knew it built muscle and the wood smelled good. Compared to real loggers I was never more than average-minus with an ax, but I was equally "fair" swinging either left or right-handed. So I was surprised to learn when I started to set chokers in the big trees of the Pacific Northwest that even some experienced loggers could only chop from one side. Sometimes on steep ground I would have to chop some of the notches for guylines because the other chokermen and even the rigging slinger could only chop from the right side while the only place to stand required left-hand chopping.

Idaho Hand Logging

I was better with a crosscut saw (maybe it was my long arms). I was very pleased when in 1942 an old sawyer, that's what an Idaho timber faller was called, One Armed John, said that if I didn't want to go back to college he thought we could make some good money falling white pine for the Ohio Match Company. Ohio Match (later Diamond) was logging on their holdings near Magee where I was working for the US Forest Service. At the time, we were spending a week falling big snags (dead trees) for firewood.

One Armed John was a wizard at getting logs to roll down the hill and land right on the road where they could be bucked into firewood length. He would have us roll the log in a certain way from it's bed (where the tree had fallen), using a cant-hook (a C-shaped steel hook, pointed on one end and fastened to a four-foot ash or hickory handle) or a Peavey (like a cant-hook, but usually with a longer handle and always with a spike on the working-end of the handle). John would aim the log so that it would hit a stump or two and a couple of wood chunks in a certain way so as to lose speed and change direction and fall right on the road. This was quite an art since some of these logs were three feet or more in diameter and weighed a couple of tons.

Note: This method of moving logs is called hand logging. In the early days of logging in Alaska and the Pacific Northwest, one strong savvy faller with some hand-operated jacks and wedges could get a lot of logs into the water where they were put into rafts and towed to a mill.

The hillside was pretty steep, maybe 60 percent (60 feet of rise in 100 feet of horizontal distance) and the road was cut into the hill making an 8-foot or so cut. With John's direction we had had logs roll about 150-200 feet and

30

drop-dead on the road. Gravity did all the work after we had rolled the log out of its bed.

One day John couldn't be with us so he said, "Just fall and buck a couple of snags — don't try and roll 'em." You know what happened. My partner Bob von Neuman, from Minnesota, another 17-year-old and I felled a couple of snags across the hill. The last was a larch (also called tamarack, Larix occidentalis) that was over 3-feet in diameter at the stump and about 70-feet long, and we bucked it into short logs from 10-to-16-feet long. The butt log was about 10-feet long and looked like it would roll easily to the road with a little help from us. We pooled our intelligence and carefully plotted out the route. After we got it started, the large end of the log was to hit a high stump, then hit a big chunk (piece broken out of a tree or log) on an angle that would route it into another high stump. It would then drop-dead on the road. We had 150 feet to go. Using language loosely you could say we were partially successful. The log, weighing about 3,000 pounds hit both stumps and our chunk. However, it was going about 20-miles-an-hour when it hit the road once and plunged down into the canyon about 600 feet below. The next day John asked no questions and we didn't volunteer anything.

I Became a Westerner Fast

From the time the streamliner train the Empire Builder left Chicago for Pocatello, Idaho in early June 1942, I was glued to the window during the daylight hours. When we reached Idaho, I had seen my first wild coyotes, a bear, many antelope and prairie dogs and became dedicated to moving west at the first opportunity. I really became a westerner after experiencing the beauty of Northern Idaho with its gorgeous sunsets, bountiful forests, scenic beauty and friendly people. Idaho is that way today, but the friendliness has dropped a little, inevitably, as the population has increased.

My pre-forestry classes at the University of Illinois quickly give me an overview of the role of forests and foresters throughout the world. Trees became almost an obsession. I wanted to learn to identify them, especially those of the western states where I knew I would work if I survived the War. I would detour just to walk past the pines near the armory. Just looking at those Ponderosa and white pines gave me a pleasant feeling that was almost sensual.

Pearl Harbor had been attacked during my freshman year. I learned about it on a train traveling between Chicago and Champaign-Urbana. When I reached the fraternity house, a couple of students had already packed their clothes and gone home to enlist. It was that kind of a war.

Tree Heights, Special Interest

Beginning the summer of 1947, when I measured redwoods for the forest service, I had a special interest in tree heights. The volume of wood in a tree is a function of its diameter, height and shape (often shape is called form-class by foresters). Therefore, height has a scientific and economic value, but that really doesn't account for my bent toward being conscious of tree heights wherever I go in the world. If there is a practical reason, it mostly relates to the fact that tree height is one measure of the productivity of that particular site. But it is just a way of getting a little more enjoyment out of looking at trees. Over the years here is something that I may have discovered that would interest a tree-person.

The southern US is a great tree-growing area. Loblolly pine (Pinus taeda), the principal industrial tree in the south, makes rapid growth in its early years, even faster than our western Douglas fir and far faster than Ponderosa pine, the major pine species in the west. I have spent several hundred days in the south and talked with dozens of old foresters about tree heights. The old foresters often had some experience with southern pine areas that still had old-growth timber. My conclusion thus far is that the south, despite its tree growing capability, very possibly never grew a pine that was 175-feet tall. No one I have talked with has ever measured a native southern pine that was over 150-feet tall.

Note: One of the nice things about writing a book is that if there has been a 175-foot southern pine actually measured, a reader is liable to write and tell me about it. That would be fun.

Douglas firs over 300-feet-tall have been found on Vancouver Island, British Columbia and in Coos County, Oregon. I talked with a Weyerhaeuser cutting foreman who scaled seven forty-foot logs (plus trim of about six inches out of a tree felled in the Mattson Creek drainage) and it was only about 150-years-old.

I've seen the lob (loblolly) that scores the highest in the record Big Trees list compiled by the American Forestry Association. (See photo.) It is preserved on Potlatch Corp. land near Warren Arkansas and is about 145-feet tall. Since southern pines are relatively short compared to Pacific Northwest species, the volumes per acre are also low compared to the west. The heaviest volumes per acre are in the coast redwoods, where 500,000 board feet) is not uncommon. In Del Norte County, California, Craig Giffin and I mentally laid out a circular acre that contained over one million board feet. I've never heard of loblolly or other Southern pine on 40 acres that averaged over 25M per acre (Scribner).

In 1968, my crew logged well over 200 MBF per acre from 122 acres of a Weyerhaeuser Section 21 on the north side of the South Fork of the Toutle River, near Mt. St. Helens.

Hardwoods

Australia claims the tallest hardwoods, eucalyptus that are over 300 feet. There are dozens of different species of eucalyptus. In this book there is a picture of Norman Brocard taken near Valdevia, Chile in May of '96. Norm is standing by a three-year-old plantation of Eucalyptus nitens. The taller trees are 10 meters (34 feet). In the US, the tallest hardwood I recall was a yellow poplar in North Carolina that measured over 200 feet in height. A coast redwood (Sequoia sempervirens) is the tallest known tree in the world at 369.3 feet.

Russia — Many Trees But Short

Russia has about one half of the softwood sawtimber in the world. But due principally to being in far northern latitudes, the trees are relatively short. The bulk of the old-growth trees probably average less than 80 feet in total height. On good sites in New Zealand, Radiata pine (Pinus radiata) is often 150-feet tall at age 40, and I have seen 40-year-old trees over 160-feet tall near Rotorua, N.Z. Chile also has fast-growing stands of radiata pine, a California native known to Californians as Monterey pine.

Fun of Watching Trees Grow

My favorite time to be in the woods looking at young trees is in the spring when the new growth is about half-developed and you can almost feel the surge of tree vitality. That is one time when one of my less favorite colors, chartreuse — the color of the new growth, is beautiful as it contrasts with the darker greens of the older foliage. When examining young Douglas fir here in the Pacific Northwest, I frequently think of a phrase that I seldom use otherwise "this fecund land." Another frequent thought is that "This land wants to grow trees," and it does.

Peaceful Interlude on Luzon Patrol

During infantry combat time, I always felt comfortable when surrounded by trees, unless we were getting mortar or artillery fire. Then you were better off being in a place where shells wouldn't hit part of the tree and detonate in the air. Snipers did hide in the tops of coconut trees especially, but in the Philippines we had little fighting where that was a problem. One of the reasons the following mini happening was so enjoyable and memorable is that it took place in a forest.

Camaraderie is great, but excessive human association with anyone or group, in any unit of society gets a little burdensome at times, at least for me, especially when you sleep with a guy every night in a small hole in the ground. So, occasionally I'd take short solo hikes. Sometimes this made tactical sense as well as mental health sense. Following is an example.

One especially hot day we had an all-day patrol that took us from a brushy valley, south up a steep trail into large old-growth timber. As we reached the highest level, fog came in and then lifted. As a potential forester should, I liked the timber. So, I told the head noncom I was going to take a 15- or-20 minute solo hike to look for enemy signs on a faint trail that led off to the west. It was easy going and silence wasn't a problem, even for big-footed me.

34

The timber type was what is called "high forest." This logically meant that the crowns of the trees met each other high above the ground. The trees were well over 100-feet tall with trunks that had few branches. Light filtered down through the leaves and gave a cathedral effect. It was quiet and peaceful, an enjoyable change. After a few minutes of moving quietly, I heard a faint sound. I released the safety on my rifle, stepped behind a tree and waited. It was a tense moment.

Slowly down the trail, with apparent dignity, waddled a large bird, larger than a crow, with striking colors. It was blue and gray with a white breast. In the center of the white was a brilliant scarlet patch, magnificent. Soon it turned and waddled slowly out of sight. It was such a beautiful and peaceful happening that I've never forgotten. After the war, I learned it was aptly named Bleeding Heart Pigeon.

McHenry, Illinois age 6. I remember telling Mom she should have taken the picture the day before when I had brought home a REAL string of fish.

Gerhams Lk., Wisconsin 1933: Age 8, on red pine with Winchester .22 slide-action with hammer.

Redwood Region, Northern California, near Klamath, summer 1947: Craig Giffen and I backpacked up Turwar Ck. (flows into the Klamath River from the north) to cruise redwood for the U.S. Forest Service. We laid out (mentally) a one acre circle that had over 1 million board feet (Scribner); enough wood for 100 big homes on a circle with a 117 foot radius . Camped next to a 14 foot plus diameter redwood that was goose-penned (base hollowed out by natural fires). If it had rained we both could have slept inside the tree. Yes, (smile) this was an Ancient Tree. As I recall, the largest tree we measured that summer was 14 feet in diameter 20 feet above the ground. The volume tables were based on the 20 foot diameter to avoid the wide variation in tree volume caused by butt-swell. The tallest tree was just under 300 feet — not REALLY tall in redwood terms. A few coast redwoods (Sequoia sempervirens) go over 350. The tallest is 369. It is in Redwoods National Park that cost around $2 billion dollars when it was established in the 1960's. Redwood Park is one of the least used national parks in the U.S.

Loblolly pine champion, preserved on Potlatch Corporation land near Warren, Arkansas, 59 inches DBH and 145 feet tall; and Ernest Sangster, Woodlands Manager, 1973.

The War Years
1943-1945

My War

After taking infantry basic training and some advanced training at the Infantry Replacement Training Center, Camp Croft, Spartanburg, South Carolina, I was ready to go overseas. Rumor had it that we were all headed for Europe—wrong. Our unit, primarily infantry replacements, left New York Harbor in December 1943. The ship was an old Grace Lines freighter the U.S.S. Santa Cruz—no convoy, just a lone ship. About 800 of us were on this old clunker that took 45 days to get to New Caledonia via the Panama canal. Beautiful sunrises and sunsets helped take our minds off the food, which was awful. I had been issued a canteen cup (the canteen nested in it) that was so corroded I couldn't get it clean. I used it for drinking what was called coffee. In a few days, because of the "coffee," my canteen cup shined like new. There were two meals a day. We waited in line up to three hours to get fed. Army food is uneven in taste, but nourishing.

Our bunks were in the holds below deck. They were stacked up six or eight high and someone close by was usually seasick, had B.O. or both. So, many of us slept up on the steel deck with a single woolen blanket as a mattress. The trip wasn't bad. I read about 10 books in the 45 days *(Lust for Life* — a Vincent VanGogh biography and *Life in a Putty Knife Factory* by H. Allen Smith (humor) were the two best. Conversation included exchanging life stories with new friends Bob Dvorak from Chicago and Howard Labbe.

After seeing the changeable beauty of the ocean, I understood one of the reasons why people choose to be sailors.

The monotonous pace was broken one morning in the Pacific when someone shouted, "There's a mine." Sure enough, less than 100 yards away was a spherical mine about three feet in diameter, complete with seaweed and horns. If anything hit one of the horns, the mine exploded. The mine just drifted off. The rumor was that our captain decided not to detonate it with rifle fire for fear that an enemy submarine might hear us. The troops thought it was dumb, that is, to risk having another ship run into it in the dark.

Soon after leaving the Panama Canal, there was trouble with a boiler and we slowed almost to a stop. After we had been slow-belling it for about a day, we got a laugh. A huge turtle (Hawkesbill, I think) swam slowly past us, heading our same direction. We joked that the war might be over before we got into it — not to worry.

Our arrival on New Caledonia was livened up by a hurricane that began just after we anchored. It gusted to 70 and 80 miles per hour. At gusts of 60 or 70 the only way you could move around on the dock was to get in a long single file and hold on to someone, conga-line style. Sailors did this on the dock to secure some ship lines. In a nearby lumberyard, lumber was blowing around like leaves.

One night, four of us took a flashlight and climbed up a rocky slope for a mile or so to explore some caves. It was eerie. We were about 30 or 40 yards into the cave, feeling spooky, when we came to a place where the roof had caved in so there was only a hole five or six feet wide and two feet high. All of us were side by side and I shined the light into the black hole. There was a loud screech and a huge bat flew right at the light. We fell over backwards and I dropped the light. When I finally found it, I looked around — I was alone. That ended cave exploration.

New Zealand

In early February 1944, some of us headed south to New Zealand to join the veteran 43rd infantry Division as replacements. It was great to leave the humid heat of the tropics for temperate and gorgeous New Zealand and its friendly people. I continue to associate this experience with the lines from Kipling's *The Song of The Cities*. He said of Auckland, New Zealand,

> Last, loneliest, loveliest, exquisite, apart —
> On us, on us the unswerving season smiles,
> Who wonder mid our fern why men depart
> To seek the Happy isles.

I'm sure that about 99-plus percent of servicemen who have been there still have a deep and continuing affection for New Zealanders and their beautiful country. Tourists also love it. Here is a tribute.

In 1973, I was in Lewiston, Idaho and met the owner of a travel business who had been in the business over 25 years. We were chatting about nice countries to visit and she said, "You know, the only place in the world where every single person I've sent there wants to go back is ...," I interrupted with, "New Zealand," and was right.

Yanks were almost universally popular in New Zealand, but not all was sweetness and light. A few Kiwis probably had the same complaint as an Englishman who said, "Yanks are okay except for the three "Over's." When asked what he meant he said, "They are overpaid, oversexed and over here." Most of the young New Zealand men were overseas, so the Americans cut quite a swath with the ladies with the occasional predictable results.

One morning we lined up for reveille at daybreak and two of our veterans of the New Georgia campaign (possibly sober), looked as though they had just refought it. Prickett and Burgoise were blood-spattered from head to waist. And their eyes were blackened and blue, and each had six or eight oval bruise marks on their faces that doubtless perfectly matched someone's New Zealand army boots. They had been too friendly with somebody else's Maori girls. No real harm done though.

Harry Nash

Some people that you know only briefly make an indelible impression that lasts for the rest of your life. Soon after joining L Company, 103rd infantry, 43rd Division in New

Zealand as a very green 19-year-old buck sergeant (three stripes, no "rocker") I had that happen. This started when a thoughtful act by a veteran Sergeant greatly increased my enjoyment of our first weekend pass.

A couple of us were waiting near camp for the bus to Auckland, when a grizzled veteran machine gun sergeant, Harry Nash, walked up to me, stopped and pulled out his wallet. I knew who he was but that was about all. I'd only been in the company a week or two. Harry opened his wallet pulled out a couple of big bills and said, "Gruenfeld, I know you men haven't been paid for a long time and must be about broke (he was right). So take this and pay me back when you get paid. You'll be doing me a favor 'cause I'll just spend it if I keep it, and I have more." I accepted with many thanks and had the warm feeling you get when someone does you a favor in exactly the right way.

Harry was popular with the troops and had done well in combat. He wasn't very big, but looked wiry and strong. He had a heavy bunch of muscle high in his back that some people get from doing manual labor. (For instance, now I know that is a typical physique for a cable-logging rigging man). Harry had been a pulpwood logger in Maine before the division was activated.

A few weeks later at a weekend dance at a Grange Hall, he and another noncom argued over who should dance with a certain lady and decided to settle the issue with a fist fight. It looked like Harry was overmatched since his opponent had been a CYO boxer and was the regimental light heavyweight boxing champ. When they were about to start, the other man said he was afraid he would hurt Harry, who was outweighed about 20 pounds. They did finally have to stop the fight. Harry had knocked the champ down three times and might have really hurt him if they had let it continue. Quite a guy and a nice guy.

Last I heard about Harry was that he had been wounded on Luzon during the battle for Hill 600. Hope he has had a happy life.

Humor With History Of The 103rd Infantry Regiment

Soon after beginning our New Zealand combat training, all the replacements were assembled in a big barn-like building to learn the history of our veteran regiment. The 103rd had recently performed solidly in the New Georgia, Solomon Island campaign that ended with the capture of the Munda airstrip.

The 103rd Infantry began as the First Main Volunteers in the Civil War where it did well. In World War I, it distinguished itself in some hard fought campaigns. The orientation was given by an articulate tech sergeant who had been in public relations prior to the war and had a professional voice. Things were going well through his telling us that the regimental motto was "To The Last Man." That registered positively and was followed by a thoughtful silence. It ended when a loud voice in the back of the room yelled, "Yeah, the Colonel." This brought the house down with uproarious laughter and terminated the orientation. Note: Joe Cleland, the new regimental commander — a Westpointer, was seldom the last man, and in the Korean war commanded the 40th Infantry Division as a Major General. In Korea, Cleland mentored Colonel David Hackworth, USA retired, currently our most decorated living soldier.

Self Appraisal of Combat Potential

Few of us replacements had a firm opinion on how we would do in combat. After completing the live ammunition firing problems at Rotorua I figured to myself I had a good chance to be OK in combat. Pfc. Louis Magrames was eager to get to where he could, "kill some Japs" and knew he would do well (more on him later). A significant minority of us replacements were eager to see action. Of the veterans in L Company, the only one who told me he was looking forward to getting back into action was a squad leader named Moody. He was busted back to private in New Guinea for fighting with some MPs, but was made a squad leader soon after the Luzon beachhead. He did well in combat.

Some of our battle maneuvers took place in young plantations of radiata pine (Pinus radiata). Revenues from radiata products are now an important part of the New Zealand economy. Radiata is native to California, where it is usually called Monterey Pine, since it's found on the Monterey Peninsula southwest of San Francisco.

I've been back to New Zealand several times since the war, mostly on business. When they know you trained there in World War II, the wartime impact on the girls is occasionally mentioned. The funniest comment to me was made when I was playing in a New Zealand tennis tournament at Otorohunga in 1990. (I had given a talk at a forest industry conference in Rotorua). I was visiting with some other players, when up bounced, always effervescent (I learned later) Allen Robinson from Tauranga. After knowing me for 15 seconds, and learning I was a returning vet he said, "Come back to see the kids, Jay?" A riot. He then kind of blushed. I assured him there were no kids.

Since I did spend much time during six months in 1944 with a pretty 17-year-old Warkworth girl, Elra Brakenrig (now Mrs. Rufus Chessum) it's worth adding that I didn't even come close to creating any "kids." I was nineteen, and a virgin — though "interested." My squad of 14 men was very disappointed in what they judged was my lack of progress with Elra. They saw her as a very attractive objective. She was. She and Rufus visited us in 1993, and I've seen them a couple of times in New Zealand — great folks.

Goodbye New Zealand

After six months of solid training, including much use of live ammunition on maneuvers near Rotorua, we sailed for New Guinea and combat. It was July 9, 1944 and my mother's birthday. Through cheering spectators, we marched down the streets of Auckland to the ships. There were many teary eyes — marchers and watchers both.

New Zealand June "44" 43rd Division 103rd Infantry "L" Co. 3rd Platoon. McAllister, Platoon Sergeant; Garmany, Fecser, Cook, Gruenfeld, Prickett, Brammer as indicated.

New Zealand 1944: Elra Brakenrig, 17, now Mrs. Rufus Chessum, Warkworth, N.Z.

WWII at an Infantry Replacement Training Center (IRTC) James E. Cook Missouri, at the end of basic; later rifleman in my squad 3rd Platoon, "L" Company 103rd Inf. 43rd Division Pacific Theater. He looks like what he was, a bright, studious, church going, high school graduate. But notice that he had qualified as Expert (top rating) with three infantry weapons and sharpshooter with two more. Cook was a fine person and first-class soldier. Was wounded after I left the squad. His mother sent my Dad this photo.

48

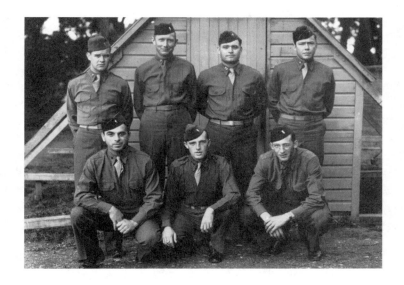

Early 1944: Kaipara Flats near Warkworth, New Zealand. Officers of "L" Company 103rd Infantry, 43rd Division. Kneeling from left: Lieutenants Vilano, Fletcher (transferred out), Ditkoff (transferred out); standing Thompson (3rd Platoon), Dooley (Texas A&M), Capt. Chase (had been a private detective, Atlanta, GA.), Foell. Foell and Thompson KIA (Killed In Action). Chase, had at least one Purple Heart and Dooley did too, I think. They averaged very good. Note hutment for four non-coms, or two officers.

Combat

Our Division left Auckland, New Zealand on July 9, 1944, and headed north to New Guinea. We were in a small convoy. Our ship was the Torrans — a Norwegian freighter that was later sunk by the Japanese. As we arrived in Aitape, New Guinea, now Papua New Guinea, on about July 16, there was a distant rumble of artillery fire. This was my first sound of actual combat.

The early New Guinea campaigns in 1942-43 had been tough and bloody. When we arrived, a battle around the Driniumor River was winding down. Our division was involved in fighting but had only minor casualties except for parts of our 169th regiment. They, a regiment of the 32nd Division and the 112th Cavalry (Regiment), author Norman Mailer's outfit, were badly mauled. Though nearly starving, the Japanese, led by General Hatazo Adachi, made a ferocious attack on our defensive line along the Driniumor. They broke through in several places and could have gone almost unopposed to the harbor at Aitape where our ships were unprotected. But they milled around, exhausted and decimated by casualties. The defense stiffened and our air corps and artillery destroyed thousands of the attackers. This was the last major Japanese attack in northern New Guinea.

Our operations were mostly patrols, manning the pill-box perimeter around the Aitape harbor, and intensive training for the next beachhead. For me it was a good introduction to combat. Especially the combat and reconnaissance patrols where I led patrols of eight to fifteen men. On one patrol of about five hours, for the entire time we were in a sago palm swamp in water from ankle to waist deep. The only wildlife we saw was a small crocodile and a swarm of bees. Without a compass and map I would have been lost in 20 minutes.

Because the jungle was often flat and dense, one man in our regiment, reportedly headed for a latrine 100 feet from his pillbox and got turned around. It took him 24 hours to find his way back.

Early Emphasis On Communications

In warfare, business and life, communications are required for efficient operations. For example, the army manual on Scouting and Patrolling emphasizes how important it is that everyone understands what the mission of a patrol is. But, in the army, as in business and life generally, there are many communications failures. At the beginning of one all-day patrol that covered 9 miles, I spent about 10 minutes explaining to the patrol where we were going, and why. After the patrol, a veteran of many patrols told me that was the first time he had been on a wartime patrol that he really understood the mission. I was surprised.

Memorable Non-Battlefield Incidents

Being a somewhat normal guy, I've been afraid many times in my 71 years. Perhaps I have been most afraid at certain times under heavy mortar or artillery fire in combat with the Japanese. But the single incident where I had the greatest momentary, fear-shock-surprise-terror combination wasn't in combat, though I was in the Army in Northern New Guinea when this happened.

One of our men had been wounded and was in the Aitape Army Hospital, so one afternoon I hiked a couple of miles to see him. We were inside a very well fortified perimeter so were not allowed to carry weapons unless on duty. Since enemy soldiers occasionally infiltrated our lines, I was uncomfortable not having my rifle. This added an element of tension. Also, I took a shortcut on an unused new graveled road built through a sago palm swamp. The vegetation in parts of the swamp was heavy and very dry and was inhabited by various lizards, snakes, birds and other jungle creatures. Significantly, in this episode I was alone. There was no leader role for me to play. My emotions were not under the constraints generated by being with others.

Talking with the Americans and Australians in the hospital kept me there till well after dark. There were no lights on the unused road and I considered taking the longer route back, that had traffic, but decided to return through the swamp though it was pitch black dark, with no moon and only a few stars. I did not have any kind of light. It was creepy.

As I walked slowly down the road I immediately became tense. The wind rustled the dead palms and other vegetation. Animal noises added to the stress. Finally, after about a half an hour, while right in the middle of the swamp, the hair on my head started to stand up. Later in the war I would have recognized this and the accompanying feeling of extrasensory tension, as a sure indication that something big was about to happen. I even stopped and considered turning back. But young soldiers, who aspired to courage, weren't supposed to do that, so I cautiously continued.

Suddenly, a big animal hit my leg, all around me there were loud snorts, squeals and thundering hooves. I was terrified. I jumped straight up in the air, I yelled, I ran a few steps, then stopped, realizing what had happened.

A herd of wild pigs had heard me coming and stood motionless on the road until I walked right into them. They then stampeded while I panicked in complete terror. I finished the hike thankfully and without much emotion, since I had been feared-out.

Based on this encounter, I concluded that I wasn't going to have to worry about soiling my pants whenever I got hugely scared. I was right. No event since, has come close to that instantaneously high level of fear. The incident was a good conditioner. It prepared me for the following happening.

Stranger In The Night

About a month later we were dug in on our main defense line along the Driniumor River, east of Aitape. We had been sleeping in damp foxholes for about three weeks and one night finally had a chance to sleep off the ground. We found some communications wire and laced it between a couple of poles as a makeshift bed, a couple of feet off the ground. Instead of a mattress we had a layer of cardboard from ration boxes. A pancho was rigged over the two beds to keep the rain out. This structure was against a five-foot diameter fallen tree. Our shelter was pretty crude, but it looked a lot better than a foxhole. I was to sleep with the tree brushing my left shoulder. My buddy commented on the tree being a logical highway for snakes, lizards and other things that crawl in the night.

New Guinea was a snake paradise, but I only saw a few. The SOP (Standard Operating Procedure) when nonhuman things crawled over you at night was, "Don't grab them, just let them crawl off." Good thinking.

I have never been a good sleeper, except in combat. In combat you were nearly always tired, often exhausted and never had enough sleep, so most of us were quickly asleep when the opportunity came. Someone in the next foxhole had first guard duty (sitting in a foxhole). So when it was dark I lay down on my back, closed my eyes and was instantly asleep.

A couple of hours later I was wakened by a large snake crawling across my neck and face, in that order. I instinctively grabbed it and threw it out from under the pancho, as I yelled, "Snake." So much for the SOP. As my buddy described it, "You then did something that was physically impossible, you sort of levitated up off the cot and then shot out from under the poncho, feet first, without knocking it down, and ended standing up." I didn't know where the snake was, so crawled back on my pad and after we had a few laughs was instantly asleep. If that happened tonight, I probably wouldn't be able to sleep for a couple of days. Don't know whether the snake was poisonous or not, but it was about two inches in diameter.

Infantry Rifle Squad

Our primary weapon was the M1 Garand, a .30 caliber 8-shot semiautomatic rifle loaded with a clip that held eight rounds. A superior weapon, then, the best military rifle in the world. Firing the M1 at targets, about man-size, at 500 yards was a standard part of marksmanship training. If there wasn't much wind, a good shot from the prone position could hit the 30-inch bull's-eye regularly. When I fired for record, it was dead calm. I had six bulls in a row, but dropped a point on each of the next two shots.

In each rifle squad, we also had one Browning Automatic Rifle (BAR) with a 20-round magazine which was a good weapon, but a holdover from World War I. We also had a recoilless rifle, called a Bazooka. It fired a specially designed shape charge and was good on pillboxes and light vehicles.

Three different types of hand grenades were our in-house artillery. The fragmentation grenade was the most common. It weighed 20 ounces, had a 4.6 second fuse and broke into fragments when the TNT exploded. Second, was the white phosphorus grenade that produced concussion, white smoke and burning bits of phosphorus that could not be extinguished with water. This was a deadly weapon in caves. Third, were various colors of smoke grenades. They were good for concealment and signaling.

No one had taught us, but we soon learned that when working on caves or pill boxes the optimum sequence, sometimes, was first a white phosphorus grenade with its smoke and fire followed by fragmentation grenades. In the smoke it was difficult for them to find the second grenade to throw it back.

Considering the importance of hand grenades, recruits in our 17 weeks of basic training surprisingly received very little grenade training. You usually only threw one grenade in basic training. In my case it was at a mock-up mortar position. The army was concerned about avoiding injury in training, so when you threw the grenade they created unnecessary fear; that is, treated it like it had the power of a big artillery round. So, fresh replacement were often aghast when they saw how casually veteran combat troops often treated grenades. Many men could throw a hand grenade further than I could. But, like nearly every American soldier, I had played some baseball, killed (sorry) quite a few birds with rocks until I knew better, and had a pretty strong arm. I could just barely throw a grenade far enough so that the hang-time was enough, that is, over 4.6 seconds, to get it to detonate in midair. In this time it covered a maximum of about 50 yards.

Rifle grenades were available, fired from the rifle, but we didn't use them very often. If there had been more pill-boxes, we would have.

We trusted the quality of the fuse in our grenades. For example, to avoid having a grenade thrown back by the recipient, it was usual to hold it for a second or two, or even longer before throwing it. I remember crouching outside a cave with a green replacement immediately behind me. I pulled the pin on the grenade, held it a couple of seconds behind my head, then threw it into the cave. When I turned my head away from the blast I saw that my partner was deathly white. Said he darn near wet his pants. He wasn't prepared for such treatment of grenades. I was slightly wounded twice by enemy grenades which weren't as deadly as ours.

In late December 1944, we headed for the Philippines.

New Guinea, September 1944 Four of the 14 in my squad, from l. Fecser, age 19, Fraley 18, Tinker 25 (veteran of New Georgia campaign), Waller 19; hidden in background, Garmany 19.

55

Aitape, New Guinea, Sept. 1944, the squad leader (author) ,19, sago palms in background were the primary vegetation.

The Luzon Beachead

The Luzon liberation invasion was the largest amphibious operation of the Pacific war. (Source: *U.S. Military War History - Triumph in the Philippines*). Over 1,200 ships took part. Our company of about 220 men went from New Guinea to Luzon in an LST (Landing Ship Tank a.k.a. Large Slow Target). It has a bow door that exits amphitracks and other beachhead equipment either onto a beach or into the water.

On the way up, in the Southern Philippines LST 225 (?) a couple of hundred yards to our left was attacked by a kamikaze plane. It looked like every antiaircraft gunner within sight was shooting at the doomed plane. For a couple of seconds after the plane disintegrated, just above the water, some gunners kept firing. They caused several casualties in I Company that was on the LST. Not our first experience with friendly-fire, nor the last, by a mile. Friendly-fire is just part of war. It can be reduced, but not eliminated in an efficient large scale battle. The troops, on average, get pretty philosophical about it after a while — as you do about a lot of repugnant things — in order to remain sane.

The Sunset

Sunset watching has been a favorite pastime of mine for as long as I can remember. Jan, my wife, is also a sunset watcher. I found that out on our first date (December 17, 1972) and it was one of the reasons that I went home that night knowing I was going to marry this superb gal. Speaking of ego.

When you are an adult and have spent most of your life in the Pacific Northwest, and aren't blind, you have seen many magnificent sunsets. But the most beautiful, most unforgettable sunset that I have ever seen wasn't in the Pacific Northwest. It happened as we sailed in an LST on our voyage from Aitape, New Guinea (now Papau New Guinea) to make the beachhead at Lingayen Gulf, to help liberate the island of Luzon.

The day this occurred it had rained much of the day, but as we sailed to the west, with small islands on each side, the rain stopped. Dark clouds started to open and the sun started to gradually break through. We were sailing right into the sunset. As the sunlight burst through the clouds, every cloud for maybe 20 degrees each side of the sun, was edged in gold. The violent purples and reds changed to pinks and magentas and grays, back and forth. Within minutes men were crowding the rail for a better look. The boat bobbed and swayed gently, not interfering with our enjoyment.

Some sunsets are at peak beauty for a brief period, but this one went on and on. At least eight times someone would say, "Well, it can't get any better than this — but it did. Finally, 360 degrees of beauty.

Accolade To The Sunset

Yes, due to the situation we were more than normally receptive to beauty. Anyone with half a brain knew that there were people in our rifle company who wouldn't see many more sunsets in this life. And many would be in hospitals for a long time where you would rarely see a sunset. But, even allowing for my being especially sensitized to beauty, this sunset, which lasted over an hour, was clearly the best I have ever seen.

It may strain my credibility with the veterans (of any war) reading this, but I can truthfully make a statement that is the ultimate testimony to the sunset's unsurpassed beauty. This sunset was so gorgeous that it broke up every card and dice game on the ship which was carrying over 300 soldiers and sailors — impossible as that might seem to a veteran. Note: I can personally only vouch for the games on the deck, but was told that the below deck games were also suspended.

A Tough First 30 Days On Luzon Island, Philippines

Our 43rd Infantry Division (about 14,000 strong) landed at 0930 hours January 9, 1945 on the left flank (east edge) of the four Division beachhead at Lingayen Gulf. This is about 120 miles north of Manila the capitol city. Our landing at the small town of San Fabian was unopposed, but as we moved off the beachhead the resistance stiffened and our casualties were heavy. For the first 30 days of fighting, we had many more casualties than the total for the other three beachhead Divisions (6th, 37th and 40th Infantry). This was because the 43rd Division with help from the 158th Regimental combat team and a regiment of the 6th Division operated against an entrenched enemy holding the high ground, while the other divisions were usually on easy ground against light resistance.

After six weeks of combat, a very moving and sad ceremony was held on February 17 at the temporary cemetery where the Division's over 600 fatalities were buried. To get to the ceremony on time we left our camp at daylight. (During the truck ride we saw Filipino kids sound asleep on the backs of the big caribou they were herding. It was nice to see a peaceful scene.)

This number of fatalities meant that the infantry rifle companies that did most of the fighting, had averaged well over 50 percent battle casualties. L Company, mine, had 65 men left out of about 220 after 30 days of combat. We were lucky compared with "I" company of our regiment that had 24 men killed and only 28 left after 30 days. Fifteen had been killed in our company. Usually there were three or four wounded for each fatality, but it depended on the weapon type.

Artillery usually caused a higher ratio of wounded to fatals than machine guns. The rifle platoons in our company had sustained about 50 percent battle casualties plus more lost as non-battle casualties. The non-battle casualties from sickness, disease, battle fatigue and other causes often run from 25 to 100 percent or more of the battle casualties. Usually, the longer the battle the higher the non-battle casualties. It took a pretty bad wound to get sent home. Despite the casualties our morale was good, but we knew there was much more to come.

We were finally relieved by elements of the 33rd Division in early February and had a few days to rest and receive replacements. Many wounds are relatively minor. Some of the wounded return within a couple of weeks.

Letters

(Note: Letters, only a sample, are reproduced exactly as they were written. My dad saved every service letter I wrote.)

15th January, 1945
Phillippines (sic)

Dear Folks:

Everything is going along fine. Can't really say I wish you were here but we're doing O.K. You will probably not hear from me very often for a while but don't worry. No matter how tough she gets it doesn't bother me too much and I know I got myself in and hope to get myself out.

It really makes a fellow feel like he is doing something. The people here really are glad to see us. There was one old man about 70 I guess. The fellows asked him if he knew where there was any water. Old as he was he took their canteens and ran down to a little well and filled them. Whenever a vehicle passed he would wave both hands and bow. The people, especially the kids say, "Moning Suh." We get a big kick out of it.

I received many packages before we left New Guinea and it really filled out my shipboard diet. Thanks for the razor Dad, it's in my pack now. (Boxes 12 and 22 came before I left.)

Please don't worry about me Mom, no matter what, there is always a bright spot and I can pick them out.

Lots and Lots of love,

Jay

PS   Thank Uncle A for the sardines — they were good.

Good Soldiers Àre Of Many Types

I had a great background to help make me a solid combat soldier. First, I volunteered for combat, I didn't have to be there — at least at that time. Also, I was physically strong (6 feet and about 185 pounds), had been well-trained, had a happy home life, solid religious belief, believed deeply in the rightness of our cause and was accepting of the political-socio-economic system in the US. Despite all these positive attributes, I often didn't find combat all that easy. So, I would say to myself, "How in hell can so many of these other guys, who lack many of my helpful characteristics that make this relatively easy, still hang in there and do the job." I developed a great respect for "the troops." My personal feelings are expressed in the following eloquent quotation, the best I've ever read, from a WWI English infantry officer, writer and poet.

"I was rewarded by an intense memory of men whose courage had shown me the power of the human spirit . . . that spirit which could withstand the utmost assault. Such men had inspired me to be at my best when things were very bad, and they outweighed all the failures. Against the war and its brutal stupidity those men had stood glorified by the thing which sought to destroy them."
Siegfried Sassoon, 1930
"Memoirs Of An Infantry Officer"

Feelings and memories like those described by Sassoon are one of the rewards of combat. They apply to all good combat troops whether they are New Zealanders, Aussies, Japanese, Germans, Russians or whomever.

Some Fought From Hate

A rifleman in another platoon of our infantry company was such a man. His name was Louis Magrames and he was from Mishiwaka, Indiana. A big guy, maybe six-foot-one and 220 with sloping shoulders, 19-years-old. Not too many men made it perfectly clear that they were eager to get into combat, so they could "kill some Japs." However, that is the way Magrames was from the time I first met him in New Zealand in January 1944. When I asked why he was so eager to get into combat all he would say was, "I've got a grudge." So, I wasn't surprised when he performed magnificently in combat.

For example, one day two different times, he kept firing his rifle to keep an enemy down in his foxhole and then stuck his bayonet in him and lifted him out of the hole like he was forking hay. His platoon leader, Don Shaw, California, who had been in three campaigns said, "Magrames is the best combat soldier I've ever been around." Maybe we should make even more effort to have our infantrymen develop grudges against the enemy.

My only personal contact with Magrames, in combat, was positive. Here is what happened. Though I was a relatively eager combat soldier, my morale did have ups and downs. One day I was way down. A good friend, Gifford, had been badly wounded and perhaps killed the day before; I had had only a couple of hours sleep a night for a week or so, was exhausted —and mainly, we had been getting a lot of incoming artillery. Between shell bursts, I ran and dove into a small dry creek bed for shelter. Suddenly, from the few yards away, came a loud and joyous, not-a-care-in-the-world, "Hey Jay, great to see you, how've ya been?" — Magrames. Right away I felt better and, of course, told him everything was just right.

A Combat And Life Highlight

My 72 years have had many exciting, memorable times but the following, in its way, is the highlight.

After twenty days of pretty intense combat we were put into battalion reserve for a couple of days and had dug our foxholes in a coconut grove on the edge of the village of Pozorrubio. Filipinos came in and said three Japanese had been seen near the edge of town. The C.O. called for volunteers to look for them. Volunteers were used not because of any special danger, but probably because the officers knew what we had been through and the search was not mandatory.

Brammer and I decided to go along. Ten of us went out. He was a first scout and PFC (private first class) in another squad of our platoon, I was a squad leader and we had become friends during our time in New Zealand and New

Guinea. Bram was a tall lanky, happy-go-lucky kind of baby-faced Texan, age 20 years and about three months — a month older than I was. We had been in the Army almost two years and overseas about a year. We had joined the 43rd Division as replacements in New Zealand after being in a Replacement Training Center on New Caledonia.

As usual, it was sticky-hot and it had rained the night before so we were able to move very quietly. After about an hour of searching, the other eight guys went over to a nearby village to try and get some eggs. We had been on canned and boxed army rations for over three weeks. Bram and I kept searching. We were about 75 yards apart when I found very fresh tracks made by split-toed shoes. These shoes were made for Japanese, but Filipinos sometimes wore them. I followed them for about 25 yards along one side of an elevated square of foot high grass, bordered by banana trees. This 25-yard square was raised about three feet above the adjoining rice paddies. The paddies were on two touching sides of the square. The other two sides merged with land the same elevation as the square. When I reached the corner of the elevated area and entered the rice paddy, the tracks turned at right angles and I could see that they went to the next corner about 25 yards away. This made me very cautious. If I continued to follow the tracks I might turn the corner and be face to face with enemy soldiers. So, instead of following the tracks, I continued straight out into the paddy which, of course, was flat and had little vegetation, so I could see clearly. I was out past the corner of the elevated area about 30 yards and looking back at the corner of the elevated area where the tracks turned the next corner, when I saw something that didn't look right. I didn't know what it was, but it wasn't right. (Later I learned it was the light reflecting from the corner of a leather ammunition pouch.) So I retraced my steps and then crouching low, slowly crept through the grass. I was on the center line of the elevated tract headed toward where it joined the rice paddy on the side of the square I hadn't seen.

Approaching the border of banana trees, I became very tense and the hair started to stand up on the back of my neck. This happened several times to me in combat and others have told me it had happened to them. I knew that something special was going to happen. It was as though the music in a scary movie was building to a climax.

Crescendo

A Japanese soldier was 10 or 12 feet away on the edge of the rice paddy. His back was to me. His head was about level with my knees and he held the barrel of his rifle in his extended right hand, with the butt on the ground. He was gazing out over the rice paddy — maybe thinking about home. I looked at the back of his head through the peep sight of my M1. Our men sometimes wore Japanese equipment — though I'd never seen anyone with a Nip helmet — and I didn't shoot for fear that it might be one of those knotheads, though I had never seen them wear a Nip helmet. Then, Brammer whistled (not yelled, thank God) and the enemy started to turn his head. I saw he was Japanese, shot him in head and he plunged forward. There was noise, so I knew he wasn't alone. I dropped back about five steps, pulled the pin on my only hand grenade and let the lever fly, held it for two plus seconds and lobbed it toward the noise. It went off and a groan followed. Bram ran up, I told him what had happened. I am not sure of the exact words, but I know we told each other that this did NOT necessarily mean we had two down and one to go.

He didn't have any grenades, so we moved out into the paddy with me leading and Bram about 12 or 15 feet away. We were in about three inches of water. A grenade popped, meaning that an explosion was coming in about five seconds and we kneeled in the water and briefly put our heads down. The grenade went off and a body rose up out of the tall weeds at the edge of the rice paddy, turned end for end like a rag doll and dropped to the ground — a suicide. We began firing rapidly at a range of 40 to 50 feet. They threw a couple of grenades but ineffectively since in water, a grenade just blows up a big column of water and you are usually safe unless it is right on top of you. They were firing at us through a heavy screen of weeds and rice and we were doing the same at them. Our fire was coordinated so that we never had two empty rifles at the same time.

This was done with yells like "Three to go." Soon we had fired over a hundred rounds between us and the enemy fire had dropped to virtually zero. Bram started to go in close, got within 10 or 15 feet of them and started to fire rapidly and yelled, "There are a lot of them." I honestly think his grammar was right. He didn't say "there is." Not welcome news.

The Memorable Quote

This is hard to believe, but in the middle of the fire fight Bram shouted to me. As I remember it, his exact words were, "Hey, Jay, this is all right, (bang, bang) just like the movies (bang, bang)."

(Present comment: Yea Texas!) After 40 or 50 more rounds, I moved in close at the other end of their position. Soon we had each fired about a hundred rounds — easy to do in a short time when you have a semiautomatic rifle with eight shots to the clip.

Someone moved, I shot him, we fired a few more rounds and it was over. Nine Japanese lay dead, nearly touching one another. If all seven survivors from my first shot and the grenade had stood up together I think they would have had us. Lucky again.

There was a shout, and our other eight men came across the rice paddy in a skirmish line, weapons ready.

Finale

For some reason we were both pretty excited. Neither of us wanted to spend any time really looking for souvenirs and intelligence information (probably in that order). Looking at nine people you have just killed wasn't enjoyable for us. I remember being surprised at how little blood there was despite all the wounds. I grabbed a saber and we left the rest of the chores to the other eight. Our outfit was already moving out when we got back to the coconut grove, so the recounting of the tale took place mostly as we marched along.

The person that said, "Rather lucky than smart," had it right.

Postlude

When I read what actually happened it seems unreal. Especially since in the three weeks just before this scrap, we had endured some nerve-shattering combat, where it was so bad that a time or two I looked at the dead and felt that maybe they had a better deal — but only a time or two. But we had been given a couple of days of rest and were young and resilient. If this had happened a month or so later I would have fired the first shot, thrown the hand grenade and run for help.

When the fight was over, I had an eight-shot clip in my rifle and two more clipped on my shirt front. This meant I had fired nearly 100 rounds. Bram did about the same. Recently I learned from Bram, that because of our heavy volume of fire, the battalion was thinking of sending tank support

Pozorrubio, Luzon January 1945: When the Filipinos heard I was a veteran, looking for where Bram and I had fought the 9 unlucky Japanese 50 years earlier I drew a helpful crowd, everywhere I went. The police provided transportation. Never found the exact site but made a couple of new friends.

The Infantry

**"I give you the combat infantryman, the guy who finished
what others began."—Anon.**

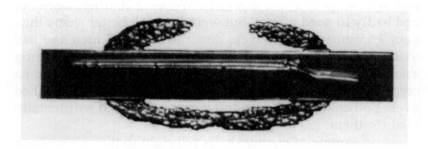

Combat Infantry Badge

One good thing about being a combat infantryman is
that most of us got so we half-believed the old saying, "All
combat infantrymen go to heaven, because they've already
been through hell." But there were other good things besides
the assurance of heaven. The camaraderie, being part of a team,
fighting for a cause you believed in, knowing you were doing
more than your share — all these things made for positive
feeling that offset much of the negative. But it wasn't easy.

The Great Equalizer

In combat, most of us liked the down-to-basics standards on which you were judged. In combat a person's social
status, education and looks didn't matter much in how you
were judged by your peers.

67

You were judged on the answers to questions such as "Will he be there when I need him? Does he know what he is doing? Is he honest? Does he take his fair share of the risks? Is he really trying?"

The Mount Alava Spectacle

Our company of 220 plus men that made the beach-head, was down to about 70 and we were manning a defensive perimeter near the top of Mount Alava — a prominent cinder cone near Lingayen Gulf. Company I of our battalion was going to make an attack on entrenched Nips, using five tanks. We were going to have a near-perfect view from our mountain top, at a range of about one mile. We were shot-up, worn out and badly in need of rest, but were in much better shape than poor I Company. They were down to 30 or 35 men and had over 25 men killed in less than 30 days. Yet they were being asked to make another attack. As we watched, those few men crept from their fox holes and went slowly forward crouched over. You could see they didn't want to do it, and we mentally bled for them.

A couple of enemy shells fell right in the infantry and we saw there were casualties. One of our tanks was hit and burst into flames as they often did when hit. The attack bogged down.

One of the seven or eight men left in my squad came up to me as I stood quietly watching the spectacle through binoculars. It may have been Frank Fecser. He said, "You know it sounds crazy, but I kind of wish I was over there with 'em." I had been thinking the very same thing.

Amazing but true. Note: Of all my war stories this one is the hardest to tell without tearing up. I guess the tears come partly from despair over what humans are asked to do in war. And part is from admiration of the power of the human spirit.

When male bonding could produce actions like the above, no wonder some men went AWOL from hospitals to get back to their unit, their buddies — their family. And these were civilian soldiers, not regular Army. The human spirit is powerful.

Sure there were some self inflicted wounds, legitimate battle fatigue, faked battle fatigue and cowards, but most of the guys did their job. Frequently it was a tough job.

Role Playing

    In the Army being a combat leader often required being out in front. The field manuals didn't encourage this, but it was frequently necessary if objectives were to be taken. And it was a way to compensate for mistakes you were bound to make.

    Note: An interesting statistic from the battle for Saipan, in the Western Pacific, where both Army and Marines participated, showed a significant difference in officer fatalities for the two services. This was despite having about the same percentage of officers, of total manpower, in each service. On Saipan, the Army had one officer killed for every eight enlisted men killed. The Marines lost one officer for each 12 enlisted men. (I believe this statistic came from an *Infantry Journal* article). This should have been expected since the Marines place much more emphasis on being aggressive, due to the shorter time they expect to be engaged and the frequent necessity for taking an objective quickly. Also they are heavier to volunteers, who tend to be somewhat more aggressive, on average, than draftees.

The Cost Of Role Playing

    Shakespeare said, "All the world's a stage, and all the men and women merely players:" We are role players much of our lives. This is especially true when young men and boys are playing a role in the deadly game of war.

    When I became a combat infantry soldier I quickly adapted, as most of us did, to the combat situation. This included trying to appear to be tough. Being tough included appearing unconcerned in revolting situations. For example, the first time when you dragged a dead enemy out of a cave and part of him trailed as much as eight feet behind his main body, you pretended that this was all in a days work — later, it was, but not at first, for most of us.

    When enemy (or friendly) artillery hit terribly close it lifted you off the ground and slammed you down hard enough so you had trouble breathing and were often stunned. After being pounded like this for a while you were pretty much speechless. And, it was just as well because the words that would have come out might have been a prayer, and that wasn't being tough. Actually veteran troops often admit fear readily, but usually only in acceptable situations and sometimes only when the fear is put in the form of a joke. Here is an example.

Robert Garmany of Anniston, Alabama was a good soldier, but funny. Always had something wrong with his uniform. A legging under one pant leg instead of over it, steel helmet on crooked—you know the type. Garm joked about his playing the role of combat soldier.

Garmany's Quote About His Role in Any Attack

After we had been in heavy combat on Luzon for about a month, we had a quiet period and were able to have a bull session where almost the whole squad, by then maybe seven or eight men left out of 14, joined in. We talked about the sometime problem of determining how aggressive you should be in an attack. There were questions such as where to draw the line between being cautious and being cowardly and where courage became stupidity. Garm brought the house down when he said in his slow drawl, "Well I know one thing. When we are in the attack and there is a man behind me, I call that man a coward."

Prayer in Combat

Life has taught me that zeros and 100 percents are nearly always wrong when used as generalizations, especially when applied to human behavior and objectives. So, I don't believe, and didn't believe the old army axiom, "There are no atheists in foxholes." My modification, based on experience would read, "There are darn few atheists in foxholes."

One day, for example, we were laying behind Sherman tanks, one squad to each tank, while our artillery pounded the enemy position. It was noisy and scary and we were going to have to attack when the bombardment lifted ... had my Bible out and so did the four men I could see. One of our squad couldn't read but I'll bet he had memorized appropriate verses. Especially popular were the 23rd Psalm "...Yea, though I walk through the valley of the shadow of death ...," and the 91st

Psalm "... His truth shall be thy shield.... A thousand shall fall at thy side, and ten thousand at thy right hand; but it shall not come nigh thee...." Even though most of us eventually figured that, unless we got sick, it was just a question of what kind of wound we were going to get, it was comforting to read the Bible.

Having had a Lutheran upbringing I was no stranger to prayer. Early on in New Guinea combat I stopped praying to come home alive, because in my idealism, it seemed to me that this could mean someone might die in my place and that wasn't very Christian. So, my prayers were usually asking for strength and guidance to be able to do my duty, not be cowardly and so forth. Later in the Luzon battles I would occasionally weaken and pray for a wound that would get me home. This always happened under heavy mortar or artillery fire. I suspect civilians don't realize how many soldiers pray to do their duty rather than for survival. I guess that the duty-prayer is more frequent with increase in rank, while the spare-me prayers decrease with an increase in rank.

The Other Side Prayed Too

One morning I had taken a long shot (maybe 200 yards) at a Nip going up a trail through a coconut grove. You couldn't tell for sure if I had scored, but my hand was resting on a downed tree when I fired, so I had been steady as a rock and the rifle was zeroed for that range. A Nisei interpreter was with me as I shot. That evening as we sat in our foxholes the interpreter came up. He said, "Lieutenant that was great shot; you got him." The guys responded as usual with "Way to go Jay." "Score one for our side." "File another notch," and some unrepeatable encouragements. But, there was deathly silence after he finished with, "Yes..., you shot him through the lungs, and he died reading his Bible."

For a week or so after that we were almost normal humans, but gradually, over the next week or so, most of us again acted unconcerned as veteran combat troops do, complete with an almost impervious shell over our true feelings.

Note: In 1982 in Winslow, Maine at a reunion of our 103rd Infantry I heard more about this incident. Apparently, Minor, one of the riflemen had fired at someone in the same area, so might have been the shooter. At the time the troops gave me full credit, probably because of my undeserved reputation as one of the greatest rifle shots in the history of the Army of the United States.

Combat Humor

Escaping from combat stress, predictably, takes some funny forms. For example, to help stay sane you try and laugh a lot — even in situations which would normally not be regarded as funny. For example, one day we laughed as enemy machine-gun bullets chased Robert Garmany across a rice paddy because he was a humorous and cherished guy who ran funny and "couldn't" get hit and he didn't. Bullets actually went between his legs.

Foster And Friendly Fire

One of the real cutups in L company, third platoon, was a slender New Englander by the name of Foster. He had a great sense of humor, but had also soldiered well in the rugged campaign on New Georgia Island (Solomons) for the Munda airstrip.

On a mission in New Guinea we came under some moderate rifle and machine gun fire from our own troops. We were hugging the ground when someone said, "Look at Foster." For a laugh, though lying on the ground, he had raised his rear end up as high as it would go — like an ostrich is supposed to do when it hides his head. He got his laugh and everyone felt better.

Basic Training Generated A Lot Of Jokes

Infantry basic training was pretty rough on the recruits in the Army and even worse in the Marine Corps. The Army took raw civilians, and in 17 weeks of training usually transformed them into something that resembled soldiers. You never had enough sleep and there was much physical and mental stress. Near the end of training, on the infiltration course, you crawled through barbed wire and explosions simulated artillery, while heavy machine gun fire was a foot or so over your back. If you panicked and stood up you were nearly sure to get hit. This was usually done in the mud. Needless to say, many post-basic references to basic training showed respect for the process.

For instance, one time in the battle for Luzon, in the rain, we were pinned down in a particularly nasty mix of incoming artillery, machine gun fire and mortars. Some GI yelled out, "Holy shit, this is nearly as bad as basic training!" Sometimes you had to laugh or cry, and tough guys aren't supposed to cry in that situation, so there was a lot of laughter, some of it not forced.

Mac And The Booby Trap

Nearly every place we dug foxholes we would put out booby traps just before dark to warn us of any approaching enemy. Hand grenades were most commonly used, but ration cans full of stones, flares and so forth were also popular. Everyone knew you didn't go outside the perimeter near nightfall without asking about the location of the booby traps. Platoon Sgt. McAllister failed to do this one night and hit the trip wire on a grenade. When it popped, Mac knew he had 4.6 seconds to find cover. He had an audience as he spent about 3.6 seconds running in one spot, trying to get up a muddy bank. As he finally made it and hit the ground, the grenade went off. His wildly churning legs and waving arms were a funny sight. There were gales of laughter, even before we knew he was okay.

My personal experience was that we had just about as many casualties from our booby traps as the Japanese did. But it did give us early warnings.

Battlefield Commissions

Most Army commissions are received after attending officers candidate school, from a military academy, or by completing a Reserve Officers Training Corps program in certain colleges and then graduating. The phrase "90-day-wonder" was often used to describe the second lieutenant who became an officer by completing basic training, sometimes other training, and then going through a physically and mentally demanding 90-day training program at Officers Candidate School (OCS). For the US Army infantry, this was usually done at Fort Benning, Georgia. After my basic training, I decided not to go to paratrooper jump school or officers candidate school (which was an alternative). Like quite a few others, I was eager to get overseas and was already tired of training. I didn't know how I'd do in combat, but I wanted to find out.

I was a rifle squad leader with the rank of Staff Sergeant when we made the Luzon beachhead on January 9, 1945. There were normally 12 men in a rifle squad, but we had 14 when we made the beachhead.

During wartime, in combat, some non commissioned officers are given a direct commission on the battlefield because of casualties among the officers and the need for combat experienced officers. The first American battlefield commissions were awarded in the Civil War. Napoleon did it regularly in his campaigns.

After we had been in combat on Luzon about 21 days, we were dug in on Mount Alava. The company commander called me to the CP (command post)) and asked whether I would like to be an officer. I had just turned 20 two months earlier, but was a combat veteran of two campaigns who had been overseas for about 14 months. However, I told everyone I was 22, you know, old. I replied, "Sir, honestly, I don't know, I haven't thought about it, and I like my squad a lot."

He said, "Well, think it over, you don't have to decide now."

I told some of the men in the squad and most of them urged me to take the commission. One, Frank Fecser (Cleveland, Ohio) said, "Think how proud your Dad and Mom would be." I didn't give it any more thought during the next days of combat. Then our unit was relieved and we hiked to a rear area. It was a vast improvement — we even had tents.

On February 15, the First Sergeant came in to our tent and said, "Gruenfeld, go down to Regimental Headquarters and get sworn in."

I said, "For what?"

"To be an officer."

So, I did. There were four of us and the ceremony took about 10 minutes, including time to pin on my gold bars (donated by an officer in our company). As I left the building and passed a Filipino soldier guard, he presented arms — my first salute. I learned later that, according to custom, I should have given him a silver dollar.

When a unit had heavy casualties, battlefield commissions were not uncommon. My platoon sergeant Loren (Mac) McAllister, (North Anson, Maine) was also commissioned. He had led the platoon when we made the beachhead. But I was somewhat unusual in being barely 20, a replacement and only a squad leader. Most field commission were given to veterans who had gone overseas in November 1942 (27 months earlier) and were Tech Sergeants or First Sergeants and were usually older. Mac was 25 or 26.

Now that I was an officer and "gentlemen" the usual procedure was move you to another part of the regiment. At first it looked as though I would lead a weapons platoon (machine guns and 60 and 81 millimeter mortars). But I had been a rifle squad leader in a rifle platoon, so want to stick with what I knew best.

The commander of the First Battalion (my new unit), Lt. Col. Lloyd E. Barron, (a fine leader) knew me, listened to my plea and gave me the last rifle platoon available in the 1st Battalion, (Second Platoon C 'Charlie' Company). Some thought I was making an unwise choice, because rifle platoon leaders, on average, have the shortest combat life of any infantry position. I suppose I disregarded this partially because the law of averages was already saying my chances of coming through unscathed were "damn slim and none" regardless of my rank. I had already been bandaid-wounded by shell fragments.

Mac, my platoon sergeant got a weapons platoon and didn't seem to mind. He had been in the army over three years, been through the brutal New Georgia campaign (Solomon Islands) and had been wounded on Luzon. Mac, though my superior in rank, was commissioned four days later due to alphabetical listing. I kiddingly commented that I was therefore senior to him. He remarked that he understood that "rank among Second Lieutenants was like virtue in a whore house." So, I was not a "90-day-wonder" from Ft. Benning, but I suspect some people thought it would be a wonder if I lasted 90 days. But I did — exactly.

Feb. 18, 1945

Dear Dad,

Please send some food, like sardines, crackers, etc.

This is just a short letter to you. As you can see by the return address it is Lieutenant Jay now. I was given a direct appointment without going to O.C.S. I guess it is a little more of an honor that way. Now the responsibility is greater. I (1996 note: should have said often) led my squad by being at it's head, but you can't control a platoon when you are lead man so that will be one difference. Just wish you were here so I could hear your's and Mother's advice and encouragement. We did a good job, Dad, and are damn proud of our outfit. (1996: See photo — Mom in new hat and infantry crossed muskets pin.)

Went to church this morning for the first time since leaving the ship, and really enjoyed it a lot.

Glad Uncle Frank shows some signs of improvement.

When I get the dope on exactly what the details are I will write them to Mother.

She sure looks great in her new outfit.

Thanks for your letter or the 22nd Jan., Dad, I enjoyed it and the clippings. That sure sounds like a real job that you have now. Dad, the Legion Post on N. Damen sent me a $3 money order. Thank them will you please.

Lots of love,

Jay

PS   Heard Giff had died, but he pulled through. He was shot up pretty bad. Sure am glad. He deserves a break.

1996 note: Giff, a squad leader and close friend was later killed by "friendly" — 155 artillery. War sucks.

Some Of The Humor Was Rough

This humorous episode happened after we had sustained very heavy casualties on Luzon.

One night we were being moved from one part of the line to another. Our promised three days of rest had been shortened to one and a half and the men were owly. They had seen how well the rear echelon troops had it; clean clothes, zero danger, beer and women and now we had to go back into combat while they had some time to play. I was riding in the cab of the two and a half ton truck with the rest of the platoon in the back. We passed through a small town that was crammed with rear echelon troops standing under corner street lights, all dressed up and carrying-on with the Filipino girls.

Suddenly there was uproarious laughter and cheers and shouts from my men. This went on for so long that I stopped the truck and went back to see what was going on. Some of the guys were nearly in hysterics but I finally was able to get the picture. There had been some pointed and shouted dialogue between my troops and the support troops at several lighted road intersections where the partying was going on.

Finally, at a lighted main street intersection, just as we were leaving the town, someone, I never found out who it was, stood up, yelled, "Grenade," and threw a hand grenade into the guys and gals. He had removed the TNT, but they didn't know that, and it popped like a live-one as he threw it. The place exploded into action. Men and women dove into drainage ditches, fell over each other as they tried to get away, ran like rabbits, and generally created a comic scene that the troops enjoyed immensely. And I mean immensely! The boys needed a good laugh and they got one. No one reported the truck number or we would have gotten chewed out, but good.

Looking back on it, now, it isn't nearly as funny. I hope no one got seriously hurt, took it personally or soiled their pants.

The New Platoon

Like anything human, platoons vary in quality. I was lucky and inherited a good one. The 1st Battalion had not been decimated in the Solomon Island campaigns so the noncoms were mostly young but very experienced soldiers. It wasn't unusual to have a 22 or 23 year old Sergeant who had been in the army four years, overseas 27 months and seasoned by two campaigns before Luzon. These were combat tested noncoms. Maybe a quarter of the enlisted men were also veteran, the rest being replacements of various vintages.

The platoon received about twenty new replacements at the time I arrived. One of them (Virgil Brumfield, Huntington, West Virginia) immediately made a positive impression on me, in an unusual way. Brum was relatively old, 22, had a wife and three children and had only been in the army about 6 months. He was a medium height, well-built blonde, German looking.

In my first group orientation meeting of the platoon with the replacements, naturally, most of the talking was done by the veterans. But when I related an incident where a soldier had run instead of standing fast, it was green-as-grass Brumfield, six months in the army, who said, "Why, that yellow son of a bitch." The old timers were taken aback that a tenderfoot should make such a comment. Over the next couple of days, I watched Brumfield show great physical strength and leadership while disassembling a stout fence (to get building material), and show

79

in other ways he was a pretty tough, savvy guy. He looked like he might be a first-class soldier.

First Patrol With The New Platoon

After about a week with the new platoon we moved back to a combat zone and I was told the second platoon would be reinforced and would be making a major patrol. I began thinking about the patrol.

As I have gone from age 20 to 72, I'm surprised that my basic thought patterns haven't really changed that much over time. (There will be more about the significance of this later in the section on Communications.) So, as I now remember what went through my mind when I learned about this first patrol, I suspect it probably wasn't all that different from what my thoughts would be now. Sure, now that I'm a well-trained, experienced business manager, and older, the thought format would be a little more complex and formalized, but the basics would be similar.

I knew that my future as the leader of these 40 veterans and green replacements was going to be strongly influenced by how I performed in our first combat assignment. And they knew their performance was going to impact their future relationship with me and with each other. Most of them, especially the replacements, doubtless spent considerable time hoping they would survive. As the leader, I spent considerable time hoping and praying some, that I would do a good job and our casualties would be low or zero.

The Patrol Objective

A battalion intelligence officer gave me a map and explained what we were to do. The enemy held the high ground, as usual. Their defensive positions were called the Shimbu line. My platoon, reinforced by a 60 millimeter mortar squad of 5 men, was to start at daylight and reconnoiter to the south a couple of miles, then turn east and try to cross a steep hill range. After turning east it was a couple of miles to a blacktop road. Our forces controlled the road to the south. If we got that far, trucks could bring us back. They expected we might make some contact with the enemy and we were to determine the strength of any positions we encountered. It sounded familiar and a little spooky, especially since we were covering a lot of distance and would probably return well after dark. The starting point was south of the town of Antipolo and the main terrain feature was Bench Mark 7, a high rocky hill held by the enemy. The Japanese were firing big rockets from BM 7 and we were to try and pinpoint the launching site.

I was able to brief the whole platoon on what we were to do. This logical and important part of patrolling was too often done in haste in a half-baked manner and sometimes not at all. Communication is important in any human activity. It's too bad that in combat, business and families, communications are seldom given a high enough priority.

It was a clear, hot and humid day as we started out. The leader of the lead squad leader said Brumfield and Joe Brionis, his buddy, wanted to be scouts, "Was that OK?" I said.

"Sure, we might as well see what they can do they do."

The two scouts were usually the closest to the enemy and there usually wasn't too much competition for the positions. We were in a loose single file (squad column) and the scouts were out 75 to 100 yards ahead since the country was pretty open.

We had gone about a half mile when we started to receive a few rounds of long-range rifle fire. They sounded a little like a cap pistol as they cracked overhead. Then you would hear a pop that told you where they were coming from. The pop was from the discharge of the rifle.

It didn't take too much experience before you could tell from the time between the crack and the pop how close the rifleman was. If the crack-pop was one sound, he was close. These shots were coming from 600 yards or more and we just kept walking. About 6 or 7 rounds had gone off when Brumfield said, "What's that?" I was about fourth in line and told him that was a sniper. He said, "Where is he? I'll go get him." This was pretty naive, but again showed he was an aggressive guy without much apparent fear.

After hiking for an hour or so, there was no more sniper fire and we had a nice interlude. Some Filipinos, three men and a women, were gathering cashew nuts and fruit. I had had a year and a half of pre-forestry at the University of Illinois and had seen drawings of the cashew fruit and nut. The fruit is peach-like with the nut sticking out of the end.

We seldom were around any friendly non-Americans in a combat situation and the troops enjoyed watching the harvest. So, we put out guards and took a break. To this day, I remember this refreshing change of pace with pleasure.

Action

The country we had been traveling in was gently rolling and fairly open with no roads and a few trails. As we approached a wide-open grassy area with a patch of trees behind it, I had the feeling that this was a place to be careful. We stopped about 300 yards from the timber. This was a lucky decision. After talking with the platoon sergeant (second in command), Johnny Herrick, and the platoon guide Larry Daley (3rd in command), both from Maine, we decided that Brumfield and I would scout the area before having the platoon cross the opening. The platoon was positioned so it could give us fire support if we had any trouble.

There were some small grassy mounds that provided good cover and Brum and I started out. I would cover him as he moved forward 10 or 20 yards at a time and hit the ground, and then he would do the same for me. It was hot and very quiet as we did this. As Brum approached the tree line the hair started to stand up on the back of my neck and I knew something was going to happen. Suddenly, while lying prone he brought his rifle to his shoulder and fired a couple of shots toward the trees which were about 30 yards away. I fired my eight rounds and reloaded. As soon as Brum fired, the platoon put a wall of fire into the trees. I yelled at Brum to come back and after he passed I followed him back to the platoon which was still laying down heavy fire.

Now I knew the Second platoon wasn't one where the men were reluctant to fire their weapons. Not firing was often a problem with green units.

After another brief strategy meeting with Herrick, Daley and the squad leaders we adopted the following plan for a probe of the enemy position. It was agreed that we would try to avoid a prolonged fire fight. Once we had a good feel

82

for what they had and where they were, we would pull back on my voice signal or Herrick's the platoon sergeant, in case I was put "out of service."

Most of the platoon would provide a base of fire from the left flank. I would be the extreme left man in the attack of Harlow and his squad. (Harlow was reputed to have killed more Japanese than anyone in the battalion). Herrick decided he would go with us, although we talked about his staying back so that there would be a senior guy in charge in case I got pinned down by enemy fire. We attacked in a wave with about five yards between men. The line used me as a guide and the right side of the line stayed slightly behind me, to avoid getting hit by our own fire. Our mortar squad was accurate with about 10 rounds of mortar fire right into the tree line as we advanced. The rifle fire from our support was accurate and heavy.

Soon we were within a few yards of the tree line and firing hard to keep them down. In the orientation talk to our new recruits, I had told them how important it was to count your shots so that you knew when your rifle was almost empty. I hadn't. On my left, out of the corner of my eye I saw a Nip rise up in a foxhole. I immediately jerked off a quick shot without really aiming. This would give me time for an aimed one. I aimed quickly and pulled the trigger, nothing happened. My rifle was empty! Others were firing at him and he ducked down as I dove for cover. He was about 20 feet away. I reloaded. Then pulled the pin on a hand grenade, let the handle go, counted two and then tried to delicately drop the grenade into his hole. I thought, "Oh shit, it's short", my exact thought, then it rolled straight and dropped into the hole and went off. Suddenly the air was full of pieces of equipment and man, I clearly saw a pack strap fly through the air. There were some cheers from our side who were now lying on the ground seeking cover and firing. Hand grenades kept going off and the rifle fire was heavy.

On my right, I saw someone dive behind a log and right after him came two Nip grenades. It was Sgt. Harlow. He had been ready to shoot a Nip who was in a hole and had his arm cocked to throw a grenade when his rifle jammed. Harlow dove for cover behind a log. Unfortunately for Herrick, he was behind the same log. The two grenades went off and I figured we had at least one fatality. But they were both only wounded.

Someone from behind us yelled, "Cover me," and I looked up to see our medic, Sgt. Harry Horne, running across the open ground and drop down beside the wounded men. It would have made a nice scene for a movie. In the bright sunshine with his medical aid pouches and equipment flopping it was a fine and welcome sight.

I had been told that Horne was "one fine combat medic, though a little different." It didn't take me long to tell he was different. When I met him, he was wearing shorts, sun glasses and a green Australian army officers shirt complete with grey epaulets (Gen. Patton never would have allowed that). And he always seemed to stay clean no matter how dirty the rest of us got (Patton would have liked that).

Harry patched Herrick and Harlow up. In a few minutes, he again yelled, "Cover me," and lurched off with his arm around Harlow's waist and Harlow's arm around his neck. Herrick made it out under his own power though hit pretty badly. No one else had been hit except Japanese.

It was time to pull back. So I yelled some orders, made sure there was plenty of fire support and we pulled back a few at a time with me last. The wounded men shouted to us that they had left their rifles behind the log 30 or 40 feet from the Nips. I wasn't thrilled about going after the rifles. However, the platoon was putting down so much fire that I felt pretty safe as I picked up the rifles and ran back crouched over lugging three rifles (30 pounds). It's usual in tense combat situations to say some strange things. Sometimes they are funny. As I got near our fire base I was yelling, "Rifles for sale, rifles for sale," it got a laugh.

We radioed back to battalion headquarters to report what had happened. I asked if they wanted us to try and take the enemy position or continue on our mission, hoping they would say "continue the mission." They said to continue and we all breathed easier. We still had a long way to go. The wounded were left with litter bearers and a few riflemen. Battalion was going to send a patrol down to assist them.

We had turned east now and were headed into some steep country that looked like a good defensive position. We saw a couple of enemy run into the jungle. While the platoon waited, Daley and I scouted downhill through an area of waist-high grass and drew enough rifle fire from 200 to 300 yards away that we hit the ground and started to crawl out. It was sticky-hot as hell and no wind. Larry said, "Boy it's hot, why don't we make a run for it?" I said, "Okay, who should go first?"

"You," he said, and I took off running back up the hill.

There were a few shots but nothing too close and I reached a covered position and hit the ground. Now they knew he would be coming, and were ready. As he ran up the hill there were bullets cracking all around. He dove to the ground about four yards from me and began pulling at his equipment. The first thing I saw was that a bullet had cut one of his pack straps and it was dangling loose. I said, "Are you okay?"

"Yeah, but look at this." He opened up his shirt front and there was a red line across his chest, that looked like it had been drawn with a piece of lipstick. The bullet had also broken his pipe. Close!

This near miss with Larry Daley was ironic. Daley was one of the veterans who had seen very little combat just due to the luck-of-the-draw. Only a couple of days after the beachhead, he was wounded. This was his first combat since getting out of the hospital. Later he told me that after this happened on his first day back, he didn't think he had a chance of surviving the war. But he did. Another thing about Daley's wounding was told to me by Harry Horne. Larry had a couple of pieces of mortar fragments in his stomach, but didn't want to leave the line. So, at Larry's urging, Harry went into his stomach, through the wound, three or four inches trying to find the fragments, but failed. (Note: Horne, like nearly all medics was not a medical doctor. He had taken infantry basic training and then transferred to the medics where he was trained in giving first aid.) Our medics were great.

There were a few soldiers that faked injuries, or even shot themselves to get off the line. But the great majority did more than their share of work under exhausting and dangerous combat situations. It would have been easy to get off the line. All you had to do was stop taking atabrine and malaria chills and fever soon would put you in the hospital. But few took this way out partly because each noncom was responsible for seeing that his men took their yellow bad-tasting pills.

We put the scouts out again, Brumfield and Briones, and sent them on a course just south of where the firing had come from. There were about two miles to go through the steep hills before we would hit the road, and it was well past noon. (See photos.)

Over The Mountain

We headed east. Harry Horne was feeling pretty good and when silence wasn't required, he was quoting snatches of Kipling poetry to me as we walked along behind the lead squad. I quoted some back, mostly from *Gunga Din* and *The Young British Soldier*. Kipling really captured the attitude of the soldier. It's a rare book on warfare that doesn't include Kipling quotes.

From *The Young British Soldier*

When yer officer's dead and yer Sergeant looks white,
Remember it's ruin to run from a fight.
Just take open order, lay down and sit tight,
And wait for supports like a soldier,
A soldier of the Queen.

After the war, Harry and I briefly collaborated on some pretty bad but sincere poetry. Here is the verse I wrote about him —

"If ever you were wounded and needed extra care
Our crazy Johnstown medic would reach you anywhere.
Many had the Silver Star for doing less than he
And if the wounded gave em' he'd sure have more than three."

The Japanese might have withdrawn since we weren't fired on as we passed near the source of the fire that had been directed at Daley and me. Soon we were in thick jungle climbing steeply uphill, often on jagged rock. The surface of the rocks was a series of broken blisters. The fractured edges of the blisters were sharp enough to cut shoe leather if you weren't careful. It was tough going, steep ground, heavy with vines and brush and we were tired and hungry. (Note: This year I learned from the radio man on this patrol, Corporal William (Mitch) Mitchell, Somerville, Massachusetts, that he did the entire patrol on a bar of emergency ration chocolate.) We took a break after a unique and kind of funny event.

I had moved up near the front of the platoon, just behind the scouts and the squad leader. Briones came back with a strained and sheepish look on his face, nearly in tears. He had part of his rifle in one hand and part in the other. Apparently, a vine had caught in the trigger guard of his rifle and pulled the trigger group out. The rifle held together temporarily but the next thing Joe knew his rifle was in two pieces. They couldn't find the missing piece. I had never heard of this happening before, or since. From behind a scowl, that was partly fake, (Joe was the kind of guy it was hard to remain mad at), I told him to have the medic tape his weapon together, put on his bayonet and pray that we didn't get in another fire fight. I suspect he did pray.

More Contact

Brumfield came back and whispered to us that he had heard voices. I thought, "Nuts, here we go again," and crept forward with him and the squad leader. By this time we were over the crest of the Mountain (steep hill to someone from the Western US, see photo) and thought we were within a half mile or so of the road. Soon there were loud voices shouting at each other and a dog was barking. It was Japanese. So we turned a little more south and continued, trying to be especially quiet.

About a half hour later we came to a blacktopped road. We had made it. Soon, one of our scout cars came by and a soldier told us they were expecting us at a road junction. We arrived at the junction just about dark.

Truck Ride In A Blackout

After we ate some rations, a Lieutenant oriented us on how we would be trucked back to our camp. He must have said at least three times that six bridges (not five or seven) on our route had been blown up by the enemy and the truck would have to leave the road and ford the creek or cross a dry creek bed. We were going to be paralleling a big fresh water lake (Laguna de Bay) on the south end of the Morong Peninsula.

Somehow we got the entire 40 or so men and equipment into one 2½ ton truck and started out. All we had for light were the little slits of blackout light from the truck headlights. A rifleman rode on each front fender.

It was slow going but we were well-fed, pretty content and on the way back to our base. And, no one had been killed. Our patrol had achieved it's objectives and we knew we had completed a tough but worthwhile job. The creek crossings took time but were without incident. Finally we came to the 7th bridge and the driver started confidently across, but slowly in the black night, thank God. Our men on the fenders started waving their arms and yelling for us to stop. We did. I got out and walked a few steps ahead of the truck and stared straight down about 50 feet into a dry creek bed. Seven bridges had been blown, not six. Such is war.

Note: Harry Horne said, recently, that he was sure that the tough- looking armed Filipino men who surrounded our truck at bridge seven were going to try and shoot us to get our weapons. I hadn't given it a thought.

We reached camp after midnight and staggered off to find a place to sleep. There was level spot with protection from small arms fire and we flopped. Another unit had sentries out, so we could just sleep. Maybe I should have had us dig foxholes but I didn't. That night we got a little incoming artillery fire but most of us slept through it.

Before dropping off into a deep sleep of exhaustion, I reflected on the day. I felt that my relationship with the men in combat was off to a good start. And it was obvious that the 2nd platoon was a honey. I was content. If an unlucky round of artillery had dropped on me, I would have died happy.

Postludes To The First Patrol

Non-infantry people reading this might not recognize that our performance on this patrol reflected that we were a well-rested, proud unit, recently brought up to full strength with high-quality replacements. Just three weeks before, we had been a battle-decimated, exhausted group of survivors. If I had led that group of survivors on the same patrol three weeks before, it would have had a different outcome. First, we would not have gone back to the Japanese position the second time. Second, I doubt that we would have had the physical strength to complete the patrol. On the lighter side, no one's rifle would have been taken apart by a vine.

A few days later, based on our information, our company of two hundred patrolled to the Japanese position we had probed. The enemy had pulled out.

The infantryman I had killed had been buried in his foxhole. His comrades had left on his grave a hand-size little silver saber wrapped in a cloth. The troops muttered a few words that acknowledged this was a nice touch. But that didn't keep someone from collecting the saber as a souvenir.

Our company dug in for the night after forming a perimeter on a trail just north of the vacated enemy position. Second platoon (ours) was on the southwest part of the perimeter. Just before dawn an enemy unit walked right up to the north edge of the perimeter. They were practically to our foxholes when our unit opened fire. It was a massacre. In the morning we scouted the area. I saw at least 30 bodies and we hadn't had a single casualty. A couple of the men said they wished the Nips had come in on our side of the perimeter. In an earlier engagement, I had collected a saber, and here added another one. It was a beauty. Neither of them made it back to the States with me.

Brumfield rapidly developed into a fine combat soldier. He was the only man I knew who, remained an aggressive rifleman, even when he had dysentery so badly that he just took a knife and split his pants to save time on the BMs.

Briones also became an excellent soldier. And had the best sense of humor in the platoon. He and Brum remained a pair on scouting assignments. Joe named the platoon "The Fighting Deuce" and many of the men called it that. On patrols I wore an olive-drab handkerchief knotted at the four corners, with the knots tucked out of sight. A poor man's beret. Many of the platoon did the same.

The platoon had good luck and went from success to success. Our casualties were low but many Japanese died. Our success was partly because we were used almost entirely on patrolling where our skill could be used to best advantage. We tried to be silent and careful and really knew how to use our weapons. The already good reputation of the platoon improved.

Compliment

About a month after the first patrol, probably the greatest compliment I have ever received in my life occurred due to another platoon having liberated some Nip sake. Two excellent combat noncoms in another platoon, which we considered the second best in the company, after drinking much sake, came up to me in a half-smashed, (make that three-quarters smashed) condition. In front of a couple of my noncoms they said they wanted to transfer to our platoon and would even take a reduction in rank. One of them was Francis Hitt, Reading, Pennsylvania a superb combat soldier and squad leader. The other was the platoon sergeant, Lew Olmstead. Transferring was of course impossible and they knew it. I was touched and a little proud, though I knew luck had a lot to do with our success. Hitt survived the war, but died in 1989 of cancer.

Return To Luzon, 1995

On January 13, 1995, I was able to re-walk a couple of miles of the First Patrol route. Appropriately, by the end of the day I was dog tired. The small mountain ridge that we crossed still looks rugged though only about 600 feet high. (See photo.) Some human habitation now exists where there was only rangeland. The vegetation has changed some, less grass and more woody vegetation. For instance now there is more cover where Daley and I were shot at. This time I noticed that there was a small mimosa-like plant that closed its

Luzon: The first patrol (dashes indicate patrol route) with The Deuce climbed this rocky hill headed east (from right to left). January 1995 photo looking south. Joe Briones lost the trigger-group out of his M1 Garand rifle in the dense jungle hear the top of this hill. Note bamboo foliage framing picture and big leaves of banana tree near home. There is no road here, just a trail.

leaves when touched. We had seen a similar plant in New Guinea.

There were many memories but no desire to make the First Patrol again it had been nearly perfect.

April 2, 1945

Dear Dad:

You ask about the cuts and scratches, Well, I've been nicked three times. Twice by grenades and once by artillery shrapnel. They were just nicks so did not accept the Purple Heart. I think its not right for a real wound to receive the same decoration as a scratch.

I didn't lose any time on the line they were that minor. On the last one they were throwing grenades from a cave and on about the 15th grenade I just turned sideways and ducked my head and a piece (2 little pieces) hit me right in the tail.

We really had a big laugh about that when we returned to our lines.

Dad this is The Enlisted Man's Prayer:

"Dear Lord, please divide the bullets
The way you do the pay
Mostly among the officers."

HA HA

Will write Ruth now. I hope to see this town soon. No time as yet. There is a Catholic Church built in the latter part of the 16th century.

Loads of Love, Luck and Good Health, Dad.

JAY

Thank Uncle A for the swell pinup picture will you. Its a LuLu. Don't tell Mom. That's one of the reasons I didn't take the Purple Hearts.

1996 Note: Dad said this was to be just between us men. But he told Mom right away.

Sympathy From An Artillery Major

Much combat humor is flamboyant and often gross. It's a part of communicating in a way that reduces combat stress as in the following happening.

Usually there is good rapport and mutual respect between the artillery men and the infantry they support. There was in our unit, but there are many incidents that strain the relationship. One time my platoon was alone on a hilltop outpost coded "Lively Lady." At night, the Nips controlled the surrounding ground. That day our 105 millimeter howitzer artillery had fired various concentrations of fire around us. Each separate concentration was given a letter designation so we could call for fire on a specific location. But powder temperature varies and what hit in a certain place at noon might not at midnight. That night we were getting enemy machine gun fire, so asked them to fire concentration "G." The shells were short and the first five-round salvo, all shells fell in or very near our perimeter, instead of on the enemy. But no one was hit. I knew the artillery major in charge, who was a pretty good guy. After we radioed and got the firing stopped I leaned on him some with comments like, "I know you guys really don't know where your rounds are going to hit, but next time would you please try and put some of them on the enemy." Also, when bullets were cracking just inches over our foxhole, instead of talking, I put the speaking end of the phone where he would receive a big earful of machine gun sound. After a minute or so of serious talk, including my description of how rough it was at outpost "Lively Lady," he said, "Gruenfeld, wait, do you hear that dripping sound?"

I bit and said, "No, what is it?"

"That's my ass bleeding for you." The guys liked that.

My Role

Just Getting The Job Done

I liked leading my platoon the "Fighting Deuce," as Joe Briones had named it. And, under false pretenses, I had part-time rather willingly assumed the difficult role some of the men had assigned to me — the role of fearless leader. Much of the time I was scared. But as I worked at trying to be a good platoon leader, the fear of dying was replaced by more time spent trying to determine how to do the job right. How to get the job done with minimum casualties. Finally, as with many others, certain combat situations ceased to bother me. If I knew that a small fold of ground shielded me from rifle and machine gun fire I was really pretty unconcerned even when the bullets cracked a few feet over my head. Even when in the open, sometimes it was easy to disregard small arms fire because you couldn't do anything about it, and fearless leaders and good soldiers were supposed to disregard it, in that situation. Mortar fire, since it came straight down on you was a different matter. I never got so I could relax under mortar fire. It was the worst ordeal to endure, with artillery fire second.

Fear was often less a problem in actual fighting than in the lulls between fights. Many times when in hot combat, throwing hand grenades and firing my rifle in face-to-face combat I wasn't afraid. You get charged up, the adrenaline is flowing, it's exciting. You often don't worry about much — for the moment — except getting the job done especially if you are fresh. However, once you become exhausted it's a different story. You finally become a zombie, almost without feeling.

94

Audie Murphy, our most decorated soldier in WW II, on page 243 of his book *To Hell and Back*, has a great description of combat exhaustion. This happened just after intense combat that earned him the Congressional Medal of Honor.

> *"As if under the influence of some drug, I slide off the tank destroyer and, without once looking back, walk down the road through the forest. If the Germans want to shoot me, let them. I am too weak from fear and exhaustion to care . . . except for a vague pain in my leg, I feel nothing: no sense of triumph; no exhilaration at being alive. Even the weariness seems to have passed. Existence has taken on the quality of a dream in which I am detached from all that is present. I hear the shells bursting among the trees, see the dead scattered on the ground; but I do not connect them with anything that particularly concerns me."*

Since I sometimes had to censor the platoons outgoing mail (only when no other officer could do it), I knew what was being written about me. Also, I'd get reports from men who had heard others talking about my performance in combat. Some of the men obviously didn't know that most of my occasional apparent lack of fear was an act. I suppose some of them thought, "well at least he is a good actor." And I have to admit I liked being with a fine group of combat soldiers, some of whom thought I was "not afraid of anything."

There was real physical danger in playing the role of fearless leader. Many men unnecessarily died or were wounded in the role, or had close calls, because the role playing overcame their common sense. Here is a personal example.

A Bad Decision

The platoon had been holding a hilltop for over a week. We were dug in a perimeter (rough oval) on one end of a horseshoe shaped ridge. The other end of the ridge, to the northeast, was dense jungle and slightly higher than we were and a rifle shot (150 yards or so) away. A couple of the men had heard that our new artillery FO (forward observer) had never seen a live enemy. So, without asking me, said they would take him out on the ridge and show him some Nips that were in foxholes about 500 yards to the north. They could be seen from a small saddle in the ridge just west of the other end of the ridge we were on. Since they were going out anyway I said I'd go along and we could take a look at the end of the ridge, where one of our men had though he heard digging. We reached the saddle with the FO and he enjoyed seeing live enemy.

Ed Barker a squad leader (Staff Sergeant) and I told the others in the patrol that he and I would scout out to the east on the ridge top trail. Ed was a tall lanky deer hunter from East Stoneham, Maine (the troops called him Abe). He had been in the Army since 1941, when the National Guard 43rd Division, had been activated. I had already had our machine gun squad in the perimeter alerted to what we were going to do, in case we needed support fire.

The foot trail, east from the saddle, was just a foot or so wide and ran through dense cogan grass, over eight feet high. Visibility was limited to, at the most, 10 or 15 yards. It was dead calm and hot as hell. As we moved quietly along the tension started to build up and I again had that feeling that something was about to happen. After we had gone about 150 yards the trail gained elevation and made two sharp switch back turns. As I slowly and carefully rounded the second switch back crouching over, I straightened up and could see fairly fresh dirt around a foxhole about eight feet away and slightly uphill. I signaled Ed, who was a few yards behind me, about the hole and that I couldn't see if there was anyone in it. Past the foxhole, to the east, the ground leveled out, but I could only see a few feet beyond the hole because of the dense grass and a bend in the trail. If I stood where I could look in the hole I would be shootable for anyone just up the trail. There were now a number of alternatives to be evaluated.

One option was to simply turn around and go back, and perhaps call for artillery or mortar fire on the fox-holed ridge, and come back later. But this was costly and it was very possible there wasn't anyone on the ridge. Or, I could drop a grenade into the hole, probably. But that would alert any enemy and the hole might be empty. Dropping a grenade in the hole and running didn't seem the right action for a fearless leader — I might miss the hole — and so forth. It was possible any enemy had heard some talking from our men at the saddle. Ed and I had been totally silent on our approach, I hoped. All this and much more ran through my brain. Maybe I wanted to impress Ed who was a crack soldier. So, by pantomime I signaled Ed that I would look into the hole, while being prepared to shoot at anything that was further up the trail. He came even closer to me where he, too, could see the foxhole. With great care I plotted exactly where I would place my feet, hold my rifle, pivot and even breathe as I took the three steps it would take to look into the foxhole. I was as tight as a drum.

In a split second I took the three steps, and as I pivoted to be faced up the trail I looked into an empty hole and looked up. Bang, a Nip in another foxhole shot at me from about 20 feet and missed. I shot him twice in the upper chest and fired a couple of more rounds up the trail. Anyone but an Ed Barker would have run, but as I ran the couple of steps back to where he was he fired about five quick shots up the trail. When I came even with him he ran and I stopped and emptied my rifle. I yelled so our men would know about where we were and because I usually yelled a lot in a combat situation. A lot of us did. The machine gun opened up in covering fire and we ran out unhurt and yelling like mad. One of the riflemen at the perimeter thought we were attacking the men in the saddle and shot once right at us. He missed. My luck held again.

17 April, 1945

Dear Dad,

Will start a letter to you before noon chow. Please send a length of fish line and some hooks.

Received your letters 189 & 190 day before yesterday. Well Dad, as I look at what we've been through the past couple of months I guess on the mental and physical end of the deal I guess I've done all right so far. You read about how we had to dig the bastards out. They are tough when dug in, and have support, but we lick hell out of them on patrol against patrol and man to man. They (as a general rule) are second rate shots.

Please send a deck of cards with Contract Bridge scoring.

Well Dad I'll sign off — keep giving me the old "haswasser" advise because its good.

Naturally do all you can for Mother.* Dad get a big bunch of carnations for Mother on Mother's Day will you?

Your Pal and Son
Jay

PS   Remember how I told you all the evenings I threw grenades after hours at Croft? Well its really paying off.

*   1996 Note: Mother's brother had died, she had been with him in California for several months.

Last Day As A Combat Effective
On May 15, after I had been a rifle platoon leader 90 days, we had "one of those days." The Division was driving to take Ipo Dam (40 percent of Manila's water supply) and as usual the Japanese weren't cooperating. There were casualties but, again, the Deuce had been pretty lucky.

Another platoon in our company got into serious trouble in an attack. They were on a steep, open ridge without cover, stopped from going forward by machine guns and being shot up from the rear by a large force of Japanese riflemen. Captain Galyea had replaced Captain Taylor from Wyoming. Taylor had been killed two days before. Galyea radioed for me to send over a squad. I didn't really consider not going along. We were down to two squads so I took Staff Sgt. Hollis Morang, Eastport, Maine, who had replaced the wounded Harlow, his assistant, Sgt. Harris Choate, and the other six or seven men and went over to help out. It was a mess, but we helped them out. The cost was too high. When it was over, Briones was dead from multiple wounds. He may have died in my arms as I gave him first aid. Brumfield got hit twice — the second time while being dragged out, and won the Silver Star in addition to the Purple Hearts. Dan Broderick, a solid soldier from Chicago, was also killed and others were wounded.

After we were engaged, the captain asked me to send a non-com and four men to another part of the fight. Morang and the four others who went were all either killed or wounded.

Microcosm Of True Feeling

This last day as a functioning warrior provided a microcosm of true feeling behind the role I was playing. In the middle of the red-hot fire fight, Morang dropped into my foxhole. He had two ugly purple-edged holes in his face where a .31 caliber bullet had entered and exited (in medic terms, he had a through-and-through wound). It was ugly but not serious. He told me, "You gotta get over there. Lt. Mullins is hit and nearly everyone is hit. It's a mess."

"Staying calm" I opened a sulfa packet and prepared to shake sulfa into the holes — it wasn't necessary to shake — I just held the packet above the wound and my hand was shaking so much the powder came out easily. After I got "over-there," I tried to help, but just added to the mess by being hit twice.

Note: Mullins survived a head wound that caused a fever of 108 degrees. Jan and I visited with Hollis in 1975 at Eastport, Maine and he looked great. Just a couple of extra little wrinkles in his face.

Pfc. Bert Johnson, the medic who had replaced Harry Horne, (hepatitis got Harry) got hit, but kept giving first aid to about seven wounded under fire. I wrote him up for the Distinguished Service Cross (see below), but he got nothing, not even a promotion. This is a rare sore spot from my combat time, since an officer who reportedly did far less got the Silver Star. Unfortunately this wasn't all that unusual.

Most vets will agree that medals, especially among the officers, don't mean that much. And most men that received medals will tell you that there were many who deserved it more than he did — but got nothing, especially those who died.

I was glad to leave. Over four months of nearly continuous combat had exhausted me mentally. Maybe I would have stayed on the line if the arm wound had been the only one — but it would have only been an act.

May 20, 1945

Manila Hospital

Subject: Recommendation for the Award of Silver Star or DSC to Pfc. Bert Johnson (Medic).

In the Ipo Dam area Luzon, 15 May, time 1700, the 2nd and 3rd platoons of Company C 103rd Infantry, were in the attack. Casualties were heavy. Pfc. Johnson, 2nd platoon medic, while exposed to heavy enemy small arms fire risked his life time after time in giving first aid to seven wounded men. Johnson also supervised and took part in the evacuation of the severely wounded men. Although wounded in the shoulder early in the fight, Johnson stayed in the fight and continued to give aid to the wounded.

Johnson's daring actions doubtless saved the lives of some of his fellow soldiers and he was a magnificent example for the men around him. His heroic behavior was far above and beyond the call of duty.

Being one of the severely wounded men I was an eye witness to PFC Johnson's actions and certify to the truth of the above statements.

J. Jay Gruenfeld, 2nd Lt.
Platoon Leader, 2nd Plt.

On my last day as a functioning warrior, I was hit at two different times. The first was what we called a "Golden Wound," — the type that got you off the line or home without doing any severe damage. It was through the right arm just below the biceps and missed the bone and caused only a little nerve damage. I probably could have continued. But, as Bert started to work on me I was shot through the hips. A rifle bullet entered my left hip, jogged around my spine and exited my right hip after shattering the bone.

My Near-Death Prayer

The shot through the hips was the first time I had been knocked out, and I was falling downhill from the grasp of a medic (Pfc. Bert Johnson, Richmond, CA) who had started to treat a bullet wound in my arm. It was as though I was getting a massive electric shot as I floated down into a dark void. I said, rather unemotionally to myself, "So this is the way it feels to die," and then spontaneously began to recite the Apostle's Creed, "I believe in God the Father Almighty ...." At this point, I regained consciousness and immediately tried to move my legs. They moved, even though I couldn't feel them.

By coincidence, the first six words US Army retired Colonel David H. Hackworth used to describe his thoughts when death appeared eminent were the same as mine. He said, "So this is the way it is, what an uninspired way to go." (*About Face*, page 179 — a great book on Korean-Vietnam Combat.)

Luckily for me, the arm shot was from a .31 caliber bullet and the through-and-through hip wound was .25 caliber. The doctor who looked at the X-rays said that if the bullet hadn't jogged it would have cut my spine. Talk about luck!

Johnny Herrick had returned from the hospital so he was now the leader of the badly depleted 2nd Platoon. In 1981, at the only regimental reunion I have attended, I learned that after my last day only eight were left out of the forty plus who had started and we had received a couple of additional replacements. But there were a substantial number of non-battle casualties, especially from disease and infections.

It could have been much worse. A replacement in the platoon had a mortar or artillery shell explode in his foxhole with him and wasn't scratched.

May 19, 1945

Dear Folks,

My arm is kind of beat up so excuse the writing. Mail will be a long time catching up with me so I won't have anything to answer. I am as always doing OK. A couple of Jap bullets put me out of shape in a hurry. However, I am lying on my side on a cot so I think the handwriting is pretty darn good.

I might as well tell you I am hit in the right biceps (no fracture) and another one caught me through both hips so I have a long rest ahead of me. I am in no pain and the medics are swell. I feel fine mentally too. I just played with fire and got burnt that's all.

Mom please send 1 $1 bill every other letter for ten letters, I'm broke.*

Don't worry and I'll write when I can.

Loads of Love & Kisses

Jay

I will let you know as soon as I get a semi permanent address.

* 1996: Prior to an intra-platoon poker game at the beginning of the Ipo Dam campaign I had $32. My non-coms won it all.

1995: At Annual Reunion of the 43rd Infantry Division, from left Ed Hoe, New Jersey, commander of C Company 103rd Inf. Regiment during Luzon campaign, Bill Mitchell, Somerville, Massachusetts, radioman, Harry Horne, Jennerstown, Pennsylvia medic. Class veterans. All have at least one significant war wound that merited a Purple Heart medal, Mitch has two. See text about Mitch's last combat day and Nip saber.

Luzon: looking north, Ipo Dam in next valley; site of last day (May 15, 1945) as an effective combatant. Part of the ridge where The Deuce was decimated. Mitch staggered through this area after being wounded. That night it took eight hours for Filipino litter bearers to carry us wounded to where we could be loaded on a jeep that was then towed by a dozer to a road and an ambulance. No choppers then. July 1964 photo, grass was even shorter in 1945.

103

April 15, 1943 with Dad: had just been inducted into the Army at Ft. Sheridan, Illinois.

U. of Illinois 1945 soon after V J Day with cousin John F. McMahon Alpha Phi Sorority House (Ruth's). John ran high altitude chamber at San Antonio Aviation Air Cadet Center. He used to say "There's no flak at SAAAC." Great guy.

1945 Mom in new outfit. This photo was enclosed in letter to me received soon after Luzon beachhead. Dad's note on back of Mom's picture: "This was taken at the lake. It was a dark Sunday. In the first part of Jan. '45. Gee she is a swell Mother Jay and a real soldier. She always will say to me our Jay boy is a real soldier and we must be also. Dad" She was, as were millions of other mothers.

Luzon January 1995. On Hill 600 where our usually helpful air corp blew C Company off the top of the hill after we suffered many casualties to take it. Robert Garmany L Company, as mentioned in the text, ran across one of the rice paddies in the background, pursued by bullets from a Nambu machine gun — while we laughed, because he ran funny and we "knew" he would make it. He did.

Manila April '45: Three members of "The Deuce" 2nd Platoon, C Company, 103rd Inf., 43rd Div. Ray McGrath, Pottsville, Pat Patterson, DesMoines, Iowa, Pat Chiaccio, New Jersey.

My guide on Hill 600 was a veteran of the Bataan Death March.

With Filipino veterans from Pozorrubio at Lingayen January 9, 1995, 50 years after the beachhead.

Tokyo, 1995 author and friends: I was returning from the Lingayen, Luzon beach-head 50th Anniversary Celebration. Doing business with the Japanese is a pleasure, especially after hours. What a change 50 years makes.

107

Reflections on the War

Dropping The Atom Bomb

I think the atom bomb should have been dropped on Japan, but not on Hiroshima. When the atom bomb was dropped in August of 1945, I was lying in an Army Hospital bed in Louisville, Kentucky, recovering from wounds. My immediate reaction to the announcement of the bomb drop was, "Why did they drop it on the women and kids?"

Mostly this spontaneous reaction came from having read, in the middle 1930's, a fictional account of a future World War. This was a serialized story in a magazine. The final chapter in the story told of the discovery of an atom bomb by the United States. We were fighting the Germans, Japanese and the Russians and were almost licked when we discovered the bomb. Our scientists convinced the Germans that we did have the bomb and they surrendered. But, the Russians didn't, so we dropped the bomb. Unlike the 1945 actual happening, in the story we dropped the bomb, as a demonstration, in the Russian steppe — and probably killed only a couple of jackrabbits.

I must have been about twelve when I read this and remember thinking that the author had it right. Americans wouldn't drop the first big bomb on a bunch of women and kids.

If my combat infantry units had been asked whether the first bomb, of the two we had, should be dropped on a purely military target rather than a city like Hiroshima, I'm sure that the vote would have been overwhelmingly in favor of sparing the women and kids from

108

the <u>first</u> bomb. The vote might have been 5 or 10 to one — even if we had been told the US had only two bombs. As infantry, we were mostly in our late teens or very early twenties and largely idealistic on the subject of unnecessarily killing women and kids. The vote would have been hugely in favor of dropping the second bomb where it would do the most to shorten the war. Recent conversations with McAllister and others confirms this. To provide a basis for my opinion on how such a vote would have come out, here are two examples of our idealism and yes, perhaps foolhardiness.

Idealism

In early February 1945, our 3rd platoon of L Company, 103rd Infantry Regiment, 43rd Division, was a veteran combat infantry unit. We had suffered heavy casualties. I was a rifle squad leader.

A Filipino civilian came to our outpost, as they often did, and reported that three enemy soldiers had just been seen entering a sugarcane field nearby. Ten of us volunteered to go out and try and get them. When another rifleman and I arrived at the place where the enemy had been seen, the other eight, including our platoon sergeant, Loren McAllister, a relatively old guy of 25 or 26, had already agreed on a plan.

The sugarcane, which hid the Japanese, was nearly mature and would burn well. In addition, there was a brisk wind. So burning the field to flush the enemy was an alternative. But since the Filipinos were desperately poor and this was their only crop, our men decided we would make a pass through the sugarcane, without burning. I agreed to go along with the plan, but was glad I hadn't had to make the decision.

About six of us got in a skirmish line (wave) spaced about five yards apart. We walked as silently as we could through the field while the others waited to fire at any Nips who ran out. Visibility in the field was a maximum of three to thirty feet and we were all pretty scared and tense. What saved us was the wind rustling the dry parts of the cane and covering our noise. Mac and I each made a kill and we had no casualties. We emerged, shaken, from the cane to learn that eight enemy had run out of our field and across a thirty-yard wide open field into more sugar cane. This time, four men

109

went to the upwind end of the field and set it on fire. We eliminated six more and there were two suicides. A large group of Filipino farmers cheered. We had no casualties, but had taken a big risk.

Another Example Of Combat Idealism

Chalmus Brammer, a fine soldier and good friend mentioned previously, was a rifle squad leader in another company of our regiment when I heard he had been badly wounded. It was because he and his patrol were trying to protect a couple of women. A Japanese unit was in a grass house. The normal tactic would have been to grenade and burn the house and get the enemy as they came out. But there were also women in the house. So Bram and another soldier tried to sneak in at night and use only rifles. They made some kills but were both seriously wounded. Chalmus still walks with a bad limp and is lucky to be alive.

I wrote this atom-bomb piece for two reasons. First, to criticize where the first atom bomb was dropped, and second, to see if any of my readers have read that same piece of serialized fiction that I read in the middle thirties. I want to read it again and see who the author was, but I can't locate it.

Lesson For The U. S.

Dropping the first atom bomb on women and kids cost the United States a good part of its worldwide idealistic image, needlessly in my opinion. If such a mammoth decision is faced again, God forbid, let's hope the troops whose lives are to be saved are consulted for their input. (Want to bet?)

Combat Wounds

As I think back on the injuries, the memories are bittersweet (see photo 1995 of Hoe, Horne, Mitchell). One of my favorite stories is about Bill Mitchell, Somerville, Massachusetts. It occurred the day we both received our last wounds. This was verified by an eye witness. Mitch was hit hard by a bullet that entered the front of his right shoulder and exited to the left of his backbone. The enemy fire was intense and you could see bullets hitting everywhere since the only ground cover was short grass and it was a very steep hillside (see Ipo Dam photo). There was a dead Nip officer in a foxhole who had a nice saber. Despite the heavy fire Mitch, stopped, bent over and tried three times with his left hand to get the sword. But each time his rifle's sling slipped off his shoulder and he finally gave up and staggered to safety, with his rifle. Talk about combat-crazy. He stumbled by me looking mighty gray. I thought he had had it. Note: From a soldiering standpoint, Mitch's effort to get the saber was unprofessional. But it showed the kind of spirit that most of us civilian soldiers admired, and professionally he didn't leave his rifle to get a saber.

Two weeks later Mitch and Brumfield walked up to my bed at the hospital on Biak Island, Netherlands East Indies. We had gone there on a Dutch hospital ship, the Maatesuuker.

Mitch was walking fine, but still looked gray and had a cough. I turned him so the bullet exit and entry holes were lined-up and using my limited knowledge of anatomy said, "Are they sure that bullet didn't get your lung?" He said the X-ray didn't indicate that. When he got back to the States, they discovered he had been walking around with a collapsed lung and had pneumonia.

Brum had been shot through the knee and after he had been treated, a bullet put two big ugly holes in his back — not serious but painful. He then in shouted expletives complained to the Nips about hitting a poor guy again. I was lying within a few feet of him, having been hit twice, and thought something that, had I been an officer in an English regiment and an Oxonian might have come out, "Really ole boy, don't complain, this isn't a bloody cricket match you know." But his being strong enough to shout made me feel good.

Brum was on crutches and said the knee "hurt like hell." Back in the States they put him in a cast. The bullet had broken a bone.

Note: These are not complaints, just facts. Our medical treatment averaged excellent — probably the best in the world. Combat medics must have been one of the most revered groups in the war. Their casualties were very heavy as they treated the wounded. And some of these men were conscientious objectors who did not carry a weapon. Harry Horne, our medic, wasn't exactly like that. He carried a weapon, used it, and was the demolition man for the platoon.

Don Brookhart, another member of the Deuce wounded on that bad day (May 15, 1945), came in, maybe the same day, also on crutches. As he was running, a bullet went through his foot just below the ankle and didn't hit anything important. After the war I learned that Brookhart had been a rodeo cowboy before going into the service. All I knew was that he had been a fine replacement and nice guy. Too many times you didn't get to know the replacements very well and they were gone. Normally though since you checked the foxhole location and general situation every evening you at least had some contact with everyone.

Casualty Communications Lag In Combat

In heavy combat, we focused on survival and getting the job done; the latter especially if you were a noncom or officer. Sometimes people in your platoon would be missing, and until you talked with the medic, maybe weeks later, you didn't know if they had been killed, wounded or evacuated, especially on the non-battle casualties. This was more true when I was a squad leader than as a platoon leader.

In the Deuce and previously in the 3rd platoon L Company, we lost several people to blood poisoning. They would get a small cut or scratch a mosquito bite too much and then there would be flies all over the cut. You tried to keep it covered but you were sweaty, the bandage would get pulled off by the brush and sometimes white wasn't what you wanted to wear in a combat situation. The flies may have been on decaying flesh and soon you would have an infection and abscess. If a man had several of these on his hands and arms, sometimes a red streak would start up his arm and he would be sent to the rear. I saw these red streaks at least three times. Blood poisoning was serious and these men never came back while I was there. Hepatitis, yellow jaundice, malaria and dengue fever were other diseases that commonly caused non-battle casualties.

During the early New Guinea campaigns, examples were Buna and Guna, I remember reading that a medic said, "If we had taken everyone off the line who had a fever of 101 or over we wouldn't have had anyone left." Atabrine normally kept the malaria symptoms down when used regularly, but there were many other bugs. In the two platoons I was in, I don't think we lost anyone to malaria.

Lt. Evart "Hank" Henry, now Puyallup, Washington ex-37th Division and I were wounded on Luzon within a week of each other and came down with our first malaria attack within a week of each other in late June 1945 in Nichols General Hospital, Louisville Kentucky. He was in the next bed. After being wounded we stopped taking atabrine and the malaria parasite eventually caused the malaria symptoms. Hank only lasted two days after receiving his battlefield commission.

My last malaria attack occurred after the war when I was a forestry student at Colorado A&M, Ft. Collins, CO. I had a 105 fever and the shakes, but took a Geology test and then boarded the train for home and the Christmas break. Most of the students knew I was having a malaria attack. I turned my paper in early and as I left the classroom and headed for the train, in a very shaky loud voice said, "Meer-rry Chris-ss-mas — it got a good laugh. (Only a B on the test though.)

Time Magazine Reporter's Combat Visit

We were on an outpost in April, 1945 when Gilbert Cant a senior editor of *Time Magazine* spent a night with us. It was atypically quiet combat-wise. Horne wanted to simulate a night attack complete with grenades and automatic fire to give Gilbert something to write about, but I vetoed. Cant had spent a lot of time at Douglas MacArthur's headquarters at Hollandia, New Guinea. So the next morning, just before he left I asked him if the General was as much of a showboat as they said.

He put his hand on my shoulder and said, "Jay, the stage's greatest loss was when MacArthur decided to go to West Point."

The troops enjoyed that. Cant wrote my folks when he returned to the States and then wrote again when he heard I had been wounded. Good guy.

Biak Island Reflections

The Biak hospital days were quality time for me. I was safe for a while which was a relief and able to visit with a couple of my men — my-boys (take your choice) and others — even an occasional lady nurse. When the Doctor said I was going to be "evacuated" (sent back to the States) my new found combat-maturity left for a few seconds and I must have sounded like a kid as I laughed and shouted for joy. In some ways, I was nearly as mature as I would ever be but heck, I was only 20 and a half and sometimes the immaturity showed. Come to think about it, it still does.

A Bridge Too Far

Veteran troops are sometime not what you want when taking a tough objective. They know too much about what "satisfactory performance" is and sometimes can't be forced to go beyond that point. Here is a comment on green troops.

The great book *A Bridge Too Far* by Cornelius Ryan, describes the World War II battle for a bridge at the town of Arnhem on the Rhine River. The British First Airborne Division, one of the finest in the world, took the bridge after a parachute jump and heavy fighting. The Division was then almost totally destroyed when British troops failed to break through the surrounding Germans.

While at Oxford I read the textbooks on World War II used at West Point, loaned to me by a Rhodes Scholar. In one of them the British Corps commander who led the forces that failed to break through, is quoted as saying, "Oh, if I had had one green division."

His point was that a well-trained green division that had not previously suffered many casualties, might have kept attacking long after more experienced soldiers would have stopped. A more general corollary to this is that young people sometimes accomplish great things, because they didn't know it was impossible.

A Further Thought On The Arnhem Disaster

I think that if my platoon had the mission of breaking through to, say an Australian unit, we would have fought even

114

a little harder than breaking through to our own. Maybe I'm wrong, but I think national military pride is a great motivator. But the Brit-US military relations would have really ruptured if it had been a US corps that had failed to breakthrough to the British First Airborne, so I suspect the Brit-Brit tactic was best.

Hollywood Infantry Combat Scenes

My guess is that most combat veterans seriously watching a movie with John Wayne et al. in a combat situation are thinking to themselves -- "For crying out loud -- Spread out!" Because, beginning in basic training you are constantly warned that missiles are directed toward groups so to survive, keep your distance from your buddies. Wayne & company always seem to be surrounded by enough bodies so that one hand grenade would WIA (Wounded in Action) or KIA about six people. That ain't the way the crack outfits do it.

Some of our 43rd Division went through a harsh learning period on Luzon. One day we were spread out lying down preparing to attack, in view of the enemy we knew, since it was open country and they held the high ground, as usual. One of the men in another company, that we could see clearly across a shallow valley, got up and walked over and flopped down next to another man. This danger was compounded when they were joined by a third. I yelled back at several men my squad that could see this. "Don't ever do that, they are just asking for it!" In no time at all, Pow! a knee-mortar round at least wounded all of them. There had been zero mortaring before then.

Sure in a movie it's supposed to be entertaining not factual. At least they don't show John Wayne in training films -- I hope.

We had a worse example of lethal-grouping a few days later when Nip artillery that had been silent that day, watched a 3rd battalion command post meeting assemble. I witnessed the following incident from about 300 yards. It is described in the official Army history volume *"Triumph in the Philippines,"* page 150.

"An incautious grouping ... brought down fifteen well-placed round of 75mm artillery fire. Within minutes four company commanders were killed ... seven enlisted men were killed." Over 39 were reportedly wounded. There were foxholes but too few. Trees and a rock wall combined to spread fragments lethally. I think there were only three CO's killed (including ours of L Co.) plus a battalion staff officer and it may have been 77mm. After watching and hearing the calls of "Medic!", I went over to a nearby unit and suggested that all the litters they had would be needed. So, spread-out Hollywood.

Forest Wars

Some of you may wonder at my warlike reference to the debates over the use of our public forests. But those of you who are familiar with the politicized debate over the management of the Nation's forest land know that terms like battle, war, combat, et cetera are appropriate.

Forests are dear to me. I chose forestry as a career because I love forests and wanted to be in a profession that would allow me to spend time in the forest as part of my work. The trauma of my infantry combat made me desire working conditions that would be relatively pleasant and, for example, not be subject to the hurly-burly of an attorney's life. I wanted to help improve the management of forests, and in a small way I have been successful. This desire to learn about forests is what prompted me to get two graduate degrees that had a forestry emphasis. Though the Oxford Diploma in Forestry came after my principal work had been in Politics, Philosophy and to a lesser extent Economics, I did do a thesis that had lumber trade as the primary subject.

So naturally, after the three purple hearts from World War II, and three degrees and about 47 years of experience in tree growing, harvesting and marketing I know something about the problems of forestry. And recognize that the people problems are, ultimately, more important than the tree problems. Better than most, I know what the trade-offs are and, of course, have some firmly held opinions on how forest management in the United States can be improved. But let's talk a little more about the relevance of the warlike terminology.

At age 72, it's unlikely I'll be engaged in any more infantry combat, but I will continue to be involved in the battles over how our public forests will be managed.

The loggers, mill workers and their families who have been so unfairly treated under the Endangered Species Act and other flawed legislation are the combat infantry of the forest management wars and I'm on their side.

Oxford
University Days

University Of Oxford Time
September 1949 To December 1950

In August 1949, wife Barb and I were living just north of Mt. St. Helens at Spirit Lake Lodge, just below Spirit Lake on the Toutle River. Barb was cleaning rooms in return for our rent, and I was logging for Weyerhaeuser up Coldwater Creek — a northern tributary of the Toutle. The region was thick with fine Douglas fir timber. At that time, it was called old-growth Douglas fir, over mature timber or yellow fir — the timber cruiser name for 400-plus-year-old Douglas fir that had yellow colored wood. Now, some would call them a politically astute, appealing name — Ancient Trees. When St. Helens erupted, it destroyed, in some cases atomized the old growth, and all other vegetation, in a radius that went 10 to 15 miles north of the mountain.

I often fished the outlet of Spirit Lake near the lodge and store run by Harry Truman, who is now immortalized in folk lore. He was a crusty old former sea captain. At my age, I can envision much worse ways to go than Harry's. When the mountain erupted he died in the place he loved, probably holding a partly full bottle of bourbon.

In August 1949, a telegram arrived offering me a lucrative Fulbright Scholarship to study at the University of Oxford. Deciding whether to leave my chokersetting job ($1.63 per hour, which wasn't bad) and go to Oxford, for more net money was easy. However, setting chokers on cable logging operations gives invaluable experience to a forester. You learn the basics of logging, including the language. No matter how much you have learned in another field (like the Armed Services), logging experience teaches you a lot about people skills, teamwork, leadership — and how to survive. But after five months and the inevitable several near accidents, I knew that "diminishing returns" had set in on my logging learning curve. Doubtless, I'd learn more at the University of Oxford. There, I'd have less likelihood of receiving a logging "Purple Heart" to go with those from the war.

The high regard I have for logging experience is summed up in the following.

Suggestion: I strongly urge every forestry student to try and get some logging-related experience before taking that first job out of college. It is a valuable part of the forestry experience and gives greater employment credibility, particularly if his or her ultimate work relates even indirectly to trees.

Note: Rex Allison, my hooktender logging boss and a best friend, had only a certain level of sympathy for girls that wanted to log. Late in his career, when he was Woods Manager at Weyerhaeuser's Coos Bay logging operation, he put an anvil in his office that weighed a couple of hundred pounds. He told the girls who wanted to log, to simply carry that anvil across the office. Don't think any did though some of them probably could have but recognized a no-win situation.

What To Study At Oxford

Early on, I made what proved to be a wise decision, based on a correct assumption. It seemed to me that going to Oxford, with my Masters Degree in Forest Management, and studying mostly forestry, would by like going to M.I.T. (Massachusetts Institute of Technology) and taking home economics. Even though I could get a forestry doctorate in two years, without languages, since Oxford, being Oxford assumed that with a graduate degree you "are surely proficient in a second language."

My war experience and education made it apparent the forest management people problems were far greater than the tree problems. This was coupled with the assumption that foresters were often better with trees than with people. So it was easy to decide on PPE, politics, philosophy and economics. My formal course work was entirely politics and philosophy with a thesis on an economics related subject.

One of the attractions of the University of Oxford is that the system is very flexible. You can study what you want to a much greater degree than at almost any American University. This is true at both undergraduate and graduate levels. I have to smile imagining our President at Oxford.

Bill Clinton would have had a ball at Oxford, especially since he didn't get a degree. But opportunities at Oxford University are so great that he must have learned much that helps him as president.

Oxford Stimulates

At Oxford, most students are striving hard to be intellectual. Even the bull sessions are at a higher intellectual plane than at the average American university — my opinion.

The Oxford system is so unstructured that it's possible for many to coast through and still get a degree. It might be a "third" rather than a higher class, but still a degree. As a graduate student I could have attended zero lectures, given a mediocre performance in the tutorials, spent very little time writing a poor thesis and probably still obtained a Diploma. Instead, like most Americans I'm sure, I worked harder intellectually than I ever had before or since. Never before had I had headaches from just thinking.

My Oxford college, Exeter, was founded in 1314 AD and its longevity was only seventh among the 27 colleges, which collectively are called the University of Oxford (even though most of us refer to it as Oxford University).

The system of education used at Oxford varies significantly with the subject to be studied. Training in some of the physical and biological sciences is more like the United States system than if you study principally politics and philosophy, as I did. In addition to course work I did a thesis. My thesis subject was topical, if not succinct.

"An examination of the present competitive relationship between the Lumber Industries of British Columbia and Washington-Oregon, especially regarding the United Kingdom and Eastern United States Markets."

123

An Opinion On The Thesis From Colonel Greeley In 1951

In 1950, one of the best known and most respected people in US forestry was William B. Greeley, who led the West Coast Lumberman's Association, and had been a very effective Chief of the US Forest Service. Many called him "The Colonel" due to his rank during World War I as the head of the Tenth Engineers, a forestry and saw milling unit that operated in France.

During the writing of my thesis, I had received some helpful comments and statistics from the West Coast Lumberman's Association staff. They expressed interest in seeing a copy of the completed thesis and I sent one. I was amazed and pleased when in early 1951, I received a three-page, single-spaced letter from the Colonel with perceptive comments on what I had written.

Today, 45 years later, one part of the letter is prophetic relative to timber production from British Columbia in competition with Washington-Oregon.

The following excerpted from William Greeley letter dated February 5, 1951:

There is an important factor affecting the competitive situation for the long range ahead, that you mention but to which I do not think you do justice. That is the relative progress of the two regions in forestry. I will venture the statement that Western Oregon and Washington are twenty years ahead of Western British Columbia both in protection from fire and in reforestation. This progress is partly due to the vigorous policy of sustained yield administration on the federal holdings which comprise 53 per cent of the standing timber now remaining in Oregon and Washington; also to a very vigorous development of private tree farms, intensive utilization of wood, purchases of cutover lands, tree planting on a large scale, etc. Western Oregon and Washington have close to four million acres of private tree farms, dedicated to continuous timber cropping. They are vigorously inspected and kept up to scratch, or stricken off the list. This means about one third of our private woodlands are definitely on a sustained yield basis of forest management or headed in that direction. And there are easily another 500,000 or 750,000 acres that are moving in the same direction but have not yet been accepted as tree farms.

British Columbia's progress in this direction has been much more recent and much more limited. British Columbia is going to feel, in my judgment, much more seriously than Oregon and Washington the pinch of raw material during the period when the industry is compelled to pass over from virgin forests to second-growth forests as its main source of supply.

Very sincerely yours,
W.B. Greeley, Vice President

British Columbia's forest harvest is now dropping significantly, partly due to what the Colonel had foreseen. What Mr. Greeley could not foresee was that in the Pacific Northwest political action that prohibits tree harvest on most federal commercial forest lands has largely prevented the Pacific Northwest from capitalizing on less competition from British Columbia.

Oxford's Educational Objective
Oxford's primary educational objective is to Teach Students To Think. I can't quote an official source for this statement, but it is common knowledge.

The academic system emphasizes working-on-your-own rather than requirements such as attendance at lectures. Based on my experience, most knowledge is gained in decreasing order of importance, from:
* working-on-your-own
* tutorials
* functioning in an intellectual environment
* lectures

A rather unique and very expensive method of teaching people how to think is to use the tutorial system. That is the_method used at Oxford. This is how the system was used when I was there, and things change slowly at this distinguished university.

Tutorial System

During my time at Oxford, this was how the tutorial system functioned:

The student was assigned a thought provoking subject, often in the form of a question, and given a long list of suggested references. It wasn't unusual to be assigned 10 or 15 books. (You were also expected to study during the vacations. Some did, some didn't. During one vacation, I read 2,500 pages of 19th century English history.)

The student met weekly with a tutor on a particular subject at the tutor's College — perhaps two tutorials per week. (Colleges at Oxford are both social and academic entities. Since Oxonians, gentlemen and ladies, are trained to be quality citizens as well as scholars, each college has its own pub, so the students learn how to drink properly, hopefully.) The tutor at Oxford is called a Don. It is unusual to have more than two students in the same tutorial period. In my case I was always the only student.

He or she, during the following week, prepared an essay on the question and read it to the Don. My essays usually were 10 to 20 relatively concise hand written or typed pages. Since you had to read them to the Don, the essay was usually done rather carefully. Then there was always time for discussion. My recollection is that the sessions ran for an hour to an hour-and-a-half. What a wonderful way to learn. What an expensive way to learn.

The Don might or might not suggest some lectures available on the subject. Joke: The assigned questions did not exactly lend themselves to simple answers. For example some of my assigned questions are as follows:

Philosophy (with Dr. W.C. Kneale of Exeter, who had just published a much discussed book on logic):
"Is there such a thing as a just price? Discuss."
"If we believe in moral responsibility in what sense must we accept freedom of the will?"
I especially enjoyed this assignment and came as close as I ever did to getting an outright compliment from Mr. Kneale (they didn't say Dr. Kneale). He muttered, "Now you are getting the hang of it."

126

Politics (with Dr. K.C. Wheare, All Souls College and later Rector of Exeter):

"How far have Laski's prophesies been fulfilled in the 11 years since he wrote *Parliamentary Government in England, 1938* - and why or why not?"
Note: By luck, I later met Harold Laski, the noted socialist, at Oxford, and asked him if he thought that the, then, socialist English government would ever go communist. He said, "No," and when I asked why, he said, "Writing to the Times." In other words, I guessed, communism cannot flourish where there is freedom of expression.

"Examine the saying 'Bureaucracy Triumphant' in relation to the English Government."

Testing
If you were taking Politics, Philosophy and Economics, there was at most, one test per year. The rank of your degree was almost totally dependent on the massive final examination (zero true false or multiple-choice questions I'm sure).

Ugly American's Author
Eugene Burdick co-author, later, of *The Ugly American* had this to say about anti-Americanism at Oxford.

The anti-Americanism of Oxford is complex and subtle and I, for one, do not resent it especially. When an Englishman taps me on the shoulder at a cocktail party and says, "Look, old chap, I'm not anti-American and, God knows, some of my best friends are American, but . . ." the pain is nowhere near as sharp as you would imagine. And the anti-Americanism has the sting taken out of it by the fact that it is fashionable to have an American friend. Perhaps it is for the same reason that courts used to find a muscular slow-witted barbarian from Asia a curiosity and a comfort to have about. The role is somewhat uncertain, but it is interesting.

Sports

Participation in sports is regarded as part of education. "Mornings studying, afternoons on the playing fields," is an active tradition at Oxford. I was fortunate to be the captain of the Exeter water-polo and swimming team that won the University water polo cup, and was tri-winner of the swimming cup.

My career as a member of the University Swimming and Waterpolo Team had as a high point a one week combined Oxford-Cambridge trip to Holland in December 1949. The Dutch were European Waterpolo Champions, (having beaten the Hungarians who were the 1948 Olympic Champions) and were probably the best in the world. Every Dutch team we played; Amsterdam, Rotterdam, The Hague, Delft had one or two of these world-class players. I think we won one game, tied one and lost four. The swimming results were about the same. But what a learning experience. For example, there was much talk about the Marshall Plan as we made a boat tour of the Rotterdam harbor.

As a member of the varsity you were a "half-blue" in each of these events and could wear the appropriate tie. So, a varsity member was entitled to wear a tie that was half navy blue stripes and half white. The Cambridge color is royal blue. However, two half-blues didn't make a full blue. Only major sports like rugby and rowing were full blues. Today, swimming is a full blue and the quality of the swimming has improved.

My varsity sports career ended on a slightly off-note. The season concluded with the annual Oxford-Cambridge match. I was half-sick, won 100 yard back stoke in a lousy time (for the US) but still set a record in the 100 yard backstroke, and my waterpolo contribution was below average in a tie game.

The post-meet dinner party is a real bash. They assumed I would know that evening dress was required, and of course I didn't know, so that was the final straw. I pleaded illness and didn't go to the party. My wife had had twin girls and appreciated when I could help with them, and that was a consideration. However, something did happen that seemed especially British and nice.

Soon after the results of the meet were known, I received the following handwritten letter from Harry G. Champion, later Sir Harry, the head of the Imperial Forestry Institute at the University.

June 6, 1950

My Dear Gruenfeld,

A line to congratulate you most heartily on your outstanding success at Marylebone. It is so pleasing to see the foresters demonstrating so emphatically that they can hold their own against any other university group, as they certainly have this year. It was grand to read that you had not only won the event for Oxford, but made a significant reduction of the University record. Too bad that Oxford missed the match by two points.

Yours sincerely,
H.G. Champion

(This in the usually regular artistic and slightly unreadable Brit style. No errors and nothing had been crossed out or rewritten.)

One of the reasons I was disgusted with my waterpolo performance was that not long before I had the peak sport performance of my life. In the championship waterpolo game of the inter-college University Tournament, I scored five goals and we won five to three over Brasenose, which was known for being strong in sports and had two varsity players on their team. We had a strong team, they got me the ball and I got lucky. I received many "Well done, ole boy," comments for that. Oh well, life is averages.

Rugby

I had more fun playing rugby than in any other sport. It looked so rough from the sidelines that I wondered if I could hack it. But it wasn't nearly as bad as it looked. I was pretty bad but eager, and like a typical Yank, could handle the ball

129

fairly well. I was finally even invited to play on the colleges First Fifteen (for an out of town game at Burton-on-Trent).

Imagine, in a college of about 350 men they had three eight-oared crews, two fifteen-man rugby teams, two soccer teams — they called it football, and more. If you could breathe you could play something. What a great place to study.

Other Athletes

For most of the year I hadn't practiced swimming due to bronchitis. The doctor suggested a non-water sport so I started to practice for rugby, at the college athletic field. I noticed another Exeter man running the entire time, each day I practiced. He was a lanky six footer and often ran in stocking feet on the grass. He had a beautiful stride and ran smoothly and slowly for several laps and then would go flat-out, still smoothly. It was Roger Bannister — the first man to break four minutes in the mile. He did this soon after graduating from Oxford. Roger was a sterling man and college leader. Now it is Sir Roger, and he is back at Oxford heading one of the Colleges, after a noteworthy career as a neuro-surgeon.

A Weakness Of Oxford

I attended over a hundred lectures at Oxford, some superb (like those by Isaiah Berlin the philosopher of the Labor party) but they all had a common failing. There was virtually no opportunity for discussion. This was a recognized weakness. However the administration and the lecturers seemed to think that the tutorial discussions, plus intra-student discussion was enough.

A Mini Tribute To Oxford

The beauty of Oxford is well known and any significantly worthwhile tribute is beyond the scope of my writing ability. For the family, however and close friends, I am about to quote someone who is not noted for words of extravagant praise (some English-like understatement here). On his first trip to Oxford, August 1993, to a wood-products marketing conference we gave at Exeter College, son Chris and I were in the college gardens which are beautiful. The sun was setting and the background was dominated by the spectacular dome

130

of the Bodlean Library. Chris said . . . "Breathtaking." Well said, and applicable to many places in Oxford.

The Essence of Oxford

About ten years after leaving Oxford I realized that the Oxford system of education was successful, not only because students had a magnificent opportunity to Learn How To Think, but in addition had Learned to Communicate.

Exeter College Swimming Club; author seated center

Spirit Lake Lodge cabin, by Mt. St. Helens, Summer 1949: Black bears were regular visitors. Photo by Barbara Gruenfeld.

131

Colorado, winter 47 while in forestry school, about 10,000 feet elevation, just south of Rocky Mountain National Park, a St. Vrain drainage. We did pretty well trapping pine marten but sometimes unfortunately caught a pine squirrel. I had scaled Engelmann spruce logs that summer and saw many marten. So we sought to become, as we phrased it, "The acknowledged fur kings of the Rocky Mountain Empire."

June 1949, author at cabin on Spirit Lake highway near Mt. St. Helens in Washington state; in Pacific Northwest logger uniform; tin hat, hickory-shirt (with double back), suspenders, black jeans stagged(cut off so corks, branches, etc. wouldn't catch and trip you) and corked (spiked, caulked)) boots. Douglas fir second-growth in background.

We had to snowshoe in seven miles to run the trapline. Pulled a toboggan to get the gear in and out, otherwise just a pack. Jack Remington and I made only enough to cover our costs but have rich scenic memories in addition to learning how it feels to work in a wilderness at subzero temperatures. Jack lives in Redmond, Oregon. One of his Oregon Highway Department projects was to develop a trail system for the State of Oregon. He was a WWII navy pilot.

One of the less safe things I have done was to run our pine marten trapline alone one weekend, since Jack couldn't go. This was rationalized to my wife on the basis that to be a real forester I had to improve my woodcraft skills and become as adept as, at least, the average forester who had grown up in the west. Snowshoeing in seven miles to the camp wasn't any big deal, anymore. But for some reason I was short of time so felt it was necessary to run the trapline at night by flashlight. The temperature was around 20 below zero but the snow was light and there was moonlight — gorgeous. It should have taken a maybe three hours but it took 3 1/2 hours. Some extra work was involved. One of our "sets" (traps) was in a hollow spruce windthrown tree. It held a big male marten who was mad. Usually the trap was on a tree limb or a branch nailed to the tree and the marten hung free and died quickly. You didn't want to injure the pelt in any way and reduce the value so shooting or clubbing was out, but somehow I had to get down on my belly, crawl into the log and terminate the marten. The trap had an unusually long chain and he retreated as far as he could. I could barely reach him and was hemmed in on all sides by the tree. After 15 minutes or so I wasn't sure who was going to win and the marten seemed as big as a badger. I won't go into the slightly gruesome details but we ended up with another perfect pelt and holed-gloves. It was 20 below but I was soaked in sweat when it was over.

<u>Corporate Business</u>
<u>1949- March 1997</u>

Business Management Principles and Experience

A Life-Affecting Story

Sometimes a good story has a significant influence on a life. Since 1946 when I first heard it at Colorado A&M, the following story has made me look at many situations in a special way. You will see why. It was told to a forest management class by a guest lecturer, Paul Bean, who was then the Inspector General of the US Forest Service.

Once there was an old forest supervisor, one of the grass-rootsy types, who lived in Idaho. He was famous for being able to identify, early in their careers, young foresters who went on to very successful careers. He really had the knack. But he kept to himself the secret of his ability to so accurately evaluate these people.

Finally, at his retirement party, the emcee said, "Emil, now level with us, how do you do it? How can you identify these outstanding people so quickly?"

"Well fellas," he said, "I'll tell ya. When I get that new ranger, before he arrives, I go out to the ranger station and I knock the flagpole two degrees out of true plumb. Then, when the new person has been on the job three weeks to the day, I visit him. And if he has straightened that flagpole, I know I have a top-notch person."

His method might not be statistically valid, but it's useful. Ever since, in the actions of people and organizations, I look for straight or leaning flagpoles. Leaning flagpoles are danger signs that indicate that something is wrong and so are other things. Straight flagpoles indicate that at least some other things are being done well.

The straight or leaning flagpoles are a sample. So, you can deduce certain things from just one straight or leaning flagpole. It's analogous to the timber cruiser who might look at only one tree in twenty (5 percent), but multiplies his sample volume by 20, to get a total that is often very close to the total volume.

For the half century since I heard this story, I have looked for "straight or leaning flagpoles."

A Manager Communicates

The heavy majority of my 50 years of business has been as a manager. So, it's natural that early in my career I developed a real interest in management principles. And I have some strong opinions on what is most important in functioning as a manager. Communicating is at the top of my list of what the successful manager must do well.

Communications Defined

The definition of communications that I have found most useful is "the art and science of conveying information." Conveying information requires a sender and a receiver. When either the sender or receiver doesn't function properly, or there is interference, you get a communications failure.

Good Communicators

The list of all-time great communicators probably ranges from Jesus Christ, Socrates, Shakespeare and Lincoln to Adolf Hitler and Franklin D. Roosevelt. Saul D. Alinsky, a Viet Nam era radical, also appreciated the importance of communication.

Mr. Alinsky wasn't someone I liked, but I certainly respected his ability to get things done. In his book *Rules for Radicals* (a Random House publication) he gave this tribute to communications. "One can lack any of the qualities of an organizer — with one exception — and still be effective and successful. That exception is the art of communication. It doesn't matter what you know about anything if you cannot communicate to your people. In that, you are not even a failure. You're just not there."

138

Even specialists in the art and science of business management seldom put enough emphasis on the importance of good communications. Here is one example from my 18 years with Weyerhaeuser. In the half century I have known Weyco, it has always been known as a great trainer of people. While there, I received formal management training from many different courses. The best training was given principally by the American Management Association.

Eighteen of us spent one week a month in 1964, for four consecutive months receiving instruction in Business Management Principles. Our class was called Alderbrook 3 since the meeting place was Alderbrook resort on the shores of Hood Canal in Washington state. Ours was the third class. I was 39, and Manager of Timber and Log Sales. Export log sales were one of the most profitable things the company did then, and still are.

Functions Of Management

A keystone of the four weeks of intensive instruction and discussion was learning how to better perform the functions of a manager. These four basic functions were given as—

PLAN
ORGANIZE
LEAD
CONTROL

Communications was given as a subhead under LEAD. I objected and argued that communications (conveying information) was so important that it should be listed as Function 5. Or, even better, have as the four functions PLAN & COMMUNICATE, ORGANIZE & COMMUNICATE, LEAD & COMMUNICATE, CONTROL & COMMUNICATE — which might be overdoing it a little, but probably not.

Planes And Hill 600

In life, communications failures are a primary cause of problems. During World War II thousands of American lives were lost to friendly fire, sometimes because our military units were unable to identify themselves to other American units.

The most shocking war experience I had, personally, with a lethal communications failure involved Hill 600 near

Pozorrubio, Luzon in January 1945. Elements of our regiment had failed in three major attacks to take the hill. Our dead were scattered from the bottom to near the top of the 600 foot high hill. In the fourth attack C Company nearly reached the top. They were trying to dig-in when our Air Corp blew them off the hill with repeated attacks using napalm, antipersonnel bombs and strafing. The planes were A-20 light bombers and P-51 (Mustang) fighters. Some of our men shot at our own planes. Naturally, another attack was made a couple of hours later but it was stopped, this time by the Japanese, with heavy casualties.

During the attack by our planes, some troops cried in frustration and most of us swore in anger. But the next day it was business as usual and our major concern was that day's dangers.

A Good Communicator I'm Not

Though I recognize the importance of communications (even lecture and write about it occasionally), I give myself a B minus in overall communications performance. My speaking and writing ability is perhaps above average, but I frequently miscommunicate. That is, I fail to clearly convey information.

A recent and humorous example of communications failure involved my four-year-old grandson, Grant. I'm trying to develop his woodcraft related skills and want him to have at least a tolerance for hunting, even if I can't get him to actually hunt.

Recently, bright little Grant and I spent 15 minutes looking at pictures of elk. During this time I explained that I was going to an Idaho Wilderness Area and try to shoot a big elk. When the picture session was over, he ran upstairs and excitedly told his mother, in a pleased voice, "Grandpa is going over to Idaho and shoot a big *elf* and then bring it home and eat it!"

Deni, ever quick said, "Pointy boots and all?"

140

Weyerhaeuser Days:
April 1949 – February 1969
(Less Oxford University Time)

Weyerhaeuser Company, Almost A Model

If all companies in the United States had a corporate-citizen record as good as Weyerhaeuser's, this would be a much better country and world. Weyerhaeuser (Weyco) was and is a good place to work. Top management honestly believes in obeying the law, honest business practices, protecting the environment, fair treatment of employees and all those things a realistic nation should expect from a company — especially a big company. But Weyerhaeuser isn't perfect, doesn't pretend to be though it is gradually becoming more efficient, some say. While reading some forestry and business happenings of my 18 ½ Weyco years, some of my comments are negative. To keep things in perspective, please remember my high regard for Weyerhaeuser, its magnificent forestry program and its good people. Most of the time, if I make a negative comment about Weyco you can bet that some other companies were as bad or worse in that particular activity.

An Abstract Of My Weyerhaeuser Days

Pre-Oxford

Weyerhaeuser Timber Company was a giant well before I was born in 1924, but I don't believe I heard of it until going to Colorado A&M in 1946 as a junior. An Assistant Professor there, Walt Schaeffer, had worked for the "Big W" pre-World War II and liked it. He touted Weyerhaeuser.

141

By the time I had completed a Masters Degree (Forest Management) in early 1949, I knew that Weyerhaeuser was for me. They were leaders in their forestry practices.

Since I had done pretty well in my schooling and the War, they were able to find a "special job" for me — setting chokers on a cable logging operation. This was fine by me and I've never regretted starting "on the rigging." In fact, that was my preference. It was not all fun. Later, I could relate easily to a couple of phrases written by Buzz Martin, the singing logger, that went...

> *"I'm sick of settin' chokers in this doggone rain...*
> *an a coupla a times I was darn near kilt."*

But I learned a lot, enjoyed nearly all of it, made a lifelong friend, Rex Allison, and have never been in better physical shaped than I was in late summer when I quickly accepted the offer of a Fulbright Scholarship to the University of Oxford. Weyerhaeuser said they would have a choker setting job for me when I returned — how nice.

Note: George Weyerhaeuser, the present Chairman of Weyerhaeuser did time on the chokers. I'll bet his rigging slinger immediate supervisor heaved a sigh of relief when an unhurt G. H. W. left the woods. It shows how important his parents regarded on-the-job training. George had already had a life-threatening experience as a child when he was kidnapped.

After Oxford

When I returned from Oxford to Weyco in early 1951 I couldn't take another chokersetting job. I'd torn some ligaments in my left hand playing rugby and the hand was weak for a couple of years. But I could do the less physically demanding work as a logging railroad section hand. Bill Bowers was the foreman and treated everyone well, but expected good production. Section hand work ($1.50 per hour) gave me additional and invaluable insight as to how workers think, communicate and interact.

When I left after a couple of months to become a pre-log scaler, I missed the section gang even less than the opportunity to set chokers.

The fallers, who fell the small trees that were pre-logged prior to falling the big old-growth trees, were paid based on my measurement of the stump diameter. You had to keep moving. On my top day, I measured and numbered over 500 stumps.

Fallers-cutters-sawyers-choppers (depending on where you are in the west) seem to like to visit more than the average logger. As in every job I've had in my life, I learned some things from them.

After a couple of months I took a cut in pay from my hourly job and went on salary for the first time in June 1951. The pay was $350 per month as the first Assistant Forester for the Skykomish Tree Farm in Monroe, Washington working for Ted Yocom. It was a slight cut in pay since I was making $2.10 per hour as a prelog scaler plus time-and-a-half for overtime.

The Skykomish Tree Farm, As Good As It Gets

Eventually, with four other foresters, I managed the entire tree farm operation. I had profit responsibility for the 70,000 acre forest of scattered holdings in Snohomish, Skagit, Whatcom and King Counties (north of Weyco's Snoqualmie operations).

We sold logs and timber, examined and bought forest land, planted trees, ran the contract logging, thinned trees, did the public relations, cruised timber, surveyed — everything you do in managing a big forest well.

Being manager of the Skykomish Tree Farm was the best job I ever had in my life. In late 1957, I reluctantly left and accepted a promotion to the Tacoma office as Assistant Land Supervisor/Assistant Timber Engineer. (The decision was made principally because my wife and I thought our three daughters, then 7, 7, and 2 would get a better education in the larger town. This was probably not true.) For a couple of more years, I continued to have functional responsibility for the Skykomish Tree Farm. More on the tree farm later.

1955 On Weyerhaeuser's Skykomish Tree Farm: This salvage cut removed a couple of acres of alder and scattered mature trees including a single dead topped old growth Douglas fir. Trees of this ancient vintage, about 600 years, are called Yellow fir because the wood has a yellowish cast. The logged area was planted with two year old DF seedlings.

1955 at opening of Sykomish Tree Farm office, Monroe, Washington: J.P. "Phil" Weyerhaeuser (left) and author. Phil's wife Elizabeth and Annette and C. Davis "Dave" Weyerhaeuser also attended.

144

Dave Weyerhaeuser

C. Davis Weyerhaeuser was the Vice President Timberlands in the 1950's and retired early at the end of 1958 to pursue his many church-related activities. Dave encouraged intensive forest management and was a strong backer of the commercial thinning program that I was promoting.

Weyco owned the best, privately owned second-growth timber (trees up to 100 years were called second-growth) in the United States and perhaps the world. Thinning included removing individual trees that would otherwise die due to various factors, and those that would be slow growers if left until the final harvest. Not only was thinning profitable, it improved the stand.

Resistance To Thinning

Most of the logging supervisors regarded thinning as a pain-in-the-neck. They preferred logging old-growth of course. Their resistance to change underscored what we all knew; that resistance usually accompanies any significant change, profitable or not. After a couple of years of work, the program was beginning to profitably develop large volumes of wood.

However, Dave retired and without his support the expansion of the program practically stopped in 1959, '60, and '61 and then it ended, for the time being, with the October 1962 hurricane — the Columbus Day storm.

Note: I would like to include an accolade to C.D.W. Few people who know Dave Weyerhaeuser would disagree with my opinion: he personifies the phrase "Christian gentleman." The world needs more C.D.W.'s. (He will be surprised to see this.)

Beginning in 1960, I became more heavily involved with log sales, particularly export log sales. Finally, in 1963 I became the first corporate Manager of Timber and Log Sales in the history of Weyerhaeuser Co. (By then Timber had been dropped from the corporate name.) April 1963 was my first of many trips to Japan, and the log export business was booming and hugely profitable. Weyco had more logs available for export than anyone else. A natural disaster was the cause.

The Columbus Day Storm Did NOT Start The Export Log Business

On October 12, 1962 a massive hurricane hit the West Coast, mainly Washington and Oregon. Winds reached velocities of over 150 miles an hour. Millions of trees were blown down. Weyco had more private old-growth timber than any other company so was hit the hardest. Over 5 billion board feet of Weyco timber hit the ground and most of it was prime old-growth, now often called Ancient Trees. Some trees were over 500-years-old. What a disaster, what a waste — and what an export opportunity.

If all of the company's blown-down trees had been made into three bedroom homes there would have been over 700,000 homes. Note: This rough calculation assumes that from each board foot (BF) of log scale you would produce 1.5 board feet of lumber or plywood and each home required 10,000 BF. The 50 percent increase of product board feet above the log scale is called "overrun." Overrun varies with log length, diameter, taper and defect so varies with each batch of logs. The correct conversion of log scale to lumber tally is critically important in making some business decisions.

Conversion Factors

Business Note: If you are making a business decision that includes use of a forest business conversion-factor, make sure that the factors have been given or confirmed by an expert who knows, in detail, how the factors are going to be used. Most importantly, he must have an accurate description of the logs or trees involved. Fortunes have been made and lost because one party knew the right conversion factor and the other didn't.

Current example: Russian logs exported to Japan are sold based on the volume in cubic meters as determined under the GOST (Russian government standard scale), the Japanese buyers usually resell the logs, in cubic meters, based on JAS (Japan Agricultural Standard) scale. Unsurprisingly the GOST cubic meter (35.3 cubic feet) contains less wood than the JAS cubic meter. After all, it is a seller's measurement.

Fortunately, the log export trade was well established when the hurricane hit. Japan and Korea needed wood to re-

146

build their countries that had been devastated by World War II and the Korean War. Wood is the preferred building material in Japan to this day. Careful use of wood is part of the Japanese culture. Wood is highly valued for its natural beauty and for its fine structural, paper making and soundproofing characteristics — and its renewability. Wise people the Japanese. See Figure 1. Softwood Log Exports From Washington And Oregon In Total, and To Japan, 1959-95.

Figure 1

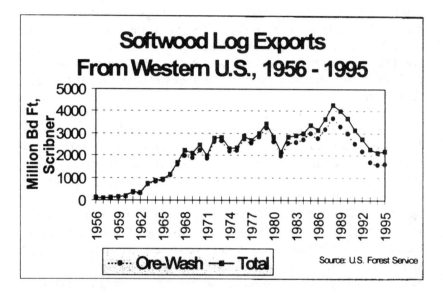

Reorganization

As Manager of Timber and Log Sales, I first reported to Jon Titcomb, a Senior Vice President for Wood Products, and later to Lowry Wyatt who had originally been Vice President of Personnel. Then in early 1966, there was another major reorganization and Harry Morgan Jr. took over from Ed Heacox as Vice President Timberlands. Ed retired soon afterward. Harry was George Weyerhaeuser's right-hand man. George was CEO.

Note: Ed Heacox, a thoroughly nice guy and excellent forester, was Chief Forester for Weyerhaeuser when I left for Oxford in 1949, and we visited briefly in Tacoma. Last month

(June 1996) Jan and I, with a couple of dozen of Ed's many friends, attended his 90th birthday party. It was a tasteful and tasty dinner at the Puget Sound waterfront home of his son Bob. Ed still shoots trap every Thursday night at the Gig Harbor Sportsman's Club.

Leaning Flagpoles

Jon Titcomb used a loose rein on me and I enjoyed working for him. I only worked for Lowry Wyatt a short time before the reorganization. We got along fine, but he was in charge of the mills and rightly saw the log-export program as being in competition with the mills for some of the best logs. In addition, "transfer prices" (the prices the mills were charged for the logs they used) were set by me. For some reason he and the mill managers always seemed to think that the prices were too high.

The log export program went very well and was highly profitable. Part of our success was due to Don Rush, Assistant Log Sales Manager beginning in 1963, who was a highly productive, outstanding person. The export log program flourished and we received many compliments and good raises.

Due to the financial importance of the export log program and our success, it seemed logical to me that I would end up reporting directly to Harry Morgan Jr. the new Timberlands Vice President. Instead I reported to Bruce Ferguson who had been promoted after doing an outstanding job on Weyco's Mississippi forest lands. Bruce reported to Harry.

Summary Comment On 1966 Personal Life Status

In 1966, my wife and I had been married 18 years. You may remember that I classified the 24 years of the first marriage in successive eight-year segments as excellent, average-and-dropping and awful. So marriage-wise 1966 was the end of the average-and-dropping phase and the beginning of awful.

Careerwise, the early 60's were the beginning of a new stage in the amount of job success I desired. Prior to then my career ambitions were to enjoy life while raising a family, and doing enjoyable forestry work in the magnificent Pacific Northwest. This required a salary we could live on and save some money. I had no specific goal such as being a the president or even vice president of anything. Money was a means to an end. I had no desire to be rich. Power was something that came with success and personal power wasn't a goal. Since I was well educated, worked hard, had some people-smarts and communications strengths, I assumed promotions would come at satisfactory intervals, and they had. But by then I was 41, the twins were 16 and would be in college in a couple of years, the marriage was in trouble. In addition, I wanted more challenge, and there had been two leaning-flagpoles (indicators) that I was not on the fastest-track for promotion within Weyerhaeuser.

The first leaning-flagpole related to the outstanding management training program that the company established for selected middle management people. These chosen few, about 18 per class, were given intensive management training by some of the top experts in the country. The training site was Alderbrook, still a beautiful resort on Hood Canal in Washington state. The training was one week per month for four months. I was not chosen for Alderbrook 1 or 2, but did attend Alderbrook 3. I was 39 at the time. Alderbrook was a typical first-class Weyerhaeuser manpower development effort. Even the food was good. We worked hard, played hard and learned a lot. Emphasis was on business management principles. Attendees represented all segments of company business, so by the end of the program, in addition to newly acquired skills, you had an improved knowledge of the company. We also made new friends. Tal Edman, then pulp sales manager and I began our friendship at Alderbrook and it continues to this day.

The leaning flagpole was that, relative to future promotions, though I was fairly young and highly regarded, there were other people who were younger and more highly regarded than I. Charley Bingham for example was in Alderbrook 1 and was nine years younger.

I was getting restless. Weyerhaeuser's ponderous method of decision making particularly began to bother me more and more. In the new organization, foresters Ted Nelson and Jack Schoening reported to me and worked primarily on standing-timber projects. Don Rush continued to work with log exports. Bill Reeves and Ken Jones worked in my department and spent most of their time in the field examining land for possible purchase. It was a good group. Ted Nelson, now retired, became a Tacoma Vice President and Jack Schoening, retired as Woods Manager for Weyco's gigantic Longview, Washington operation.

The new reporting relationship took a lot of fun out of the job. I was used to having pretty much a free hand (a rarity in Weyco) and that wasn't the new style. Bruce probably wasn't any happier than I was about the situation.

Oscar Weed, the manager of the Coos Bay operation, had always been helpful to me. He was particularly helpful when a Coos Bay log sale didn't go the way Bruce wanted it to. Oscar took his fair share of whatever blame there was and tried to smooth things over with Bruce (and with Harry Morgan). I can't remember the particulars, but know that a big part of the problem was a communications failure — as it often is with problems. Much more on communications later.

Harry E. Morgan Jr. And The High Yield Forestry Program

After nine months under the new organization, I was offered a newly created job working directly for Harry Morgan. I jumped at it. The title was Director of New Business Development, Timberlands. But the job was mostly to be an assistant to Harry. Timberlands had over 100 employees (too many in my opinion then and now) and there were many irons in the fire including High Yield Forestry. He particularly needed someone to do some of the grunt work on planning. Detailed Goals and Objectives were established and individual and group performance were being constantly reviewed. The paperwork increased.

Harry, along with a history of management success, had a reputation as being a world-class nitpicker. I discovered why after I had worked for him a couple of months coordinating the preparation of drafts four through about ten of the High Yield Forestry Report. The report for the Board of Directors was of epic importance to the company. Weyco had decided to use their forestry research information (doubtless the best in US forest industry) plus management know- how to greatly intensify forest management practices. There would be more production of genetically improved seedlings, more thinnings to increase the growth on selected trees, and fertilization of hundreds of thousands of acres. Ultimately, the result of these actions would be a greatly increased level of sustainable harvest at lower logging cost than in natural stands.

The financial justification for such a program was that it permitted the company to immediately increase the harvest of its mostly over mature forests. This would be done without being forced to dramatically drop the harvest level in the future, when the mature and over mature trees had been liquidated.

Of course, there was no law to stop the company from immediately increasing the level of cut without changing the intensity of the forestry program, which was already one of the best in the west. (Requirements of the State Forest Practice Act and Weyco's stewardship ethics prevented any significant damage to the environment.) But Weyco was a good corporate citizen, and citizenship helped precipitate the High Yield Forestry Program that would eliminate any dramatic drop in future harvest. Incidentally, a consulting company was hired to find the best words to describe the program.

Harry personally approved every single world in the final report. Never in my experience has a report, in its preparation, been subjected to such minute scrutiny by so many experts. I'm willing to bet that no one dared calculate the cost of preparing the report.

Helping on the report brought me up to date on the latest information on how to grow Weyco trees in the Pacific Northwest. As usual, George Staebler, Director of Forestry Research showed a great deal of scientific and personal integrity while probably making the largest individual input to the report.

The Board approved the report, the High Yield Forestry program began in 1966 and it's still going.

Comment: This will be hard to believe. Despite working weeks and weeks on the High Yield Forestry Program, I never heard anyone mention, in casual conversation, that the old growth cut was going to "jump up." It was as though this was something you didn't talk about even within-the-family.

The harvest level had been set on a relatively conservative sustained yield basis for many years.

The Economics Of Managing Old-Growth Timber

Anyone familiar with the biology of old-growth timber in the Pacific Northwest knew that a level of cut that could be sustained forever did not make economic sense. The bad economics resulted from the fact that generally old-growth timber has zero net growth. The stands of trees are so old that growth in some trees is offset by the death of other trees, plus the increase of defect and decay in others. The larger the acreage the truer this statement becomes.

In contrast, young trees grow rapidly. So there is an alternative of converting an asset (the trees) from zero growth to very positive growth (rapidly growing young trees) while reaping high profits from the harvested non-growing old-growth. Old growth does increase in value, but usually not nearly enough to offset the economic advantages of an accelerated harvest

Career Counseling With Harry Morgan

Harry treated me well and our personal relationship was open and excellent (in my opinion anyhow). So, I had no hesitancy, after working for him for several months, about asking for his —

* personal evaluation of my strengths and weaknesses
* opinion on what my chances of getting an Area Manager job were
* and what career advice he had for me.

He was generous in evaluating my strengths and weaknesses. Thought I had the necessary people strengths, including communications skills, was bright enough, good business sense and so forth.

Then the second leaning flagpole — he said, "You aren't quite as dedicated as a couple of the others." He was right. My working time was only eight-to-ten hours or more per day, and about half the time I took the full weekend off. The "a-couple-of-others," based on the hours they spent, probably regarded me as a shirker. But I tried to live as though the family and some recreation and other non-company time had top priority too. My war experience helped me to decide that pursuit-of-the-buck or pursuit of power wasn't the route to a happy life.

Business Note: Harry knew as others did that I had been approached by two companies including Rayonier about working for them. With Harry, as with nearly every executive I've dealt with on this issue, they regarded it as part of the system and perfectly acceptable. Others haven't been quite as fortunate in results as having bosses who felt this way.

During the discussion I told him the only positions in the company that really appealed to me were those in the western US as an Area Manager. The Area Manager in the middle 60's had direct responsibility for managing all the forest land and raw material activity (principally logs and trees) in his region. In addition, he had primary responsibility for the public relations. (Manufacturing plant responsibility never appealed to me and, here for the first time within Weyco, a person could have a really big job without the mills.)

Harry thought I had what it took to eventually be an Area Manager. His career advice to me confirmed what I already had assumed. More logging experience would shorten the time that it would take for me to become an Area Manager.

A couple of years before, I had been called into the office of the head logger, William J. "Bill" Johnson (a crackerjack guy). Before I had a chance to sit down Bill barked, "How would you like to go back to North Carolina and be Woodlands Manager?"

Still standing I said, "Bill, I'm a westerner, life is short, I don't want to do it."

He said, "I thought you'd say that," and went on to another subject.

I knew that turning down promotions often wasn't a good idea, but I knew how much the whole family liked Washington state. (Not that North Carolina isn't a fine place. Heck, I had even liked South Carolina during World War II.)

In late 1966 and early in 1967, I spent nine months reporting to Harry, doing legwork for him and doing some new business development work. Then I became the logging superintendent for a big operation on the South Fork of the Toutle River. Beautiful timber and beautiful country. Bill Johnson, the head logger for Weyerhaeuser, and the Longview Woods Manager, Amual Knutz, had found me a fine position in the Longview, Washington operation as a logging superintendent.

Logging Superintendent Twelve Road Camp

It was a good company crew. The three logging foremen John Karboski, Paul Meyers and John Zingg (who did most of the thinning cuts) were young, but experienced, hard workers. The two bullbucks (cutting foremen — Ed Bate was one of them) were old timers and knew their stuff.

Even by Douglas fir region standards, Twelve Road was a big operation. We produced about 125 million board feet (MMBF) of logs a year with 170 men. Before I left, there was a new shop that maintained the 18-wheeler log trucks and other equipment. These were off-highway trucks with 10-foot bunks that with big logs could haul about 10 M (thousand) BF. We averaged just over seven MBF on a load compared to highway trucks that were limited to a basic 80,000 pounds gross weight which would leave about 57,000 pounds for the logs. So a highway truck was lucky to get five MBF on a legal load. Depending on log length, diameter (small end) and taper, a highway load could range from about 2.2 MBF to 5.5. The smaller the log and the greater the taper the less the log scale (in Scribner scale the US Forest Service and industry standard).

Nearly all of our logging was with some type of cable system. Weyerhaeuser had stopped most tractor logging, especially if the slopes were over 20 percent, primarily because of soil compaction sometimes reducing the long-term productivity of the land.

The full truck loads of logs weighing often weighing over 100,000 pounds were transferred to railroad cars for the 30 mile (approximate) trip to the mill on the company owned railroad.

154

Great Management Experience

Any time you have 170 people producing anything, it is a challenging management task. But when the operations are always moving and scattered over about 600 square miles of territory, it's a union crew and things keep operating in all kinds of weather — it makes life interesting. Despite good maintenance, breakdowns were always a problem. The shop truck was out just about every night and over the weekends. I made sure the crew knew I not only didn't have all the answers, but that I knew I didn't and very much needed and wanted their help.

Personal: By this time the marriage was awful, otherwise my two years running Twelve Road Camp would have been two of the best of my life. One of the highlights was getting to know Amual Knutz my boss.

Communications, The 12 Road News

It seemed worthwhile to keep the men (zero ladies, sorry, remember this was the two years prior to February 1969) more informed about what was going on at 12 Road. So approximately every month, I'd put up on a bulletin board at the headquarters one or two legibly handwritten pages (each page 2 x 3 feet). This was popular. When the crew buses came in from the woods, there were usually a couple of people reading the News. Here are some samples of the content:

"Fallers Nate Johnson and Buzz Smith set a camp record by falling a four-foot Doug fir up Harrington Ck. and saving 216 feet to the first-break — measured by Ed Bate. If any crew saves 200 feet of tree to the first break, please let me know and I'll put it in The News." (Actual entry except for the faller's names.)

"Lowboy driver, Nick Hurry got three Canadian geese the other night, with his truck on the way back from Kalama. It was foggy and the birds had lit on the road at the top of the pass on the 2700 line." (Actual entry except for the name of the driver and the road number.)

"In June we will log 122 acres from Section 21, north of the mainline near Harrington Creek. I'm told this section has the highest average volume per acre of any Weyerhaeuser

155

"12 Road" 1967-68: Real loggers: from left, Melvin Wheeler, hooktender, Pickett, climber, Paul Meyers, Foreman and two equipment operators. They "jumped" the Douglas fir spar tree to a better location. Using guylines to keep it upright, the tree is cut off the stump as this one has-been and is skidded on top of a tree length log to the new location. Most spar trees even in the 60's were steel. But raised or in-place wood-spar trees were not uncommon.

When you are around men like these for a couple of years, it makes you feel like a real-logger even when you aren't. Note Pickett's black wool underwear and can of snoose (chewing tobacco) in the pocket of his hickory-shirt. This was January and I was helping.

My second (last) time to the top of a spar tree was with the help of Paul, a former high climber. There was still a pass block (small block) in an old transfer-tree that we were thinking of using and needed to know if it was sound. After testing the strength of the pass-line (small diameter wire rope), I sat in a climber's chain (a seat made of chain, two hooks and a ring) while Paul pulled me up about 90 feet, using his pickup in reverse gear, with the one end of the passline fastened to the front bumper. This took me nearly to the top of the tree by the top set of guylines. To test for rot I used an increment borer and extracted several cores of wood about 12 inches long. It was still sound. The view was great.

Tree before jumping. Note X on tree. In woods lingo, this means "don't-cut", except for special purpose.

Amual Knutz, outstanding logger and person, ex-highclimber, 1964 photo, Aberdeen, WA with second growth (despite size) spruce logs. Amual was Woods Manager at Longview in 1967 and 1968 when I was Logging Superintendent at 12 Road Camp. He has retired to Olympia, WA.

157

12 Road Camp January 1969: The "transfer" on left lifted off-highway truckload of logs onto railcars using giant grapples. Shop has 4 bays. Kenworth and Mack trucks. I kept waiting for that leaning western red cedar along the river to fall, background, but it never did, while I was there.

Melvin Wheeler, hooktender and "his" Skagit self-propelled portable spar-tree going to a new "setting". The tower telescopes up to about 85 feet.

section in history. It's an old cruise and shows 166 MBF per acre."

Note: We actually logged at least 200 MBF per acre, or 24 MMBF from only 122 acres. Believe it or not, 160 acres of the 640 acre section was 85 year old second growth (when cruised in the 50's) that only ran 100M per acre. I realize this is not the way to build credibility but it's a fact.

"Hooktender Melvin Wheeler, his rigging slinger, and one chokersetter set a camp record for highlead yarding on this tract. They yarded 28 off-highway loads in eight hours. This would be about 280 MBF."

Mel told me, "Jay, the trees weren't really big, you know, nothing over about five or six feet in diameter, but they were sure thick and tall and no defect." The taller trees were about 250 feet. Imagine the new stand is of loggable size now, but it will be left until it's around age 50. This is on a south slope with deep unglaciated soils.

Some Twelve Road timber was damaged by the 1980 eruption of Mt. St. Helens, but I believe this stand was spared; hope so. I plan to visit it soon. The eruption severely damaged Camp Baker on the main Toutle River and did damage Twelve Road. Nothing is left at Twelve Road now except some concrete slabs. It was no longr needed.

Getting Restless

After two years at Twelve Road I was 44, was confident about my ability to do a good job as an Area Manager and was eager for a change. The marriage verged on divorce. At my request, Charley Bingham talked to me in Longview about my future with Weyco. Charley was a Vice President by then and had corporate charge of the Western woods operations.

I knew Charley pretty well. We had worked together on a couple of Weyco projects and both served on the Board of Trustees of a United Church. His evaluation of my performance was positive and like Harry, he thought I would become an Area Manager — but the timing was indefinite.

Reason For Requiring The Additional Logging Time

I asked him why they had thought it was necessary to have me put in a couple of years as a Logging Superintendent despite my prior logging time and unusually deep and varied business experience. His answer was that he and others wondered if I was capable of making some of the tough decisions that a manager had to make. Examples were firing and retiring people when necessary.

This meshed with something Alden H. Jones had told me just before I left for 12 Road. Alden, an engineer, had been Logging Manager at Longview before going to a staff job in Tacoma. He knew me pretty well. I was deeply touched when he sat me down and gave me some fatherly words of advice just before going to 12 Road. This is an approximate quotation, "Jay, you are a very nice person. You tend to think the best of people. Please remember that in this logging job you are taking, you will sometimes be dealing with people who are not nice and will try to take advantage of you. Watch out."

He said this in such a way that I wasn't at all insulted. I actually felt it was a compliment that he would take the time to give good advice to someone who was a businessman and forester, not a logger. Alden is still alive and still a good guy. His book *From Jamestown to Coffin Rock; A History of Weyerhaeuser Operation in Southwest Washington* (1974, Weyerhaeuser Company, Tacoma) gives an excellent history of logging in Southwestern Washington.

You won't be surprised to know that I thought I was tough enough to make the hard decisions. However, I've never believed in a harsh tough-guy approach to management.

Not only did I have over 15 years of varied business experience, but more importantly I had been toughened in the crucible of infantry combat in two campaigns. In combat you are sometimes making life and death decisions under great stress. You must get mentally tough or you can't hack it. Granted that the business situation is different than a shooting-war, but there are many similarities. After all, business has its combative elements — for example competition is a type of war. And in both situations you are usually getting things done through people.

Now I knew that an Area Manager job would only happen after an indefinite period of time. It was also possible that future reorganizations would eliminate the Area Manager positions. That is what eventually happened, but not for several years. By this time I had begun a job search and had a stroke of luck.

The Brooks-Scanlon Opportunity

One Saturday I was in Portland, Oregon visiting Tom Galt, a good friend, from Army days at Camp Croft, South Carolina. Tom was a partner in a thriving insurance company (Campbell, Galt and Newlands). After leaving his office, I passed a door marked Management Recruiters. It was locked, but when I knocked the manager came to the door. When he heard I was "looking" he invited me in, though the office was normally closed on Saturday. We visited a while. Then he said Brooks-Scanlon Inc. a Bend, Oregon based company was looking for a forest resource manager and it appeared to "fit me like a glove."

After discussing it further I agreed. A week or so later, Mike Hollern, the young CEO of Brooks, offered me a chance to be their Raw Material Manager at a salary about 25 percent higher than I was getting (despite my recent raise). There was also the promise of a stock option. Brooks was just about to have a public stock sale and experts thought the price would rise sharply after the offering.

The Raw Material Manager title didn't describe the job. The Raw Material Manager would have profit responsibility for the logging and forestry on over 200,000 acres of Brooks forest in Central Oregon, plus doing all the buying of logs and timber, land activities plus wood chip sales. And Brooks was a highly regarded wealthy old-line family company that wanted to expand and had young aggressive management.

The fringe benefit that especially appealed to me was the great fishing, hunting, and skiing (Mt. Bachelor) in scenic Central Oregon. Also, the Three Sisters Wilderness Area was only 50 miles west of Bend in the Oregon Cascades. My marriage was so bad that a change of scene could only help. It was an attractive opportunity.

Decision Time

I went to Weyerhaeuser's head office in Tacoma in January 1969 and talked first to W. J. "Bill" Johnson (occasionally called the Red Fella) — the head logger and a very savvy guy. Bill was very people- smart and good to talk to. He had mentored a lot of young people including me. George Weyerhaeuser and other company executives listened closely to Bill on more than just logging. He saw the value of forestry and foresters better than many forestry graduates, and was a superb logger. I've noticed there are darn few successful loggers running big operations who aren't good with people — in addition to knowing machinery. Bill later became a Vice President, Far East and ran the South Seas operations, mainly Indonesia, for Weyerhaeuser.

Now, Bill, 80, and I are on the Board of the Makah Forestry Enterprise, a very successful Native American operation on the northwest tip of Washington at Neah Bay.

Bill didn't want me to leave and said the company would match the Brooks Scanlon salary offer, which was flattering. I thanked him but said that the decision had to wait until I checked a couple of things with Charley Bingham.

Charley was in a meeting with George Weyerhaeuser in a 10th floor conference room. I knocked on the door and he came out and we stood in the hall. He confirmed that I would be expected to be a Woods Manager for a while before being an Area Manager and I said, "In that case I'm going to take the Brooks-Scanlon job." Unless it was consummate acting Charley was totally flabbergasted, just dumbfounded. Actually it was a rather easy decision.

Leaving after 18 ½ years with a good employer wasn't without regrets, especially since I hadn't received tenure credit for the time spent at Oxford, therefore was not vested for any retirement income. The next year Weyerhaeuser lowered the time required for vesting from 20 years to 10. You can't win 'em all (some are rained out).

Some of the people who read this book will be business students or young people just starting their business careers. This part of the book is especially for them.

162

Hindsight: Critical Opinions On Weyerhaeuser Company 1949-69 Especially, But The 70's And 80's Too

There is much wisdom in the old saying "Experience is the best teacher." But greater success and happiness will result if a person recognizes that the "Experience of others is the best teacher."

Weyerhaeuser's many successes and virtues are well documented elsewhere, so I'll make a few comments here on what, in my judgment, were mistakes Weyerhaeuser made and the reason behind them. These comments will concentrate on the decade of the 60's which began when I was 35 and had worked for the Big W almost ten years.

Weyerhaeuser was highly regarded within the industry for certain activities. For example, its programs of forestry and forestry research, national and local public relations, safety and training. But there was little praise and much criticism of its overall lack of management efficiency and profit performance. In my opinion, much of the criticism was justified. I'd like to comment on what I believe caused relatively poor profit performance. Let's start with a good problem to have.

The Forest Resource Was Too Good

Weyerhaeuser had and still has the most financially valuable forest resource in the world. Beginning in the late 1800s wise people purchased primarily the best of the most valuable softwood timber in the world. The majority of these trees were Douglas fir which were old enough to be called Ancient.

Forestry Note: There is no single precise age when trees are referred to as old-growth or Ancient Trees (a modern term). Most Pacific Northwest foresters use 150 years up as the age break between old-growth and younger trees. When I started my forestry work with Ancient Trees in 1951, trees 150 years and up were put in the 200 years plus or old growth age class. Douglas fir older than 90 up to about age 140, but often higher, was often called red-fir, especially by the timber cruisers who estimate the volume and grade of timber on a specified tract. Also, the really old, old-growth Douglas fir is still called yellow-fir by some timber cruisers (the wood becomes yellow in trees several centuries old). A Weyco example of the use of timber nomenclature was the Coos Bay timber. Timber people would comment that most of the Coos Bay timber was not old-growth, it was red-fir. The timber had come in even-aged after gigantic fires — natural clear cuts.

During and after World War II, wood was in great demand, the quality of the timber was high and logging costs were so low that profits were relatively easy to come by. The mills that used the timber were not charged market price for the logs, they only paid book value. This meant that if timber had been purchased for a dollar per thousand board feet in the early 1900's, that is what was charged to the mill along with the logging cost — even though the market value of the log was much higher. So, making a profit wasn't a challenge. Even without an emphasis on marketing and saw milling efficiency, there was a profit. What was needed was an accounting system that charged logs to the mill at current market price. Doing this would challenge the mills to respond by improving efficiency — or perhaps lead to building another type of mill.

Transfer Price

Charging the sawmill or any other manufacturing plant the market value of the log (or any other raw material) is called transfer-pricing at market. It is a way of using an accounting system to substitute for the stimulation-to-efficiency that is realized when a mill is required to compete with others for raw material. The stimulus of competition is one of the reasons the capitalistic system is relatively efficient in the use of resources compared with, say, socialism. Consider timber buying as an example.

If a company must buy the timber to supply its mills in open market competition, it is under great pressure to be efficient in all phases of its operation. Otherwise profit margins drop and eventually the company could go out of business. Usually no profit eventually means the business dies. Efficient competitors eventually cause the less efficient to lose money when they compete in the marketplace.

Weyco did not start transfer pricing until 1961. If Weyco had started to transfer-price logs to the mills at market value in 1940 or even 1950 they would probably have had a different mix of utilization plants.

Late in Plywood

Weyco had made its reputation by producing quality lumber. Since the sawmills (lumber mills) were charged only the book value of the logs they sawed, instead of the higher market price, nearly every year showed a profit. When plywood was the most profitable end use for certain types of logs, Weyco too often was still putting them into sawmills.

Finally, about 1961, Weyerhaeuser began to charge all of their mills market price for the logs used. This applied to pulp mills as well as solid-wood mills such as sawmills and plywood plants.

Personal Experiences With Transfer Pricing

Theodore W. "Ted" Gilbert, a world-class timber cruiser was the first person in Weyerhaeuser to set transfer prices. Ted's title was Land Supervisor and Timber Engineer. I was his assistant. As Timber Engineer he was responsible for valuing, for Federal Income Tax purposes, the stumpage value (value as standing trees) of all Weyerhaeuser trees harvested. When a company harvests its own trees, the difference between the original purchase price and the current price was taxed at 25 percent instead of the ordinary income tax, which for Weyco was about 50 percent. So with the help of his timber cruising crew, Ted was an expert on the value of standing timber and logs. He was the logical one to set log transfer prices.

Ted had a phenomenal knowledge of timber. After he retired in 1963, I set transfer prices for two years. As Manager of Timber and Log Sales I was directly involved in the log markets, so the prices I set were hard to challenge. Although the mills usually thought they were too high, Jon Titcomb, my boss gave me support and they were never changed. When the mills were charged market price for the wood, many of them lost money. This led eventually to changing to more efficient mills.

The Engineering Department

The company had a huge engineering department and many fine engineers. But in retrospect, and even in the 1960's, I sided with those who thought the best way to design a mill was to find the best consultant for a mill to utilize that particular mix of logs and have him or her do the basic design.

Weyco's competition usually had to compete in the open market for timber, so to survive they had to have highly competitive mills. Weyco didn't have to pay competitive prices for their timber so, consequently, there wasn't sufficient challenge to force mills to be efficient.

Transfer pricing forced mills to become more efficient. But even so it was common knowledge that most of Weyco's profit came from having fine timber purchased at what were now very low cost. We were not an efficient processor of wood. The logging costs seemed to be reasonably competitive, but marketing and sales were also criticized within the industry as being high cost for what was achieved.

Pickups Versus Cadillacs

Many companies made much more use of secondhand equipment in logging and milling than Weyco which always went first class. Even for the High Yield Forestry Program, Weyerhauser had a reputation "for never using a pickup when a Cadillac would do." This was an overstatement, but illustrated that competitors thought that Weyco was made less cost conscious due to having a superb timber resource — the finest in the world. It was common knowledge that some of that timber went to the wrong utilization plant. Foresters, due to their education, placed heavy emphasis on using the forest resource wisely. Naturally, they were especially aware of the need to make better use of the tree.

Concern Over Timber Misallocation

George Weyerhaeuser knew that the company was not using some of its timber properly and in the early 60's considered establishing a new position titled Wood Supply Distribution Engineer. This would be a high-level staff position to advise on which parts of the tree should go to which plants.

As far as I know, I was the only one considered for the position and I would have taken it with enthusiasm.

When George interviewed me and asked whether I thought having such a position was a good idea, I told him it was a fine idea and would make the company millions. I also gave him an example of a horrendous misuse of wood that had happened in Everett, Washington a few years before.

One year, our Skykomish Tree Farm logging contractor, Simons and Murphy, had two cable logging sides in old-growth hemlock and white fir for about six months. In that time they produced about 12 MM (million) board feet. We were sick when we discovered that all the logs, except the cedar, had gone into the pulp mill — peelers, number 1 and number 2 sawlogs — all of it. To make the greatest profit, 90 percent should have gone into sawmills or a plywood plant, or been sold into the log market. We also knew that the Branch Manager who was responsible had received a big bonus that year. George said he wasn't really surprised.

The Wood Supply Distribution Engineer position was never filled. It would have been an unpopular spot to be in. I told George the rumor was that it would be a high-risk job, and the main qualification for the guy who took it was that he should be independently wealthy.

Once transfer pricing began, the pulp mills would complain if even a few sawlogs got into the pulp mills because that increased their cost. Incidentally, in the above case, the major mistake was not by the pulp division since the Branch Manager controlled the raw material distribution. More about transfer pricing when we get to Potlatch Corporation.

Eventually Weyerhaeuser made the Timberland Division a profit center. This further step encouraged more optimum use of the tree. Optimizing return-to-the-tree is easier to do when the accounting system provides encouragement and salaries reflect good performance in allocating logs wisely.

"Big" Is Bureaucracy

After three years in the Army and three seasonal jobs with the US Forest Service, I didn't want to work for the government. To me, the main negative drawbacks in government work was excessive paperwork, "protection of backsides" and other things that took the fun out of life, slowed things down and were inefficient. I didn't want to be a bureaucrat.

When I started with Weyco at age 25, I didn't realize how frequently any large undertaking had "officials who insist on rigid adherence to rules, forms, and routines," that is, were bureaucrats who did not act as though they believed that effective action was the primary goal in the long run. Too many people in the world regard rules, forms and processes as ends in themselves rather than as a way to get to the correct end objective. Governments and academic institutions are infamous breeders of bureaucrats but private industry has them too.

In a bureaucracy, it takes too long to make decisions — even then they might not be correct decisions. If you have people who are trying to change things or do new things, becoming bureaucratic is a good way to lose them.

Part of the reason I left Weyco was the burgeoning bureaucracy. But Weyco was not only a bureaucracy, it was a benevolent bureaucracy that was poorly managed.

Too Good A Place To Work

Even with my limited work experience, after a few years with Weyco it was obvious that the company really seemed to take good, perhaps too-good, care of its employees. Like anything else, this virtuous thing — taking care of your employees — can be overdone and it appeared that it had been, especially among the salaried personnel. Firings (down-sizing) were rare. It appeared to some of us that almost the only reason the Big W fired anyone was because the person had done something illegal or immoral. There were too many people doing too little work.

In the mid 60s, this all changed in a hurry when the Profit Improvement Program (P.I.P.) was begun. It was quickly dubbed the "pip" program. The program expanded the language. To be "pipt" was to be fired or retired early. The P.I.P was designed to be much more than just a staff-reduction program. (But it was the "pipping" that was most visible.) The number of salaried employees was reduced over 20 percent in just a few months. Mistakes during the implementation of the PIP program underlined how lax some people in the company had become.

I know of two foresters in two separate geographic locations, longtime respected employees who learned from their wives they were going to be "pipt" (in these cases, retired early). And their wives had learned this from someone outside of the company. Talk about leaning-flagpoles.

Unfortunately, the 1966 down-sizing, long overdue, had to be repeated at frequent intervals over the next two decades as thinning-down was soon followed by bloating-up.

Final Hindsight-on-Weyco Comments

Probably any group of managers inheriting such a bounteous forest resource would have had great difficulty creating a corporation that was as efficient as companies who didn't have such a resource. The have-nots must become efficient or perish. Weyerhaeuser had no such challenge so had no need to respond with efficiency. In addition Weyco had a piece of just plain bad luck at a very critical time in the history of the company.

John Phillip Weyerhaeuser the charismatic, far sighted and popular president of Weyerhaeuser Company died, unexpectedly, in 1956 at age 57 of leukemia. What a tragedy for the family and the company. His son George though brilliant and promising was only 30, then, and the board didn't believe he was ready to be president.

Soon after J.P.'s death George, who was Branch Manager of the Springfield, Oregon operation, except for the pulp mill, transferred to Tacoma to be Asst. General Manager under Charley Ingram. (*Weyerhaeuser Timber Company, Management Bulletin No. 83, Jan. 8, 1957.*)\

A Personal Comment On J.P. Weyerhaeuser

In 1977 when Vice President of Lands and Forestry for Potlatch Corporation, Lewiston, Idaho, I wrote the following letter excerpt to Elwood Maunder, Executive Director of the Forest History Society. Elwood had run across my name in J.P.'s files regarding a 1955 Weyco land deal with a

Boy Scout organization that was having financial difficulty
and wrote me, "... Question: How did Phil react to all this: Do
you have any recollections you can share with me? They might
be useful in drawing a picture of the man in the little book
I've been engaged to write. How do you remember Phil?"

I responded in part —

*"The Scouts were in a bind but were dealing with a
pro-Scout group so really didn't have anything to fear.... J.P.'s
reaction was, "Let's bail them out in a mutually satisfactory
way."*

"At age 53 I've met a lot of people and if I had to list
the six most impressive, J.P. would be among them. I knew
him off and on for about four years and had the pleasure of
spending one full day and half of another in the woods with
him. I mentioned to you his inadvertently stepping in the ant
hill and having to take his pants off and dance around swat-
ting ants, with encouragement from I believe, Ed Hayes, someone else and me. It didn't bother him a bit to be in the un-
dressed condition.

"The characteristic that impressed me the most was his
warmth and sincerity, to go with an obviously good mind and
great experience. As a junior forester (when we first met), I
was impressed when he asked my opinion on land exchanges
and other management activities.

"He died at a very critical time for Weyerhaeuser and,
despite the good efforts of the people that took over, I think
the company suffered."

Inevitably, his death was followed by a several year
period of readjustment and the company lost ground to competitors under the next two presidents. This is my personal
opinion that is shared by others. For example, Georgia Pacific
really hit its stride during the late 50's. Frederick K.
Weyerhaeuser, who was president of Weyerhaeuser Sales Co.,
based in Minneapolis-St. Paul, Minnesota and Weyerhaeuser
Timber Co., took over at the time of his brother's death and
served until 1960. F.K. was followed by Norton Clapp, the
largest single shareholder in Weyco. Mr. Clapp had an

engineering background and was an absolute stalwart for the Boy Scouts of America.

The mid 50's were a critical time for Weyerhaeuser. The company had become a bureaucracy and needed reorganization. The geographical branches had become fiefdoms. The timing was right for forest acquisitions, and plywood and pulp and paper expansion in the South and Southeast US. The problems created by bureaucracy were compounded by a management team that was not the best. A major problem for Weyerhaeuser during my time with them in the 1970's, and perhaps to the present, was an inability to decentralize — to move more decision making into the line organizations. Decentralization was a way to reduce bureaucracy and its action reducing attitudes of let's-not-take-chances-by-moving-quickly and protecting-my-butt-comes-first. Despite best intentions by top management and help from McKinsey & Co. and other management consultants, too much of the power remained in the head office. Most people within the company in the 1970s, who mentioned it to me, thought this was true. In the 70s and 80s I wasn't employed by Weyco but clearly heard this from sources inside and outside Weyerhaeuser.

Now For A Favorite subject -- Wilderness

The successful movement to establish wilderness areas by legislation culminated during my employment by Weyerhaeuser Company. Though the time period covered in the following seciotn on Wilderness goes beyond my Weyerhaeuser days this seems like an appropriate to discuss wilderness, which is still the place of my favorite outdoor recreation.

Wilderness

"The excess of any virtue is a vice." Author

My conception of Heaven includes Wilderness and time to use it. If I ever have a tombstone (I won't) it could be inscribed, "These things he loved." On a short list, one of those things would be Wilderness; in paradox, another would be people.

At age five, my parents noticed that I seemed to especially like the woods, swamps and other untrammeled places. When I graduated from grammar school in June of 1937, each student had a rhyme by their photo in the school book. Mine, done by a 13-year-old girl read, "Jay Gruenfeld a Frank Buck (the explorer-wildlife collector) will be and to see his cargo, you'll pay no fee."

The desire for a vocation where I could work outside in nature and beautiful country, led me to choose pre-forestry at the University of Illinois, when I was a 16-year-old freshman.

This appreciation of wild places was one of the reasons I wanted to be sent to the Pacific in World War II. Most other soldiers preferred Europe. I wanted to see the jungle. Another reason was that a serious infantry soldier had a little better chance to influence the odds of his survival in the Pacific campaigns, where there were fewer mines, less artillery and mechanization than in Europe. (I still believe this, despite my lack of expertise at dodging Japanese missiles.) Others preferred Europe because the Japanese, highly effective soldiers, almost never surrendered and routinely killed our wounded. Germans, when in a hopeless position, often surrendered and usually didn't kill the wounded.

Note: In combat, I was present in four separate engagements where thirteen Japanese soldiers committed suicide rather than surrender.

After surviving World War II, which often meant sleeping on the ground in New Guinea and Luzon wild places — creepy-crawlies included — I was certain that forestry was the right profession. And, the western US with its vast areas of untouched wilderness was "the place."

My use of US Forest Service wilderness began in 1946 when I took a short hike into the Rahwah Primitive area in northern Colorado. At the time, I was studying forestry at Colorado A&M, Fort Collins (now Colorado State U). Now, 50 years later, I remain an avid user of Wilderness and expect to do so for the rest of this life.

Legal Definition of Wilderness
Wilderness is defined in the Wilderness Act of 1964, Section 2c:

"A wilderness, in contrast with those areas where man and his own works dominate the landscape, is hereby recognized as an area where the earth and its community of life are untrammeled by man, where man himself is a visitor who does not remain."

To me, these are beautiful words about the places I enjoy most for outdoor recreating. To others, this describes places "that they wouldn't be caught dead in." This difference of opinion is one of the reasons there is intense conflict over Wilderness Area establishment. More later on the conflict.

Public lands that meet, or nearly meet the Wilderness definition, and are so designated by Congress, are called the Wilderness Preservation System. From this point on, when I am talking about land that Congress has voted into the Wilderness Preservation System I'll capitalize the "W." When referring to an area that includes lands that meet the definition, but are not be in the Wilderness System, I'll use the small "w." This is usual.

In practically all Wilderness Areas, access is only by foot or horseback. In a few places, plane and canoe access is legal. Mining can be done under certain stringent conditions, but they often make it uneconomical.

Wilderness Is A Relative Term

A general definition of a wilderness area might be — a place where a person can have a "wilderness experience." But this is very relative to the individual. Some can have a wilderness experience in Rock Creek Park, Washington, DC. But, by most standards, I'm a wilderness purist who must be at least a couple of miles into a huge area where the only access is via foot or horseback.

In my "purist" days, when I was younger and stronger, hearing aircraft, or even seeing satellite trails in the night sky slightly interfered with having a total wilderness experience. Now, at nearly 72, I'm more tolerant. I even allow some of my wilderness elk-hunt partners to use battery powered radios, even GIS (Geographic Information System) hand-held little gadgets that, literally, use data from 12 satellites to pinpoint their exact latitude and longitude at any time; plus giving a bearing and distance to camp. A horror of progress.

My early wilderness use was for hiking, fishing and hunting, sometimes with the family, often with a partner or two and frequently alone. Now, it's mostly on an elk hunt.

My hunting partners know that I will never stoop to using radios or any of these other gadgets to get me back to camp. I still sometimes rely on partners who get to camp before dark and bring extra ammunition. Then, occasionally as I stumble around in the pitch-black night, and become a little desperate, no that's too strong — impatient is better, I swallow my pride and fire my rifle and they fire theirs to pinpoint the direction to camp. Finally, I drag in and tell a tale of picking mushrooms by flashlight or tracking an especially big bull too long, etc. Occasionally, I *have* come into camp after dark because I have downed a bull too late to finish dressing him out before dark.

One unkind guy, said, "When you hunt elk with Jay, take what ammo you need to get an elk, and then take that same amount to get Jay into camp after dark." I think this was Dave Price, ex-Chief Forester for Potlatch in Idaho.

Story: A Partner Not to Have

One time, an old hunter arranged that his new, green hunting partner would be sure get into camp before dark so he could shoot and guide the old hunter into camp. The arrangement didn't work and old hunter was out all night. Next morning green partner explained, "Well, I kept shooting until I was out of arrows." This story could also be used in the Communications section. In defense, I can say I have only had to sleep-out twice (in the snow). For about 40 years of hunting that isn't too bad — and coming in late has deepened my after-dark appreciation of wilderness.

My penchant for coming in after dark, and a couple of times having partners who also came in after dark, on the same night and after me, hence couldn't shoot and guide me in, has led me to carry elaborate emergency gear, including extra ammunition. My pack is now pretty big.

Perhaps it will be lack of strength to carry the required survival-gear pack that will finally end my wilderness elk hunts.

Weyerhaeuser Company Wilderness Days And The Skykomish Tree Farm

By October, 1959 I had become Weyerhaeuser's in-house authority on wilderness. At the time, I was still giving direction to the Weyerhaeuser's Skykomish Tree Farm, Monroe, Washington.

Monroe is on the Stevens Pass highway (US Route 2), east of Everett. My salaried days with the "Big W," as it was called then, began in June 1951 as assistant to the forester, Ted Yocom, who had been working alone. I transferred there from my hourly job as a woods scaler at Longview, Washington. From 1952-57 I was manager, due to having the good luck of having Ted leave to be the first Chief Forester for Ketchikan Pulp in Alaska and having his successor, Don Dowling choose to leave and become Chief Forester at Weyerhaeuser's Snoqualmie Falls operation. After Don left, the responsibilities and activity expanded. As manager, I eventually had total responsibility, including profit, for over 60,000 acres of mostly forest, the Skykomish Tree Farm. Our lower elevation lands were principally regeneration in the 10 to 60 year age classes. But the country I loved the most, the high country, included several thousand acres of old-growth timber, that was mostly wilderness. Our old-growth very often adjoined large areas of US Forest Service and State old-growth. In 1957, I became assistant land supervisor in the Tacoma office, but continued to direct the Skykomish Tree Farm operations. They were managed by my replacement Carl Garey and three other top-notch foresters, Neill Bowman, George McAninch and Jack Palmquest with assistance from hourly employees Dick Craven and Jim Stansberry .

Glacier Peak, proposed for inclusion in a big Wilderness Area, was near our ownership around the Darrington, Washington area, and I had done some hiking and fishing in the area being considered for Wilderness designation. What follows is the statement I made, as an individual, at a Forest Service public hearing on October 16, 1959.

Glacier Peak Wilderness Area Hearing, Wenatchee, Washington

I appreciate the opportunity to spend some of my vacation listing and talking about wilderness. I am a lover of the out-of-doors, particularly of wilderness-type recreation. I have hiked, camped, hunted and fished in Colorado, Idaho, Washington, Oregon, New Guinea, Philippines, Scotland, and, for a short period, in Europe. I make this personal reference only to show that I have a deep and sincere interest in this problem, from the standpoint of a "recreationist" but also as a forester. I have worked in my profession for 10 years and completed over six years of college training in Forestry and the Humanities.

I sympathize with the large majority of the proponents of large wilderness areas, who are completely sincere in their beliefs. However, the 'mudslinging' at the Forest Service by some of these people is unjust. The personnel of the Forest Service have, to a large degree, sacrificed any great economic reward for a career in conservation, where many of the rewards come from working with nature in beautiful country. Most of these people are not only technically trained land managers, but are also devout believers in the non-dollar values

176

to be found in an out-of-doors career. If they did not feel that way they would not be working for the Forest Service.

The constant cry that the proposed boundaries of the Glacier Peak Area show that the Forest Service has sold out Wilderness to the timber industry. This is a big laugh to industrial foresters, who realize that in leaving over 40,000 acres (62 square miles) of operable timber land within the proposed boundaries, the Forest Service has certainly stopped far short of 'eliminating every last big tree.'

I have read about and listened to some of the previous wilderness hearings and would like to discuss a few points, some in rebuttal to statements that have been made, and to add other comments.

The statement is often made that cutover areas are an unsightly scar, that the only true beauty is in the glorious virgin timber. I feel sorry for people who regard virgin timber as the as the only beauty. In the same way, I feel sorry for those who like adults, but can't stand children: and for those looking at newly hatched chicks, who see the litter of the egg shell and not the chicks. These people would find greater total beauty if they would learn to look at and appreciate young reproduction. Clearcutting, although unsightly, is the most satisfactory method for regenerating many of our Northwest species.

Large areas of old-growth timber are regarded by many recreationists, including many wilderness recreationists, as an obstruction barring the way into the high country where the real beauty lies. Granted, you must include some prime timber in a wilderness area — huge areas as proposed by some more radical wilderness advocates are a definite deterrent to use of the area by everyone — as well as being unwise use of a resource. The less mobile recreationist is, of course, in the far greater majority. I understand that of 18,000 tourists surveyed this past summer, not a single one was going to pack into our primitive areas — their loss, but still an indication of what the majority does.

The establishment of American Wilderness areas is actually, in some respects, an international problem. Karl Marx, Friedrich Engels, Khrushchev and other prominent communists, have stated that the ultimate conflict between communism and other ways of life will very possibly be an economic conflict; that our system of democracy is most vulnerable along economic lines. With the economic cold war in mind I'm sure Mr. Khrushchev would like to see the entire Cascades range, plus the Sierra, put into one huge Wilderness Area.

1996 Note: Because of this statement, a couple of Sierra Club members said that I had called them communists. Soon after making the statement, at the request of The Wild Land Research Center, Berkeley, CA, I served in a wilderness recreation opinion-group with Dr. Olaus Murie, the great wildlife biologist, then the Director of the Wilderness Society — a fine man. He thought their comment was ridiculous.

The boundary controversy is primarily on west-side types. Many people are not aware of the growth potential of the west-side forest. For example a growth rate of 100-board-feet per acre per year is very satisfactory for ponderosa pine, an east-side species. For many stands of west-side Douglas fir or hemlock, 1,500-board-feet per acre, per year is common. (1996 note: It would have been more accurate to say "some stands.") So great is the growth difference between the east and west side that the volume in west-side trees dying, due to normal suppression, will often exceed the total growth of east-side species by 200 to 400 percent. The Forest Service people are aware of these facts — most wilderness recreationists are not.

To conclude, this boundary problem is being considered by Forest Service people. These individuals are fully aware of non-dollar values. They have sacrificed, in many cases, a better economic future to work in conservation where many of the rewards come from making wise use of the Nation's resources; who are technically qualified in land management; and who have conducted public hearings to gather facts an opinions. As an ardent wilderness recreationist and a professional forester, I think that substantial amounts of productive forest land can be excluded from the proposed wilderness area without seriously impairing the wilderness values. However, whatever the decision, I am personally satisfied that it will be given by an organization of technically and spiritually qualified men (only men then), who will make a completely honest and objective effort to establish a boundary that will provide the greatest good for the greatest number in the long run. Thank you.

This testimony was given when I was 34. Today, after 37 more years of "wildernessing," I feel basically the same, but would not give the current Forest Service such generous accolades.

The above was a personal statement. Three years after I had given it, I had an article printed in the April 1962 Weyerhaeuser News. It was titled "Wilderness: A Problem We Face." The message was similar, but was directed at proposed legislation (Senate Bill 172) and is more political. Bernie Orell, the Weyerhaeuser VP, Public Affairs, a forester, approved an article containing the following quotes, even though he and I had discussed the positive effect on the value of Weyco timber if all National Forest timber was put into Wilderness.

"I am a member of a minority group. It is not the usual minority group identified by race, color or creed, but a small group of people who actually visit our magnificent wilderness areas."

"In 1960, a minority of all the people in the United States enjoyed recreation in our National Forests. Of these, only one out of every 150 visited the 22,000 square miles (14,080,000) acres of wild, wilderness and primitive areas —those areas where activities of man, other than wilderness recreation are not permitted."

"The major issue in the wilderness question is not whether we should have wilderness areas, but rather how much there should be, how it should be established and who should manage it."

"The main conflicts over S. 174 are principally between two different groups of recreationists and two different groups of conservationists. Most recreationists want their recreation reasonably near roads so do not use wilderness areas. They would like to have easier access to the splendid scenery and other values available in some of the wilderness areas."

"The conservationist conflict has most of us who believe in wise multiple use of our resources opposing those who believe more strongly in a preservation type of conservation. Certainly it's proper to dedicate some forest lands to exclusive or limited use as in wilderness. But such a dedication must be wisely made, in line with actual need. The number of people benefiting must be carefully considered when determining the values derived."

"Also most people do not realize there are millions of acres in the Western states not being considered for wilderness status that will remain wilderness, for as far as we can see into the future. Personally, I am familiar with hundreds of thousands of acres of acres of spectacular country that will remain as wilderness. Much of this is high alpine country that does not have intrinsic commercial value, or is almost completely inaccessible. Fortunately this type of country has the highest wilderness value."

Federal Testimony

On February 28, 1961, as Chairman of the Puget Sound Section of the Society of American Forests, I testified at a public hearing before the Senate Committee on Interior and Insular Affairs, in Washington, DC. Senator Anderson, Arizona, was the Chairman. We supported the Wilderness concept, but wanted areas to be examined carefully before being put in the Wilderness System.

Senator Frank Church of Idaho was on the Interior and Insular Affairs committee. In the early 70's, when I was based in Lewiston, Idaho with Potlatch Corp., I got to know him. We were the same age, both former infantry officers and liked wilderness so communicated easily.

Who Uses Wilderness?

About 25 years ago, I noted an interesting wilderness statistical fact based on observations since 1946, that is, during a 25-year period. Now, this statistic has assumed increasing validity since I have used wilderness an additional 25 years and the fact remains unaltered.

The fact is this: In 50 years of wilderness use, I have never seen a black person in a wilderness area — or at the trailheads just outside the wilderness areas. And I have spent over 300 days in wilderness areas, in the Western United States so have seen many people, especially at the trailheads. Over half of my wilderness time has been in Washington and Oregon, which have a significant urban black population.

This statistic assumed additional validity when two avid wilderness users and forester friends (Neill Bowman, Monroe, Washington and Pat Cummins, Enumclaw, Washington) said that they had never seen a black in a Wilderness Area. Neill is an acknowledged wilderness guru of the North Cascades. Pat is a past Chair of the Washington Society of American Foresters. The obvious primary conclusion, based on this fact, is that blacks make very little use of Wilderness Areas. A secondary conclusion I would make, is that this more evidence to confirm what is already known. Those of us who use wilderness are much above average in income and education level.

In contrast, blacks, have much greater need for improved housing than wilderness users. So, blacks, who make little use of Wilderness Areas are hurt more by the higher forest product prices, and fewer jobs resulting from preserving Wilderness.

The Wilderness Preservation System Is Gigantic

Currently, November 1996, there are over 162,000 square miles (over 100 million acres), in the Wilderness Preservation System. Congress has set these areas aside primarily for primitive-type recreation. I suspect that Aldo Leopold the famous conservationist, who was a prime-mover in establishing the first wilderness area, would be flabbergasted at its size. Senator Frank Church told me in 1978 that it looked as though The System was going to be twice as large as he had thought when the Wilderness Act was passed in 1964. Now it is far larger than he thought it would ever be. He had a firm belief that the country also required what he called "working forests" where the sustained production of wood was the primary goal.

Best Treated Recreation Minority

We Wilderness users are perhaps the best-treated recreationist minority in the world. The Washington-Oregon National Forest Wilderness System consists of 63 separate areas totaling approximately 4.6 million acres (7,300 square miles). This means that in Washington and Oregon in 1995 there are 2.9 acres of Wilderness for each user day, on average. The heavy majority of this area is classed as commercial forest land. Wilderness Area use in Washington-Oregon has dropped 38 percent since the peak use in 1987, based on US Forest Service records. See Figure 2 National Forest.

Figure 2 National Forest (U. S. Forest Service)

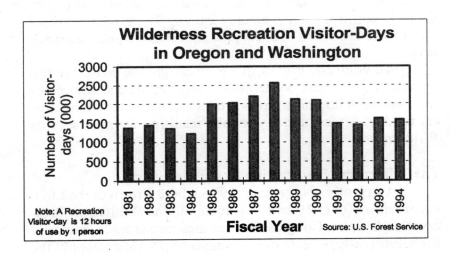

182

Wilderness Use Has Declined

Wilderness advocates are concerned at the drop in Wilderness Area use both in the Pacific Northwest and nationally since peak years in the 1980s. They should be. Massive public wealth in timber and minerals is locked up in Wilderness Areas. It directly benefits, in a major way, only those relatively few of us with the time, energy, money and inclination to use these pristine, usually hard to reach areas.

Near Seattle, Washington is the readily accessible Alpine Lakes Wilderness Area. Use of this area in 1994 was only one third of what it was in the 1988 peak. Figures 2 and 3 show a progressive and substantial drop in Wilderness use throughout the Pacific Northwest. A partial explanation of the decrease is the drop in real income, the aging of the baby-boomers, and less need for the political pressure generated by high use, since the Wilderness System is already huge.

Figure 3. National Forest (U.S. Forest Service)

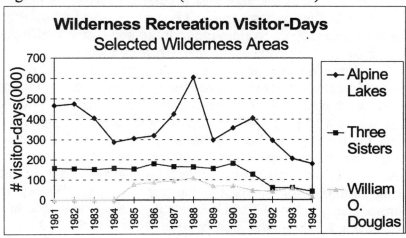

The media reports frequent complaints from users that there is too much use of Wilderness and this interferes with their wilderness experience. However there is a great deal of area getting relatively low use. To illustrate this fact see the following table where the acreage of the three Wilderness areas in Figure 3 and Washington-Oregon are divided by total user-days 1994.

Wilderness Area	User Days	Acres	Acres/User Day
Alpine Lakes	179,226	362,621	2.0
Three Sisters	285,202	40,960	7.0
W.O. Douglas	16,083	168,288	10.5
Wash.-Ore.	1,592,971	4,650,592	2.9
	(7,266 sq. miles)		

In contrast, is Mt. Rainier National Park, which is administered by the National Park Service. Mt. Rainier National Park in 1994 had 2,206,000 visitors to its 236,000 acres or .107 acres per visitor. A park visit is estimated at 3 to 6 hours. If each visitor averaged 4.5 hours, the visits in user-days would be 829,000; giving .2 acres per user-day. This indicates 10 times more use in user-days, of Mt. Rainier Park in Washington than the average of Washington-Oregon National Forest Wilderness use of 1.6 million acres. This is despite having a high percentage of the park area accessible only to mountain climbers. The following comment is one reason why I believe the Wilderness Area System is too large and is another illustration of why "The excess of any virtue is a vice."

Some Wilderness Areas include large patches of high-value old-growth timber. I have seen Douglas fir ancient trees on the west side of the Cascades in the Three Sisters Wilderness where a 10 acre patch would bring at least $250,000 revenue for the right to harvest the standing timber (stumpage value) for use in domestic mills. In the Alpine Lakes Wilderness, I have seen 10 acre patches of old-growth that would bring $500,000 for the right to harvest 10 acres, if an export permit was granted. This is because there are heavy volumes of Alaska yellow cedar that bring as much as $3,000 for a single log 26 inches in diameter by 32 feet long (1,000 board feet log scale) along side ship for export sale.

Because of my knowledge of the awesome amount of timber value in Wilderness Areas, the people-hurts inflicted on forest communities by the Endangered Species Act and related statutes, and the lack of funds to develop and maintain Wilderness trails, I proposed some new legislation in a 1991 talk at the annual national meeting of the Society of American Foresters,

The legislation was titled The Kinder and Gentler to Forest Communities Act. For the state of Washington, west side only, it provided for trial timber sales using single-tree selective logging in Wilderness Areas that removed only 25% of the total volume. Revenues to be distributed 25% for improvement of trails within the Wilderness affected, 50% to the affected counties, and 25% to the state of Washington for the poor and mentally ill. The rotation age, 200 years.

If I could get Michael Jordan, Robert Redford and Bill Gates behind it, it would pass.

Certainly, there is too much wealth tied up in Wilderness Areas, but that is not my primary forest concern in the Pacific Northwest.

Later we will talk about the number one forest problem, centered in the Pacific Northwest, but having negative impact on everyone in the United States; the reductions in federal timber harvest caused by the Endangered Species Act and related legislation. Flawed legislation that hurts the entire forest management system.

*High deer hunt, North Cascades 1959, Bald Eagle Mt.: Vegetation in the mead-
ows was primarily huckleberry, parsnip, heather and false hellebore; plus mountain hemlock, sub-alpine fir and Douglas fir trees. Neill took a buck but all I saw
was a mountain goat and we didn't have a goat permit. (Photo: Neill Bowman)
Did have a favorable, against-all-odds, happening. The bugs were thick. Black-
flies, no-see-ums, deer flies and horseflies were the worst during the day (this
was mid September) with mosquitos at night until it got cold. We were very short
of insect repellant and were going to have to ration it. Near the end of the 14
mile hike-in on a seldom-used trail as I rounded a switchback there in the grass
just off the trail lay a bottle of 6-12 repellant, nearly full. We couldn't believe it.
Later we discovered that a forest service road and trail locator, Bob Norton
(from the Skykomish Ranger Station) and his Alsatian dog had been returning,
fortunately, from a several day trip, had juiced-up and walked off without the
bottle. Lucky us.*

*Idaho Wilderness Area, '94 Elk
Hunt: Looking South down
Marble Ck. a tributary of Middle
Fork of the Salmon. Too steep to
ride. John Zingg under hat. Pon-
derosa pine primarily with some
Douglas fir. Didn't miss anything
or have to clean our rifle bores.
Collected two grouse with a .22
revolver. Great hunt though.*

186

Washington Cascades, Alpine Lakes Wilderness Area: You could squeeze a few logging and milling jobs, lumber and other home building products and profit from places like this. But most forest business workers would probably say leave it for the enjoyment of those with the time, money, desire and energy to get there; protection of headwaters and ecosystems and so forth. People dependent on the mining industry for employment and profit might not agree. Lakes: Malachite, Copper, Angeline et al. The area is administered by the U.S. Forest Service. (National Park Service Photo 4214-668A)

Brooks-Scanlon, Inc. Days 1969 - 1972

"In decision making, the real wisdom comes, when after making valid assumptions on relevant items, you act as though you believe your assumptions." Author

My Brooks-Scanlon employment time would make an excellent case history for business students or those interested in business management. Especially helpful would be the interaction between the managers. The key managers were either young or old, very few middle-aged. Example: the Logging Manager, Ernie Newstad and Chief Forester, Hans Milius both retired at age 65 or older while I was there. Both were strong personalities with long experience in Central Oregon who did their work well. In age contrast the President Mike Hollern was about 30 and a Dartmouth grad with a Masters in Business Administration from Stanford. A Stanford MBA classmate of Mike's, Bob Harrison, was in charge of land development. Two other younger top-notch Stanford MBA's, William L. Smith and Jeff D. Karl, were hired shortly after I arrived. Bill has his own land company now and is developing the old Brooks mill site on the Deschutes River.

My 3½ years with this small and fine old-line company covered a wide variety of business activity. Stewardship-minded Brooks wanted to upgrade and expand their saw milling capacity, begin a major land development program and search for merger and acquisition opportunities. I was directly involved to some extent in all these projects. There was a substantial volume of old growth timber on the 200,000 acres plus of fee (owned) land. Public timber purchase (mostly US Forest Service) was necessary to run the big pine sawmill at an economic consumption level. The mill had a 100 million board foot, two-shift annual capacity. Most of the timber harvested

would qualify as coming from Ancient Trees which were growing very slowly if at all. There was plenty of opportunity for
new ideas. Stimulating work.

Early Days At Brooks-Scanlon

Mike Hollern may have been nicest person I have ever
had as a boss. He had a streak of idealism to go with a strong
basic knowledge of how the business system and the world
functioned. Philosophically until the past decade or so, I classified myself as an idealistic-realist (a realist tempered with
some idealism especially regarding people). Now I recognize
I was probably better described as a realistic-idealist as I think
Mike was during my Brooks tenure — and probably still is.

My management task with the new company was for-
midable. Books have been written on the difficulty of change
especially when people are involved. Young managers, particularly, tend to underestimate resistance to change. I certainly did as a young manager, in middle age at Brooks and
still do, sometimes. It's a trait that is often coupled with opti-
mism, which I have.

Before he hired me, Mike described Brooks as an in-
bred, old-time company with some outdated management practices. He was right. We discussed the likelihood that I was
going to have some personnel problems in changing things,
unless I was both skillful and lucky. I was an outsider who
came from the Big-W, was highly trained in management
theory, had been-through-the-mill as a businessman and even
had a degree from Oxford. Mike is probably the only person
in the entire Brooks organization who knew that at
Weyerhaeuser my ability to get along with people at all levels
was regarded as a strength. I like most people I meet, am not a
bad listener, and most importantly, believe the number one
rule for good personal relations is to treat people the way you
would like to be treated — and I usually acted on that premise.

Primarily because of what he saw as my people-
strengths, Bill Owen, Director of Manpower Development for
Weyco, offered me the new position Assistant Director of
Manpower Development. But I had no interest in anything
which was not directly related to forests.

But Brooks-Scanlon wasn't Weyerhaeuser and I should have acted smarter than I did in my in-company personal relations.

Instant Success

C.E.O Mike Hollern hired me because I was a very experienced, profit-oriented, successful forest manager who appeared to fit unusually well with the Brooks-Scanlon needs.

Things went so well for me at first that even I was amazed. There were many opportunities to make improvements which would often show up quickly on the income statement. This was because Brooks had slipped into some bad business habits over the years. There was a parallel between Brooks and Weyerhaeuser. Each had a large volume of old-growth timber purchased at low prices. No matter how poor its efficiency, the company would usually show a profit. Without a challenge it's easy to get sloppy.

We renegotiated more profitable chip prices, made some very profitable log sales, improved communications inside and outside the company, and found new sources of logs — success after success.

Mike was very impressed and give me a good salary increase after only six months and another at the end of the first year.

The Psychologist

As the successes mounted, so did my intra-company people problems. This is the appropriate time to mention that Brooks had an industrial psychologist consultant who visited with nearly all the managers at least once a quarter and sometimes more. This was a long-standing practice of the company. He was a personable older guy, who was, of course, called "the shrink" when he wasn't around. I had no experience with psychologists and was wary despite his assurance that he was " just here to listen and help avoid problems." "I don't carry tales," and so forth. He ended up being very unhelpful.

I could have used some help. In accomplishing many good things, I was invading the manufacturing division's turf, having some communications failures, hurting some feelings and creating some distrust.

190

The Excess of Any Virtue Is A Vice

Part of my problem was a self image. I saw myself as an easy-to-figure-out, kind, well intentioned, capable, straight-arrow with Christian values, who wanted to get things done, rapidly — but not by creating a host of people problems. Also, I thought of myself as being confident, without being egotistical. Finally, I saw myself as a team-player despite my individual success.

Brooks contemporaries Leo Hopper, Marvin May and Ted Young may groan, smile or laugh in disbelief when they read this but it's true. Mike's sensitivity could pick up on the fact that I was subjective enough to believe it, totally.

My communication skills were so poor (remember that per the experts, most communication is nonverbal) that a person within the company who knew me well, told the shrink, at a critical time, that I would probably end up doing a rash act that I have never, ever even come close to doing. He told the shrink , "Some day, Jay, in a fit of temper will 'can' Tom Turner (the logging manager)." Not true! I liked and respected Tom who was a capable logger and had even been a combat infantryman against the Japanese and a fellow deer hunter to boot. Firing a good man has never been in my business repertoire. But obviously, I had miscommunicated to this fellow employee because he wasn't the type to say it for spite. But he WAS the type who would say it to the shrink.

Brookswood

Soon after joining Brooks I came up with an idea that would more fully utilize the timber resource and increase our profit. The idea was to use selected dead Ponderosa pine trees (snags) to produce a new product.

In the 1970's, parts of Central Oregon were covered by a scattering of large dead Pondersosa pine trees. In western woods language, dead trees are called snags, especially after they have lost their needles and small limbs. The most sound of these snags were used in the sawmills. The most profitable use of the older most defective snags was to make studs (usually 2" x 4" x 8', but also 2 x 6) — if your mill could do that at a low cost. But only a small proportion of the Ponderosa snags were used in this way. If one could find a new use for dead

Ponderosa more of the trees could be used, jobs would be created and the company would make more profit.

An additional benefit would be in reducing the forest fire danger. Many forest fires start when lightning hits a pine snag. When fighting fires, burning snags of any species, but especially the highly flammable pine, spread the fire and make controlling it more difficult.

We realized that snags were used by cavity-nesting birds like woodpeckers, but this caused little concern since many unmerchantable snags would be left standing.

Brookswood Paneling

My suggestion was to use some of the better snags to produce a decorative lumber paneling. The sawmill managers cooperated (some a little reluctantly since it decreased mill production) and produced lumber paneling that in most mills would have gone straight into wood chips and hog fuel because of defects.

But to certain buyers, the blued sapwood wood with varying patterns of bugholes throughout the entire piece was attractive. They would pay a premium price for this natural-looking, decorative paneling. Wormy incense cedar paneling had been sold for many years for use in recreation rooms and bars and it seemed to me that pine snagwood with some of the sapwood turned blue would be attractive. (Later Georgia Pacific manufactured a paneling they called Blue Pine).

The insects that attack dead pine made holes that varied in diameter from one-tenth inch or less (example, the Ips genus), up to one-half inch or more (various horntail borers that eventually become a wasplike insects) with all sizes in between. Horntail larvae are said to be very good to eat, especially when roasted — but you can't prove it by me. Most of the bug activity was in the sapwood, but some went clear to the heart of the tree. Sometimes, it was possible to hear the biggest larvae or beetle chewing the wood.

Ambrosia beetles are a major maker of small holes in felled timber. Since ambrosia is also the name for angel food. I dubbed the new decorative paneling "Ambrosia Pine." The name caught on and most of us referred to Ambrosia Pine when talking about the new decorative paneling.

We had Leonard Guss Associates a marketing consulting company do a marketing feasibility study and the results were very positive. Len convinced Mike Hollern and Dick Gervais, the manufacturing vice president, that the best name for the paneling would be Brookswood, rather than Ambrosia Pine — a small, personal disappointment for me.

An Opportunity

By now I was totally involved in the snag project, emotionally and otherwise. Not only was this profitable, but it enabled us to utilize more from any area we logged. In addition, pine snags were available from other owners for almost zero stumpage. (Stumpage is the price paid to the owner for the right to log timber). Brookswood became a regular grade, within Brooks, and definitely added to the net profit. In the first six months of 1971, the mill utilized 4.5 million board feet of pine snags. The delivered cost to the mill was $23.00 per thousand board feet (short log Scribner scale) and the selling price of the lumber well over $200. The pine snags were usually on gentle ground, were big in diameter, light in weight and consequently logged-cheap.

A Coup

Through some hard negotiating, luck, and other favorable circumstances I was able to negotiate a very favorable agreement to buy standing (and downed) snags from 56,000 acres of Weyerhaeuser land on the north end of the Klamath Falls Tree Farm. The agreement was for three years at a price of $1.00 per thousand board feet ($5,000 minimal annual payment). Also, there was a three-year extension providing we could agree on a new price. The agreement was effective July 1, 1971.

Remember, the best snags had probably been removed from most of the area for use in Weyco's Klamath Falls mill. But Weyco's mill was not designed to saw snags and they didn't have a high value snag-product like Brookswood. There were tens of millions of board feet of snags on the land. Weyco was paying to have some of the snags felled to reduce the fire danger.

Proposal

We proposed to Mike Hollern that we build a low-cost small mill that was designed to run entirely on snags and produce only Brookswood and studs. Ted Young did a quick study on the volumes of snags available for such a mill, from all sources, and it confirmed that we could easily "wood" the mill for six years at attractive costs. (Keep the mill supplied with wood.)

A pro-forma was prepared and using conservative costs and sales revenues it showed a Return on Investment of 12%. (The pro-forma for Black Butte Ranch showed only a 12 percent return — granted that it was a special case.) Normally 12 percent would have been a high enough return to proceed with this relatively simple project. However, the company had some serious economic problems at that time. Examples: The new small-log mill was having severe startup problems and the Glanville Box acquisition had been a disaster.

So the decision was made not to proceed with the snag-mill. I thought this was very unwise and said so, clearly, but also said I understood the special circumstances involved.

Hindsight: If the snag-mill had been built the first lumber produced would have hit one of the greatest lumber markets in history. Production would have begun when the pine stud price was 100 percent higher than that used in the pro-forma. The mill would have paid-out in less than a year. There was no way of predicting such a gigantic price spike. You can't win 'em all.

There was another major project that strained my relations with some of the other managers and Mike.

West Fraser Timber Merger Opportunity

One of the largest lumber companies in British Columbia in 1970 and today is West Fraser Mills. In 1970-71, West Fraser approached Mike Hollern about a possible merger. They were attracted by Brooks-Scanlon's financial strength and attractive young management.

Part of the West Fraser high-comfort level about the merger was due to the Brooks-Scanlon early experience in British Columbia. Brooks money started Powell River which later merged with MacMillan Bloedel and became MacMillan Bloedel Powell River. A Brooks man was on the board of directors. Ultimately MacMillan interests totally dominated the company.

The Ketcham brothers, Pete and Bill, made a number of trips to Bend, Oregon and several of the Brooks managers and I visited the West Fraser mills and licensed forest lands in interior British Columbia, principally Prince George and Williams Lake.

It looked like a natural. The management people were compatible. West Fraser was obviously a profitable and efficient lumber producer which could benefit from Brooks's financial strength and management.

Finally, West Fraser made an offer that was so attractive that I was sure it would be accepted. All I'll say about the specifics is that for a minor portion of Brooks-Scanlon stock, the companies would merge. Not everyone agreed that it was attractive. One individual was adamant in believing that West Fraser was "a one-man company, Sam Ketcham," therefore, if any thing happened to Sam it would be disastrous. I was totally in favor of the merger and thought it would be a smooth way of expanding profitably.

Mike Hollern wanted to merge, but knew they it would take a great deal of convincing to get Board approval. He was already extremely busy with the development of Black Butte and had a number of problem areas including the two mentioned above. Reluctantly, he made the decision not to proceed with the merger.

Hindsight: Brooks would have benefited greatly by merging. For example, around 1974, Brooks had the highest net profit in its history and West Frasers' profit was 100 percent higher. West Fraser is today a healthy forest products giant, and Brooks-Scanlon sold out and the name disappeared.

Mike Hollern is still active in land development. Sam Ketcham, a first-class guy and the leader in West Fraser, died in a helicopter crash a couple of years after the merger opportunity, but West Fraser continued to flourish.

Personnel Questionnaire

As a manager I needed to know how the lower level managers regarded the company, their individual positions, strengths and weaknesses. Too often managers know little about the morale and perceptions of the managers who report to those immediately below them.

The logging department and raw material division were my responsibility. With the assistance and support of the people that reported to me, we had a questionnaire prepared. It was then filled out by the twelve people, mostly managers, who reported to them.

There were no "shockers." Results, given below, confirmed that these were two pretty healthy units in the opinion of the respondents. I agreed.

DO NOT SIGN
Brooks-Scanlon Logging/Raw Materials Personnel
May 29, 1972

1. In my job I think I am:
    6 Very Secure   6 Reasonably secure   0 Insecure
2. The Logging department is:
    4 Very well run   8 Fairly well run   0 Poorly run
3. Logging department performance is:
    1 Excellent   10 Good   1 Satisfactory   0 Poorly run
4. Raw Material Division performance is:
    2 Excellent   9 Good   1 Satisfactory   0 Poor
5. The general situation within the Logging Department is:
    9 Improving   3 Stable   0 Going Downhill
6. The general situation of the Raw Material Division department is:
    7 Improving   5 Stable   0 Going Downhill
7. The unity of purpose within:
    Logging Department
    4 Excellent   7 Good   1 Satisfactory   0 Poor
    Raw Material Division
    3 Excellent   9 Good   1 Satisfactory   0 Poor
    Raw Material-Sawmill-Marketing
    2 Excellent   6 Good   4 Satisfactory   0 Poor
    Bend Division-Brooks Resources
    1 Excellent   8 Good   0 Satisfactory   3 Poor
    Whole Company
    4 Excellent   6 Good   2 Satisfactory   0 Poor
8. I am treated honestly and fairly:
    10 Practically always   2 Usually   0 Seldom
9. Brooks-Scanlon as a place to work is:
    6 Excellent   6 Good   0 Satisfactory   0 Poor
10. Improvement in the logging department profit performance could best come from (check three).
    6 Make people feel more of the team.
    7 Improved communication with logging salaried people
    5 Improved communication with hourly people.
    5 Better relations with other company units.
    1 More help with personal problems.
    5 Better logging equipment.
    1 More training of salaried people.
    4 More training of hourly people.
    0 Reorganization of the logging department.
    ☐ Other

---

11 ☐ We should hire a safety director to work for Scotty.
    12 Yes   ☐ No   ☐ ?
12 ☐ Was this worthwhile?   12 Yes 0 No
Names of those involved: Flint, Clyde, Hoover, Groshong, Russ, Holowecky, Goad, Voos, Bishop, Wyllie, Keep, Lundy

Culmination

I knew there were some hard feelings with a couple of other managers, but I knew from my performance evaluations that Mike thought I was making many positive contributions to the company. So I was shocked when he asked for my resignation. I had never been fired before. The resignation was effective in August, 1972.

Being an experienced manager I was probably subconsciously prepared for the unexpected termination. My morale returned to its usual high in a short time. There was minimal acrimony from me toward Mike and there has been little since. My divorce was being finalized and it was time for a fresh start. The trauma gave me an excuse to make several extra trips into the Three Sisters Wilderness Area, to heal.

I did some consulting in addition to a job search.

Reflections on the Bend, Oregon Years

Janet Clark Evans

Some things just seem to work out. I met Janet Clark Evans, a counselor at Bend High School on Dec. 17, 1972, and that by itself made the entire Bend tenure worthwhile. We were married on June 9, 1973 and she remains the greatest thing that has happened to me, by a mile. Not incidentally, Jan puts me in that class of people described as, "What you see is what you get." My eternal thanks to Bob Cother, her boss, who first told me about her.

Bend Oregon

Bend, Oregon is a favorite place to live for many, especially if you like outdoor recreation and dry, crisp 3,700-foot elevation air. I understand that the magnificent Mt. Bachelor Ski Development is rare in being profitable from its first year. It was started after WWII by a couple of 10th Mountain Division veterans.

Twice I had foresters come into my office looking for any kind of work. They and their spouses had seen Bend, loved it, quit their jobs in the east and moved to Bend. Then they started to look for work. We still own land in Bend. Nine months of frost limits the choices of flowers in the gardens. Bend is a petunia mecca.

Selection Logging Of Pine

Ponderosa pine, unlike westside Douglas fir, does well when harvested with a single tree selection system. This has reduced the conflict between tree-preservers and tree-users in the Ponderosa pine type. This means that the forest wars are more civilized than they are where clear-cutting is the preferred tree harvesting system. The Ancient Pine stands along the Santiaim Pass highway have been logged selectively for well over a half century and remain beautiful.

Tough Task

One of the tasks assigned to me while with Brooks related to Bill Swindells Jr., now the CEO of Willamette Industries. Brooks and Willamette, had a 50/50 joint venture. Over the years, in annual negotiations on the allocation of profit of the Redmond plywood plant-stud mill, Willamette ended up more pleased with the results than Brooks. I was assigned the task, mostly involving timber cost and value, of "returning the relationship to parity." Bill Jr. and I did a renegotiation of the methodology used. Mike Hollern seemed pleased with the results of this joyless task, and I thought it was about a draw, hence equitable. If Bill respects me, now, as much as I do him it's a good relationship.

Within the industry, Willamette has a reputation for being a tightly-run, efficient operation. So I was especially pleased that they were the top purchaser (48 copies) of our Washington State Society of American Foresters video that states strongly — "amend the Endangered Species Act to give more consideration to people." If Willamette bought that many it MUST be a good investment. More about the video later. It is STILL TIMELY and still available.

To receive a copy send $11.00 to Video, P. O. Box 2087, Gig Harbor, WA 98335.

Indoor Tennis

I started to play serious-tennis in Bend. There wasn't an indoor tennis facility near Bend. But Brooks had an old unused lumber warehouse with a 60-foot ceiling. With complete cooperation from Brooks, Mike Hollern especially, we soon had two high-quality public indoor tennis courts with good (not great) lighting. The courts were totally paid for with prepaid court time, donated work and a few cash donations and membership (optional) in the newly formed Bend Tennis Club (Jay Gruenfeld president). There wasn't any heat so winter tennis was an experience. The lowest temperature when I played was 8 degrees above zero. Dunlops were the only balls that would bounce adequately at the lowest temperatures.

This was the most pleasing volunteer project I have ever headed or been involved in and, like most Americans, I've been in many volunteer projects, church and secular, that I enjoyed. Cooperation from individuals was almost perfect. It was fun and the courts made an attractive addition to the Bend sports scene. When I left for Potlatch Corporation, since I had spearheaded construction of the courts I received some nice gifts and more importantly, many sincere "thanks." The euphoria produced by the Bend indoor court project led to a similar but much larger, not-as-much-fun project in Lewiston, Idaho.

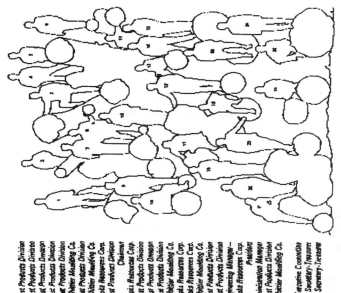

Corporate Management Group

1. Leon E. Devereaux — Purchasing Manager—Forest Products Division
2. Thomas E. Toner — Logging Manager—Forest Products Division
3. Jay Greenfield — Raw Material Manager—Forest Products Division
4. Leo M. Hooper — Production Manager—Forest Products Division
5. J. Calvin Adkisson — Plant Production Manager—Forest Products Division
6. Robert D. Whitier — Vice President—Whitier Manfding Co.
7. Frank M. Gerinacki — Marketing Manager—Forest Products Division
8. Gordon D. Whitier — President—Whitier Manfding Co.
9. C. Wendell Clore — Operations Manager—Brooks Resources Corp.
10. Harry T. Brooks — Plant Services Manager—Forest Products Division
11. Cowley Brooks — Chairman
12. Robert L. Harrison — President—Brooks Restorable Corp.
13. Harold Daley — Controller—Forest Products Division
14. John McCafferey — Personnel Manager—Forest Products Division
15. T. S. Young — Timberlands Manager—Forest Products Division
16. Frank R. Burr — Ass't Sales Manager—Whitier Manfding Co.
17. William L. Smith — Marketing Manager—Brooks Resources Corp.
18. Charles D. Austin — Sales Manager—Brooks Resources Corp.
19. Jeff D. Carl — Ass't to President—Whitier Manfding Co.
20. Bert Hagen — Sales Manager—Forest Products Division
21. Hans C. Miklus — Chief Forester—Forest Products Division
22. Robert E. McHenry — Production & Engineering Manager—Brooks Resources Corp.
23. Machael P. Holam — President
24. Marvin C. May — Administration Manager
25. E. LeRoy Maxley — Data Processing Manager—Forest Products Division
26. William E. Lambom — Plant Manager—Whitier Manfding Co.
(Not Shown)
John M. Holam — Chairman of the Executive Committee
Bernat C. Stofle — Secretary-Treasurer
Nolan J. Lea — Ass't Secretary-Treasurer

Bend, Oregon 1971 Brooks-Scanlon Corporate Management Group (from Annual Report). Brooks did most things in a class way. This photo is an example. Note: Anyone sitting on the end of a log probably got pitch on their pants.

201

Potlatch Corporation Days
1973-1979

Job Searching

In late 1972, there were quite a few jobs available for someone with my background. Weyerhaeuser contacted me about an attractive opportunity they had, based in Hong Kong, as marketing manager. Logs from their South Seas operations were the primary product, but there was some manufactured product responsibility. W. J. Bill Johnson (Vice President, Far East) and Dick Lucas, Tokyo Vice President, interviewed me in Tacoma. It looked like a fit and something might have developed, but the pending marriage to Jan took a lot of the charm out of the Hong Kong location due to the schooling of her two youngest children Lisa 14 and Christopher 12. Also, a Hong Kong location probably wasn't the best place to stabilize a new marriage and bond the new family together.

Note: Bob Rice took the Hong Kong position and did well. He has become a noted authority on the log export business, and since 1984, has been a vice president with CITIFOR, a Chinese government owned corporation— Seattle — that has worldwide forest investments. Citifor, in a joint purchase venture with Fletcher Challenge Ltd., New Zealand and Brierly Investments Ltd. recently acquired 37.5 percent interest in a magnificent New Zealand radiata pine plantation forest of 464,000 acres.

Fortunately Potlatch Corporation was looking for a Vice President of Lands and Forestry, and when the position was offered to me I quickly accepted. It was a solid company with over 1,200,000 acres of forest in Idaho, Arkansas and Minnesota. The salary and benefit package was excellent, and my location was Lewiston, Idaho although the headquarters was San Francisco. I started in June 1973. Jan and I were married June 9.

For me a real attraction was that Weyerhaeuser family members owned over 40 percent of the stock, which assured that there would be strong support for good forestry practices. At that time, 1973, this meant that the Weyerhaeuser family ownership in Potlatch Corporation, 40 plus percent, was about double its ownership in Weyerhaeuser Co.

Please understand that businesswise there was complete separation of the two companies. There weren't any family members that served on both boards.

There was one immediate, small negative to the new job. Rod Steele, the president and my boss, wasn't sure that Lewiston was where I should be based. He thought that San Francisco might be better. In complete honesty, I made a fervent case for the Lewiston location. If I hadn't, we would have had to live in San Francisco. Every single year, at least once, the question would come up. Jan and I both loved to visit San Francisco, but neither of us wanted to live there except in a no-other-choice situation. Also, daughter Deni was a sophomore at the University of Idaho, Moscow, Idaho, 35 miles away. We vowed that we would never move to San Francisco.

The company Lear jet was based in Lewiston, so transportation to San Francisco wasn't usually a problem. A nice fringe benefit for corporate officers was that extra seats on the Lear could be used by family members, kids included. The pilots, in addition to being top-flight fliers, were all fine, friendly people and it spoiled us for commercial travel. Commercial plane trips never measured-up to traveling on the company Lear.

An Attractive Job And Location

Frankly I would have preferred a line position of managing 300,000 acres or so of western forest plus the utilization plants. However, no such job was available, and I was very pleased to have the Potlatch assignment, even though it was a corporate staff position. The base salary was about 40 percent more than at Brooks and the stock options and bonus opportunities were better. An additional plus was the location relative to the boss (President Rod Steele). Virtually anyone who has had a top-level staff position and wants to be productive while enjoying life on-the-job will probably agree with me that "No matter how considerate the boss is, it is better to have him based two-hours-by-jet away rather than in the next office." Rod was easy to work for and basically a good guy. We got along well despite some philosophical differences, perhaps because of our geographical separation.

Lewiston, Idaho

Lewiston to most people doesn't rank with Bend, Oregon as a place to live, but to me it was a little better. Bend is developing a sort of semi-yuppie west culture while Lewiston, though roughly the same size, has more of a western small-town flavor. For me, the primary reason for a Lewiston preference was the availability of superior hunting and fishing while still being close to Wilderness Areas. Lewiston is only 700 feet in elevation and has a mild microclimate.

The town has a picturesque location at the junction of the Snake and Clearwater Rivers. Clarkston, Washington lies just across the Snake River.

We bought (at a very low cost) a magnificent old home in excellent condition, which had been built by the first doctor in the valley (Dr. Morris) in 1898. It had big white columns, about 5,600 square feet on two thirds of an acre, great view up the Clearwater Valley, nice swimming pool with a sauna that we didn't use once, grape arbor and a covey of quail that roosted every night in a Doug-fir in the back yard. You could leave home and in fifteen minutes be hunting upland birds (chukar and Hungarian partridge, pheasants, and quail) or waterfowl with a good chance of success. It isn't the same today. We happened to hit the peak bird populations. The commute to work was 10 or 15 minutes.

We made many friends and had an ideal social life. The kids had some misgivings about leaving Bend, but adapted quickly and loved Lewiston.

Work Responsibilities

Here is a 1978 listing of what I responsible for. It was essentially the same as 1973 but used updated terminology. One ideal feature from my perspective was that I was expected to be aware of nationwide forest management practices and their environmental and political ramifications. This especially applied to Idaho, Arkansas and Minnesota where Potlatch in 1973 owned 1.3 million acres (over 2,000 square miles): (490M, 557M and 240M acres respectively).

Potlatch Corporation
Vice President Lands and Forestry
Responsibilities
(I supplied part of this -- grin.)

1. Counsel on and help coordinate forest policy, planning, programs and operations so they comply with the corporate philosophy, therefore are profit optimizing and socially responsible. Provide technical forestry advice. Encourage the intensification of forestry practices when it is sufficiently profitable and environmentally sound.

2. Assess tree farming activities and forest management plans at each division to help determine whether the objectives and results are economically sound and environmentally acceptable. Protection of the soil and water resource is paramount.

3. Assist in the development of valid and consistent methods of economic analysis of forest management and closely related subjects, such as total wood flow and supply.

4. Monitor and evaluate major governmental legislative proposals and regulation on forest resource issues of national importance. Propose positions on priority issues and direct the corporate effort on assigned government relations projects.

5. Provide primary counsel and representation on corporate forestry subjects.

6. Provide counsel on the selection of key tree farming personnel and organizational decisions.

7. Coordinate forestry research activities so the optimum short and long range corporate objectives are attained. Assist in providing communications and coordination between all corporate research organizations.

8. Represent Potlatch in national trade associations on timber supply and land management subjects and in regional and national environmental organizations.

9. Develop and maintain professional forestry contacts with principal forestry schools, other corporations and associations; and public agencies, as requested by divisions, or when objectives are multi-divisional. The following abstract of Potlatch experience will emphasize what relates most direct to the comments made at the end of this book on federal forest management policy and legislation.

Politics
My first Washington, D. C. political experience had been in 1961 when I made a presentation regarding the proposed Wilderness Act as Chair of the Puget Sound Section of the Society of American Foresters. The Society's national position was pro-Wilderness Area establishment, but we wanted an inventory of the resource prior to establishing the final boundaries. The bill passed without any inventory of what was preserved, hence without much knowledge of the economic value of what was being set-aside. Additions to the Wilderness system since have often had a similar lack of information.
My prior positions with Weyerhaeuser and Brooks-Scanlon had an element of political action, but at Potlatch forest related politics were a principal part of the job.

The Environmental Legislation Decade — The 1970's
The early 1970s were both a stimulating and numbing time to be working on forest-related legislation in Washington, D.C. There were so many pieces of forest-impacting leg-

islation being considered that it was difficult to keep up with anything other than the top priority areas. I believe that this is why the Endangered Species Act (ESA) passed in its present well-meaning but flawed form — signed into law by Richard Nixon. The ESA never received a high enough priority rating from those whose economic interests were negatively affected and who had a mainstream value system. This included a high majority of the people in the United States.

Assignments

I chaired the National Forest Products Association (NFPA)'s Land Use Committee. Land use policy had always interested me so this was a welcome though demanding assignment. In the late 50s and early 60s, I had been on the Western Forestry and Conservation Association (WFCA)'s Land Committee. I was very inexperienced then to be serving with authorities who had the experience and wisdom of Charlie Connaughton, regional forester for the US Forest Service Region 6 (Washington and Oregon), Henry Vaux, Dean of Forestry at University of California (Berkeley) and others, but this was one of the advantages of working for powerful and well-regarded Weyerhaeuser.

The Land-Use Bill

Proposed federal legislation was an important part of our committee's work.

There was a strong movement to try and pass a National Land-Use bill that would have considerable impact on the rights of private land owners. To most of us this looked like a bureaucrat's dream and a private sectors' nightmare. Weyerhauser thought that passage of such a bill was inevitable, and urged us to negotiate with the Democratic administration to "get the best bill possible."

An Unforgettable Presentation

A former congressman from Arizona (I can't remember his name, but know he wore cowboy boots) made a brief presentation to the committee. With eloquent and forceful words he told us in a couple of different ways —

"The single biggest reason for the passage of bad legislation is that the opposition thought they were licked and settled for the best piece of legislation they thought they could get."

Ultimately common-sense politics prevailed and the legislation to create a National Land Use Planning System was defeated. My opinion is that land-use planning should be done at the lowest feasible level; probably county level in most cases, with a few basic guidelines provided by the State.

More On Bureaucracy

Russian Communism collapsed primarily because their bureaucratic government-centered system failed to provide the material things that people desire. Freedom was an objective too, but a desire for the "things" democratic capitalism provides throughout the world seems to have been the prime motivation.

President Clinton senses that most voters recognize that governments are inherently inefficient and he is ready now to act as though he favors less government. His 1993 Forest Plan, however, is a classic example of government doing things wrong. I hope that the 1997 Clinton administration will change the root legislative and administrative flaws that allowed the people-cruel Forest Plan to be activated.

Secretary Of The Interior Andrus' Plan

Cecil Andrus, who had been the very popular Governor of Idaho when I joined Potlatch in 1973, did not run for reelection and became Secretary of the Interior. I knew Cece a little because of Potlatch being the number one or number two employer in sparsely populated Idaho. Cece had been a logger so could communicate relatively well on forest management problems.

Soon after becoming Secretary of the Interior, Cece dropped a bombshell on the Forest Service and the forest industry. He said essentially. "It's stupid and inefficient for the federal government to have two gigantic bureaucracies (the Forest Service and the Bureau of Land Management-BLM) both managing huge separate chunks of public land throughout the West. What is needed is a single land management agency."

It is hard to argue with his basic premise since the amount of duplication in administrative overhead alone was staggering. But the Forest Industry pro's thought the Resource Management Agency he proposed would end up in the Department of Interior, with the National Park System and tree harvesting would be reduced. The US Forest Service leaders were afraid that it meant the end of the USFS, a proud organization. So, for different reasons, most of the forest industry and the USFS leader were opposed to the reorganization.

Since I knew Secretary Andrus and chaired the industry's Land Use committee, I was asked several times to contact him. This had little to do with any significant action. I was just a communications link. What Cece proposed had been suggested before, and floundered on the politics of the situation, and it eventually did this time. Then, I was neutral about a reorganization, but today I am totally in favor of creating a single organization to manage federal forests that are producing wood.

Note: My communications role did lead to having a nice dinner with Cece and his wife Carol. Part of the conversation was about Admiral Stansfield Turner, the head of the CIA and a good friend of the Andrus's. Turner had been a Rhodes Scholar at Exeter College which I was attending and we met there. He had played football at the Naval Academy and rugby at Oxford. I was about to play my first game of rugby for the college (on the Second 15) and he gave me some good tips. They were needed because my last football playing was as an 87 pound guard on a sandlot team.

Comments On The US Forest Service,
U.S. Department of Agriculture

My initial contact with the Forest Service was as a summer employee in 1942 fighting fire and pulling Ribes plants (current and gooseberry species), the alternate host for the White Pine Blister Rust. The summer of 1947 was with the USFS cruising timber and doing other management plan work in the Redwood Region, Six Rivers National Forest. Also, I did some part-time work compiling forest type data for the

Roosevelt National Forest while a student at Colorado A&M — 1946 - 1949. For the past 45 years, my association with the USFS each year has never been less than sporadic and usually could be rated, frequent. So I have a long experience on which to base the following comments.

Like a large majority of foresters, I had a very high regard for the people, objectives and actions of the US Forest Service for most of my career. The USFS though a bureaucracy was one of the best. In the past several years this has changed. Now I seldom defend the Forest Service. Here are some of the reasons for my change of feeling.

In the middle 70s, when in Washington, D.C. particularly, I often found myself defending Forest Service top level managers against criticism by forest industry governmental affairs personnel. Person after person, often sincere and knowledgeable foresters expressing a personal professional concern, would tell me the same basic things.

"The Forest Service has changed. Now their primary goal seems to be to survive as an agency. Instead of managing national forests for 'the greatest good for the greatest number in the long run,' their traditional role, the Forest Service does what is politically expedient. They do what they believe is best for the Forest Service, not what is good for the country. Preservation extremists who believe it is more important to temporarily preserve over-mature trees than preserve people's livelihoods, though only a small minority, are clever and well funded; and have great political clout. Preservationists more and more are calling the tune."

Now, in 1996 its obvious to me that these people who distrusted the Forest Service were right. One reason preservationists have obtained so much clout are the communications failures of the forest industry and the forestry profession. Later I'll give specific examples, but initially let's take a broader look. The following 1978 talk shows my on-going concern about the need for communications improvement.

Let's Talk and Listen More and Fight Less -- given at the 1978 Annual Meeting of the Society of American Foresters

"Communication failures, that is inability to receive or convey information, are a primary cause of forest resource problems and human problems generally. Here are two common examples of communications failures that will probably sound familiar.

"Communications on policy don't reach lower echelons or are not understood, therefore actions on the ground don't agree with policy.

"Facts are not shared between the opposing sides on an issue so the apparent area of disagreement is larger than the actual.

"The Society of American Foresters has devoted an important part of its national meeting to communications. It has acted as though communications are important and actions are needed. Our educational system also recognizes the importance of communications. The secondary education basics of reading, writing and arithmetic have two specific communications elements, and arithmetic certainly functions as a communications tool. When we criticize lack of emphasis on "the three R's," we are usually saying, "graduates can't communicate adequately."

The major purposes of this panel are to give you some forest resource oriented opinions on how to communicate, who to communicate with, and what should be communicated. Two-way communication is usually best and you will have a chance after the presentation to question or comment. Communications is an especially timely subject since public land managers are now often required by law to communicate with the public. Legislation that requires public input includes the Wilderness Act of 1964, the National Environmental Policy Act of 1970, the National Forest Roads and Trails Act of 1968, and the National Forest Management Act of 1976.

Another indication of timeliness relates to the current number one forestry issue in the lower 48, RARE II (Roadless Area Review and Evaluation). There is a common suggestion coming from Secretary of Agriculture Bergland, Assistant Secretary Cutler, Chief John McGuire, Senator Frank Church, and other legislators on how to speed resolution of the national forest roadless area issue. It's a call for consensus between various user groups. And you can't get consensus without communication.

Further, this seems to be a time when environmentalists and industry are more willing to talk and listen. The time seems to be right for more dialogue to speed resolution of major issues. As the Executive Director of the Sierra Club has said, "All parties see that it's now too easy for each side to checkmate by some legal or appellate action." Mike McCloskey should know. Checkmates hinder progress and there is agreement that more progress in problem resolution is necessary. Dialogue between the right people at the right time usually tends to develop mutual respect, identifies areas of agreement, narrows the area of conflict, increases listening ability, and is a good tool to achieve a balanced solution. But what particularly does this have to do with foresters?

The primary objective of the Society of American Foresters is "to use knowledge and skills of the profession to benefit society." Therefore, because of the overwhelming importance of communications in achieving objectives, SAF members have an obligation not only to communicate but to do it credibly. Credibility is of primary importance to successful communications. We all know this but it's easy to forget that just telling the truth as we see it isn't enough. Forestry wisdom is much more than just truth. To develop credibility the other party must understand what you are conveying and hear it in a credible context. Professionals have a special responsibility to be wise enough to be credible. The world is full of statements that are truthful but not believed.

Credible communications will help the professional forester reduce the public distrust of the forest land managers. Specifically there is distrust of the ability to manage for commodity values while protecting non-commodity values. Managing for timber and wildlife or timber and scenery are examples. To overcome this distrust and to achieve our other professional goals, we must act as though we believe that communications are important. We must communicate factually, analytically, credibly, often, and effectively. But first we must perform effectively on the ground.

212

We communicate based on what our forest lands say to the public. Public understanding is enhanced by good performance on the ground. Our credibility is obviously determined both by what we say and what we do.

Communicating usually reduces conflict. This is one reason why I am a member of the Western Forest Environment Discussion Group, which includes members of the environmental community and industry. One of the members is Mike McCloskey, Executive Director of the Sierra Club. We seek areas of agreement. Also, I recently became a member of an ad hoc Idaho group of eight forest industry people and eight environmentalists who are trying to contribute to the resolution of the roadless area issue in Idaho. Membership in these groups has strengthened my belief that talking to and listening to other forest users is worthwhile.

Perhaps I feel so strongly about communication because it's part of my philosophy that if we are "to use the knowledge and skills of the profession to benefit society," we must get into the process. We should listen but we should also speak out. We are professionals, but we are also citizens and have responsibilities in both areas, especially where the obligations overlap such as they do on public land management issues. Our obligation is to be part of the input to the decision process. I urge you to communicate two-way with the opposition on forest land issues. This results in more agreement on facts, identifies the non-issues, reduces the area of conflict, and develops mutual respect. In other words, it creates a climate that encourages a more optimum and less costly resolution. Let's talk and listen more and fight less.

Finally, to the members of the SAF. Let's assume we accept the premise that improved communications between forest users is desirable.

What organization should take the lead in promoting improved communications? Why not the Society of American Foresters? It has many of the disciplines required, represents the spectrum of land ownerships, it's relatively credible, and most importantly this would help achieve our objective of public benefit from use of the knowledge and skills of the profession. Let's communicate about this." End of talk.

Twelve years later the need was increasing.

Public Indoor Tennis For Lewiston

Despite an abundance of recreation in "The Valley," for some of us there was one major lack — indoor tennis. Fresh from the indoor-tennis project in Bend, and full of enthusiasm for Lewiston and its people, and wanting to play tennis year around, it didn't take long before Jan and I did some initial contacting to determine the level of interest in indoor tennis. We then helped form the Valley Racquet Club with me as the first president. Our club objective — public indoor tennis.

The Lewis-Clark State College had land that could be used for an indoor tennis facility and the president, Lee Vickers and his wife, Deana played tennis. A marketing study indicated that indoor tennis appeared economically feasible, maybe. So we surged ahead.

After about six months of legwork including great help from many people, but especially engineer Roger Tutty, the Friddles and building contractor Vernon Dimke, whose wife Shirley played tennis, we made a breakthrough. The club had raised $10,000 thousand dollars, most from donations and pre-paid court time. The college had some money budgeted for the facility, but we needed to borrow $100,000 and the First National Bank of Idaho, Lewiston said they would loan us money, providing we would get guarantors for the loan amount.

The Lewiston Morning Tribune provided some publicity and we began a campaign to get guarantors. Very soon it was apparent that we wouldn't get enough guaranteed money in the Valley. Wynne Blake, who did legal work for Potlatch and had played tennis, made a suggestion. Wynne said, "Fritz Jewett always liked Lewiston when he lived here, why don't you try him?"

First Public Disclosure of A Well Kept Secret

G. F. "Fritz" Jewett and his wife Lucy lived in Tiburon, California. Fritz was Senior Vice President with Potlatch and on the Board of Directors. The Jewetts were a "Weyerhaeuser" family. (Margaret Weyerhaeuser and James Richard Jewett married in 1894.) I had met Fritz and Lucy when Fritz was working at Weyco's Everett pulpmill in the 1960's.

The Jewetts were generous and supported many worthy causes, including several America's Cup entries. I wasn't

214

too surprised when Fritz said yes, with enthusiasm — but he wanted their participation to be anonymous. I assured him that the financial pro-forma looked favorable, and only requiring 29 percent prime-time occupancy to pay-out. How wrong I was in believing the pro-forma I had helped prepare.

"The indoor tennis facility would not have been built without the Jewett guarantee." The indoor court project took a ton of time and occasionally even interfered with my hunting (though never with the job).

Once the metal framework was constructed, using primarily volunteer labor, we constructed the metal building that covered the four quality lighted courts with an attached small building for the office, rest rooms and a small waiting room. It took about a year.

The first of two big disappointment's in the project was our inability to get hardly any work out of the tennis players who were in their late teens and 20s. Many of us tried but we couldn't activate them. The forty-and-fifty-year-age classes did the most work.

The second big disappointment occurred because we had believed our market survey results when preparing the business plan. Actual court use was about half of what we thought was a conservative projection. I deserve most of any blame. We were quickly in deep financial trouble.

A Silver Lining

The bank vice president who had made the loan told me that they made the loan mainly as a public relations gesture. They thought based on past experience they would eventually be stuck with any loan that the Valley Racquet Club couldn't repay.

Tennis guarantors apparently are a very moral breed. Every penny of guaranteed money was repaid with interest. Over time the guarantors ended up paying, due to interest, a little more than they had guaranteed (over $100,000 in total). It cost the Gruenfelds over $6,000, and we still have over $200 of unused prepaid court time.

But the college now has a flourishing public tennis program based on the public indoor tennis facility and the Valley has indoor tennis. It was a worthwhile effort.

215

I regard my participation in the Lewiston indoor tennis project the way I regard serving, later, on the Old Growth Commission of the State of Washington and my World War II infantry combat time.

"I wouldn't trade it for anything, but I wouldn't want to do it again."

Potlatch Communications

My contributions to Potlatch were often in some phase of communications. Some improvements were strongly supported and were new. Prior to my arrival, Potlatch, despite its diverse land ownership (Idaho, Arkansas and Minnesota), had never had a company-wide forestry meeting. The first one was in Minnesota and was well received by the attendees. I've always been a believer in the occasional use of carefully constructed anonymous questionnaires. Some people simply won't speak-up but they'll write. (See 1976 Corporate Forest Management Meetings - Evaluation Questionnaire.)

Forestry research had been expanded and the researchers wanted to have a meeting to pool and coordinate their activities.

A Potlatch Corporation Communications Success, That Should Be Standard Procedure in Industry

One of the most gratifying and productive activities that I was able to suggest and help establish was a Communications Council for the Lewiston, Idaho operations of Potlatch. All I could do was encourage this sort of thing. The action decision was made by the Wood Products and Pulp & Paper vice presidents, as it should have been.

The following excerpts from our 1992 bilingual marketing conference, "Marketing Forest Products of the Pacific Rim" in Santiago, Chile include how I described the Communications Council. This is followed by excerpts from my paper given at a general session of the 1991 Annual Meeting of the Society of American Foresters in San Francisco.

Examples Of Successful Communications Efforts

In northern Idaho, on the banks of the beautiful Clearwater River, which has a large run of salmon and searun rainbow trout (steelhead), is a 1,300 ton per day, bleached Kraft paper mill, with a tissue mill and sawmill. Lewiston, Idaho and Clarkston, Washington are adjoining towns (separated by the Snake River) with a total population of 40,000. The forest that supplies the wood is both private and public. Clearcutting is the primary method of logging. Not surprisingly, this operation of Potlatch Corporation has ongoing public relations problems. But, the problems are much less since a rather unique communications group was started in 1974 and still functions. It is called the Communications Council.

Communications Council

The council is a critical board of review, consisting primarily of people from outside Potlatch, who meet with a small group of company personnel. Some of the outsiders were severe critics of Potlatch. The members are asked to give their honest opinions on how the company is doing in its relations with the public, and on how to improve relations with the community and the public generally. It meets three or four times each year. The basic program is for the company to give a short presentation on some phase of company activity followed by a relatively long period of discussion. The discussion covers what the council members want it to cover. Sometimes the meetings got pretty emotional. However, the overall results have been the establishment of effective two way communication and an improvement in community relations. Over the years the membership of the group, both company and non-company, has been changed often enough that a significant portion of the media, Fish and Game Department and other politically strong citizens and groups, have been on the Communications Council. The council members and ax-members are credible communicators with other citizens. They are more believable than a company employee saying the same thing.

The effectiveness of the council is, of course, dependent on the support given by line management, and their communications effectiveness. Sometimes when, in a Communications Council session, listening to a person make a complaint, to which I knew there was no really acceptable reply, I recalled a statement by a very wise man.

This very successful ruler said, essentially, that when dealing with the public, it was important to give them a chance to make a complaint, even when it might not be possible to do anything about the problem. Just having someone with authority patiently listen to the complaint often satisfied the person, or group involved. This wise comment on public relations was made about 4,000 years ago by one of the Egyptian Pharaohs. It's still wisdom.

An Opinion on Changing the Communications Role of the Professional Forester and Forest Businesses, In Today's Political and Social Environment

In this paper, I will give some opinions on how the role, or function, of the forestry profession needs to change, so that foresters provide increased benefits to society, and to their employers. Also, I will give some suggestion to the forest business community that I hope will result in increased benefits to them and to society.

These are turbulent times in the management of forest land throughout the world. There is a worldwide demand for an improvement in environmental quality, and an increasing demand for forest products. Politics are very often determining the type of forest management that is practiced. Like most professional foresters, and people in general, I believe that continuing improvement in the World Environment and forest management practices is necessary and desirable.

Also, like most professional foresters in the US, I believe that the land use of our federal forest lands is heavily out of balance in favor of tree preservation instead of sustainable tree production. This is because political activists have been successful in using the public desire for environmental improvement to achieve ends that are sometimes unnecessarily cruel to people, but kind to plants and animals. The primary driving force behind these actions is a small minority of effective environmental extremists with massive amounts of money, considerable volunteer labor, excellent communications skills and an army of lawyers. (Please note: On a per

218

capita basis, I'm told Japan has about 98 percent less lawyers than the United States, or to say it another way, we have 50 times as many lawyers as they do. So, in Japan the legislative and judicial systems are much less likely to be used to stop the production of wood products than in the US. This is one of the secrets of Japan's success. (To those of you who are attorneys — pardon! Nothing personal is intended).

Though I rate our general business system very high, I see it as being much less than perfect. Here is an example.

Business Has Failed In At Least Two Big Ways In Communications

A major reason for the success of preservationists in forest land-use political battles is the miserable performance by the business community in communications — a failure to credibly convey information — a failure to educate — a failure to hear. Business has failed big, in a doubled barreled way. First, they have failed to adequately communicate the many good things they have done that are helpful to society. And second, by a relatively few dumb actions, they have very clearly communicated with the public in a politically devastating negative way. Communication failures are common to businesses generally, but I will talk principally about forest businesses.

I suspect that many of you, too, believe that business generally has failed to communicate adequately, and I believe it is an opinion shared by the overwhelming majority of forest business people in the United States.

Dumb Actions

The second general failure of the forest industry and public forest managers is they too often clearly communication the wrong thing.

An example, from about 30 years ago, was the clearcutting of about 40 hectares of giant redwood trees on an industry owned tract (at Bonny Glen) that adjoins heavily traveled highway 101 in California. This single act triggered legislation that resulted in the establishment of the Redwood

National Park. This park has relatively little use and cost the taxpayers over 2 billion dollars.

In both of these cases some partial cutting could have been used rather than clearcutting. Partial cuts would have greatly reduced the negative reaction from the public, and still regenerated the stand. Using smaller sized clearcuts and leaving uncut scenic strips for several years, would have reduced the negative perceptions of the public. Yes, it would have cost some money, but the benefits would have made it a wise investment.

Politics Are Perceptions

Politics are perceptions, that is, political actions result from what people think is true, not from the facts. Many people are offended by clearcuts, so they must be used carefully. Regardless of the biological and economic justification for big clearcuts, they are sometimes the political equivalent of spitting in someone's face. This is particularly true in the United States. Because there has been such a pathetic failure to adequately communicate key points, such as the fact that tree production is beneficial and sustainable, and how trees relate to the public's pocket book and the need for forest products.

Media

Media personnel, on average, are biased against businesses. Even my media friends agree that generally the media is biased against business. This bias increases the problem of communicating with the media. Part of the reason for this anti-industry attitude is that industry has failed to communicate the right things, on a timely basis. For example, sometimes stories are slanted against us because the reporter could not find someone who could give them the truth, in time to meet the story deadline. The media cannot use the truth if they don't know what it is. The media will seldom get truth that helps "us" from environmental extremists, who are usually capable and persistent communicators.

Communications Failures Led to Unwise Land Use

On many critical subjects, the business community has been massively outspent by environmental organizations in communicating with the voters, and other parts of the power structures that determine political action. On timber supply and other issues affecting forest industries, the voters are largely either uninformed or misinformed. The political balance is heavily weighted toward preservation rather than wise use. Unwise land use decisions are being made. In my opinion, too much sustainable public forest wealth is being set-aside and not used at all, instead of being used wisely for wood.

The Japanese, and others, are watching the forest land use debates in the United States with great interest. So far, it does look as though over one million hectares of extremely valuable public old growth forest will be set aside in Washington, Oregon and California (with no timber harvesting allowed) to protect the spotted owl, a threatened species. (Note: The annual sustainable harvest on this land is high enough that if converted entirely to lumber it would equal over 10 percent of the total US lumber consumption). The Japanese must import about 60 to 70 percent of their total wood consumption. If Japan is forced to buy more wood from tropical countries, in log or product form, it could cause environmental damage in those countries. So environmentalists would be creating more environmental problems instead of reducing them.

Time for the Forestry Profession to Speak Out

Since industry is making only a modest effort to communicate with the public on forest issues, and environmental extremists have such massive well financed strength, it is no wonder that preservationist and other environmental extremists are overly successful, and the public is suffering. Additional communications about forests and forest products are required if we are to get more balance into forest management decision making. The forestry profession can provide some of that additional truthful communications. There has been a start.

Currently I am a member of the Washington Society of American Foresters video committee which was formed in April 1991. We have just produced a 13 minute video tape that clearly and credibly urges amending the Endangered Species Act to give more consideration to its impacts on people. This, first of a kind, professionally done video has been well received. We have nearly paid for it by selling video copies, and soon revenues will go toward producing additional videos.

In my opinion, in this media dominated era, foresters and others in forest related activity cannot adequately communicate and be politically effective without using truthful, credible, expertly done videos.

In Conclusion

First, a final comment to those of you who are professional foresters, regardless of your nationality. If we as professional foresters want to use the knowledge and skills of the profession to benefit society, we must get further into the national debate, further into the process. We must listen and hear, but we must also speak out. We are professionals, but we are also citizens and have responsibilities in both sectors. Our obligation is to be part of the input to the decision process. So far we have been almost silent.

And finally I will summarize the other suggestions made to the forest related business community —

1. Expand your communications efforts with the public and with environmentalists. Be both truthful and believable when communicating — sometimes we tell important truths that are not understood, so they cannot be believed. Use videos to communicate. Listen as well as speak. Make use of your foresters — they are usually believable, partly because they are usually sincere, dedicated people.

2. Consider establishing Communications Councils that will enable your organization to develop two-way communications with key citizen groups. Some of you may have already done so.

3. Remember that politics are perceptions, people act according to what they believe — and often act emotionally rather than rationally. Therefore, be careful in the use of forestry management techniques such as clearcutting and herbicides. Education and understanding, and truth, are necessary for the establishment of good public relations.

4. Keep improving your environmental performance. What voters regard as acceptable performance is a moving target — and it's usually moving up, rather than down. So, just keeping up with public opinion requires constant improvement.

It has been a pleasure and an honor to share these thoughts of an old forester, with you. I hope they will be helpful.
(End of excerpts.)

To Industry Generally

Several times since leaving Potlatch I heard good comments from non-Potlatchers about how much benefit the company gained from the functioning of the Communications Council. A couple of times my source was the Department of Wildlife, another time a reporter.

In September '96, Judy Keller of the Potlatch Public Affairs Department said that Council had been very helpful over the years and was presently being revitalized.

Suggestion To Industry Executives (Any Industry):

Consider establishing a Communications Council — unless, of course, you don't have any public relations problems. My Potlatch boss wasn't noted for his public affairs bent, but he thought this was one of my better ideas.

The Western Forest Environment Discussion Group

Many of us who were experienced at dealing with environmental issues knew that we needed better communications with the moderate elements of the environmental community. There had to be some mutually beneficial ways to communicate with the other-side(s) in what were increasingly becoming Environmental Wars. I have a special reason for using the military term.

223

The way available to me was not with what I would normally call a moderate. It was with the Executive Director of the Sierra Club, Mike McCloskey. What happened is described in the following 1978 article from Western Outdoors magazine

Communications Reduces Fighting, So . . .

The Western Forest Environment Discussion Group has now met six times and is gaining strength. It consists of conservationists of diverse interests, industry and environmentalists, who meet to determine areas of agreement on forest land issues and take some mutually beneficial action.

On June 22, 1976 on my initiative, I had a long and stimulating talk with Mike McCloskey, Executive Director of the Sierra Club. One conclusion was that more low key dialogue between industry and environmentalists was necessary. Too often opposing sides became polarized and non-issues were mixed in with real issues and communications stopped. Two months later we met with Dwight Taylor, a Senior Vice President of Crown Zellerbach, and decided to try and form a discussion group.

At a recent forum meeting in Eugene, Oregon, I explained how important it was to avoid extremist views in a discussion group. I got a big laugh when I said that we included in the group that well-known "moderate" Michael McCloskey of the Sierra Club. Mike has been thoroughly constructive in his participation with the group. If we succeed, he deserves much of the credit.

The following general guidelines were used to organize the first meeting which was held on November 23, 1976, in Portland, Oregon

People invited would be open-minded, positive thinkers, who could impact policy in their organizations and would listen as well as talk.

Emphasis would be on discussing subjects where there was potential agreement.

The geographical scope would be the West.

Initially emphasis would be on low key discussions with zero publicity.

If the group couldn't agree on significant areas and couldn't stimulate some action as a result of the agreement, it probably would not survive.

We are in total agreement that the meeting format and guidelines are important, especially at first. There is caution to avoid giving an apparent advantage to either side. For example, meeting minutes are done alternately by an environmentalist and an industry person. Mike McCloskey and I each chair one-half of each meeting, normally meeting expenses are shared, etc. Outside experts are invited to give short presentations and join in the discussion. One presentation resulted in our being a designated oversight body for a Forest Service project on Roadless Area - Intensive Management being conducted by the Pacific Northwest Forest and Range Experiment Station.

At the first meeting a list of potential areas of agreement was developed. Agreement on certain subjects has been surprisingly easy to achieve. As a result our actions have included, for example, letters to the Chief of the Forest Service and others on avoiding the overbuilding of forest roads, and to the President and cabinet officers on our opposition to separating the research organization of the Forest Service from the land management arm. Our letters have received attention. Other actions are pending.

The group has had some modest successes, and is very much alive and generally optimistic about the future. This is due partly to the timelessness of the effort and the usual good effects of improved communications. Dialogue between the right people usually tends to develop mutual respect, narrows the area of conflict, identifies areas of agreement, increases listening ability and is a good tool to achieve balance.

Perhaps there is surprise that we should be so willing to communicate. From the industry side, I can tell you that this effort has broad support from all echelons. The most negative comments run along the line of, "Nothing worthwhile will come of it but it's worth a try" or "You will probably end up getting shafted but it's worth a try." I suspect the environmentalists hear the same thing.

Like most of industry, my company strongly supports efforts to improve communications with environmentalists and other forest land users. In the corporate philosophy booklet, "the Potlatch Corporation encourages open, two-way communications and understanding of all matters of mutual interest and concern."

Most of us are relative pragmatists and would not be involved if we didn't think there were some direct benefit for our "side". Normally most of the discussion and actions benefit both sides. Also this benefits the public, and that's a great bonus. I believe most of us honestly see in this group an opportunity to provide public benefits beyond those benefits for our particular constituency.

Perhaps our socio-economic system doesn't do quite enough in providing productive ways for expressing realistic idealism. Another way of saying part of this is that discussion groups provide a somewhat sheltered mechanism for the expression of some idealism by both sides. This usually contributes directly to the success of our particular organization and the nation.

Part of the success of the group comes from the feeling that neither industry nor the environmentalists are approaching this as some sort of subtle strategy to ultimately torpedo the other side. Naturally, primary appeal comes from the dialogue being mutually advantageous. For example, we are responding to the common sense of decreasing the strife, and benefiting our own constituencies and the public by determining the non issues. This saves time and money, speeds necessary action, and reduces frustration.

In a major step, Senator Church, supported by Senator McClure, catalyzed the forming of a coalition that developed a wilderness area - timber harvesting - nonwilderness recreation compromise. This was for the Gospel Hump Area near Grangeville, Idaho. The political-socioeconomic climate was right for dialogue.

Future

What about the future of our discussion group? There are two contrasting scenarios. In one, due to lack of obvious benefits, hence lack of interest, the organization gradually dies.

On the other extreme, due to its timeliness and logical method of operation, the group thrives, becomes a significant force in resolving and reducing forest resource problems, and the concept spreads. Currently, I think we believe it's likely the group will thrive.

If discussion groups were a worldwide activity, it would help the developing countries avoid mistakes made in developed countries. Regardless of the differences in problems and cultures, discussions between conservationists of differing points of view will usually help resolve issues by identifying areas of agreement and beneficial actions.

Current members are:

Vincent Bousquet. Weyerhaeuser Company

Rus Fredsall, Director Resources. Western Wood Products Association.

Vern Gurnsey, Vice President Industry Affairs, Boise Cascade Corporation.

John Hampton, President, Willamina Lumber Company.

Dale Jones, Northwest Representative, Friends of the Earth.

Bronson Lewis, Executive Vice President, American Plywood Association.

Cliff Merritt, Wilderness Society.

Glenn Olson, Audubon Society.

William Reavley, Western Regional Executive Director, National Wildlife Assn.

Dexter Tight, Director Government and Public Affairs, Crown Zellerbach Corp.

Henry Vaux, Professor, Dept. of Forestry & Conservation, University of California.

Larry Williams, Executive Director, Oregon Environmental Council.

Hazel Wolf, President, Federation of Western Outdoor Clubs.

Mike and I are co-chairmen.

In addition, frequent attendees are Jim Eaton of the Wilderness Society, Phil Schneider of the National Wildlife Federation, and Doug Scott of the Sierra Club.

Jay Gruenfeld is Co-Chairman of the Western Forest Environment Discussion Group and Vice President, Land and For-

227

estry, Potlatch Corporation. He was formerly with Weyerhaeuser Company for 18 years.
(End of article.)

Rod Steele's Opinion About Dialogue with
Environmentalists

After the Western Forest Environment Discussion Group had been meeting about nine months I went to San Francisco to see my boss, Rod Steele the President of Potlatch, for our periodic meeting on performance evaluation. Rod was a Certified Public Accountant, and had spent almost his entire working life in the forest industry. He had a good work ethic and treated me very fairly. I liked and respected Rod, though we didn't always see things the same way and he seemed to feel the same about me. For instance he was a conservative Republican, ex-Navy and drank martini's, while I was an Independent who usually voted Republican, ex-Army and drank manhattans.

A Steele Opinion

After we had discussed other objectives for the coming year I told him of the plans for continuing the Discussion Group. He then made two very dramatic and indicative comments. These are nearly exact quotes.

"I want you to understand something very clearly. I will let you do the Discussion Group thing because you seem to think it is worthwhile and you are doing many other things I approve of. But if you do the best job in the history of the World on it you aren't going to get a single bonus point."

"Why?" I asked, although I thought I knew what his answer would be.

"They are the enemy and you don't talk to the enemy!" he said.

"You don't really believe that?"

"Yes I do, they are the enemy just the way the Japanese were in the War."

I told him, sure that some of those who opposed us, the worst, perhaps especially a few of the professional lobbyists who were attorney's, couldn't be trusted and were "the enemy." But that many of the other-side were pretty nice folks, with a different forest-value system, who simply didn't have a clue about what was being traded off in the name of the environment and more wilderness. And these people were certainly worth talking too. For pure self-interest the forest business community needed to develop more low-key dialogue and mutual trust with the other-side(s) and were starting near zero. That certainly McCloskey personally wasn't a moderate, but he had been very helpful, doubtless because he saw some benefits for them. (For instance, the forest industry and the Sierra Club agreed that the US Forest Service tended to overbuild roads.)

Our discussion never got very heated, we just told each other very clearly what we thought. Neither of us changed our thinking and I continued working with the Discussion Group. Maximizing my bonus (a substantial part of my income) had never been my objective, anyhow. But Rod had taken some fun out the job and it's future.

After nearly 30 years in the industry, I was used to communications improvement getting a lower priority than it deserved. Not just in communications with the other-side(s), but with media, employees and within the management group.

I mention this episode especially because Rod was not alone within the forest industry in how he felt. Doubtless some of you who read this think he was right then and would be now — I hope he wasn't. If Rod were alive maybe he would have changed his mind by now — but he would still be drinking martinis.

Hindsight Opinion: If there had been Discussion Groups established in each forest in the 1970s, federal forest lands would be producing much more wood (hence, more jobs etc.) than they are now. And, today, there would be more trust between diverse interests. The group functioned for about two years after I left Potlatch.

One Of Those Leaning Flagpoles

As mentioned earlier, leaning flagpoles often indicate that other things are not what they should be. Something occurred in addition to the no-bonus-points discussion with Rod that, by itself, wasn't too serious. However, it raised questions about my ability to get things done and enjoy the work. When this event happened, I said to Jim McNutt, our forest economist, who reported to me and was involved, "Talk about a leaning flagpole...." Some background.

McNutt and I were planning the first corporate forestry research meeting in the history of Potlatch. In the six years I had been with Potlatch, the forestry research budget had substantially increased every year. It appeared that the company would benefit by holding the meeting in Denver. I had cleared the idea with all of the division VP's involved, and Rod, and we had gone to considerable trouble to have a cooperatively designed useful program. The two-day meeting was to be in Denver.

Since World War II, though seeing myself as being at least tolerant of widely varying personality types, I recognize that Napoleonic types in corporate life can bother me. One such Potlatch line division manager and I had a marginally-satisfactory relationship — though we both were usually able to disguise it. As it happened it was this person, who changed his mind about the worth of the corporate research meeting. Rod called me and said, "call it off," and of course I did. Not incidentally, if any of you younger folks think that the importance of *saving face* is limited to Asians, you are very wrong.

Transfer Pricing

Even before being hired, I shared with Rod my belief in the importance of transfer pricing wood into the mills at market value, and cited the before and after Weyco experience. But he saw transfer pricing as an unnecessary cost saying that efficiency could be obtained in other ways, which is true. But in my experience, alternatives are more costly and more risky.

Note: After I had left, Potlatch built a new sawmill at Lewiston and it had a very long, painful, and expensive start-up period plus some reconstruction. I wonder if some of that could have been avoided if the mill had historically been charged transfer price (market price) for its wood. Potlatch today does use transfer pricing. This change occurred after Rod had retired.

230

There were other negatives with the job as there always are. However, I was fortunate to be part of Potlatch's rapid progress toward intensive forestry. See table 1972-78 selected forestry statistics.

Overall Status Report

By mid 1979, six years after joining Potlatch, there had been many changes for the Gruenfelds family-wise, practically all favorable. The new family was bonded and happy. We finally were close to having only one child in college, instead of three. Financially neither of us had ever had it so good. But the job environment had changed.

Constant travel was a given. Between Warren, Arkansas; Cloquet, Minnesota; Washington D. C. and San Francisco, the major stops, I was away from home about 50 percent of the time. Also, staff work in a company that venerated line managers wasn't meant for someone with my action orientation and background.

I was 55, frustrated by lack of support for the Discussion Group and other profitable ideas (long term), the forestry program growth had matured and I was vested, financially comfortable, and Jan and I were in good health. Leaving Potlatch was easy.

Postlude To The Lewiston Years

The seven years in Lewiston, so far, have been the best seven continuous years of both of our lives. Potlatch, Idaho and its people, and the bonding of the new family can take credit for that.

Next

I've been hunting for 64 years and this seems like an appropriate place to talk about this very American and necessary pastime. By now I hope you see me as a moderate and are not surprised when I say -- the National Rifle Association is playing a necessary role in American life, but I cannot support their resistance to putting strict controls on the sale of assault rifles and similar weapons.

POTLATCH CORPORATION FORESTER EMPLOYMENT: 1972 - 78

Personnel	1972	1973	1974	1975	1976	1977	1978	% Change from 1972 to 1978
Graduate Foresters:								
Forestry, Logging, Procurement								
Arkansas	12	13	15	17	18	19	20	+67%
Idaho	20	23	34	34	36	42	55	+175%
Minnesota	10	9	10	11	12	10	11	+10%
Subtotal	42	45	59	62	66	71	86	+105%
Research								
Arkansas	0	0	0	1	1	2	2	—
Idaho	1	2	3	4	6	8	6	+500%
Minnesota	1	1	1	1	1	1	1	0%
Subtotal	2	3	4	6	8	11	9	+350%
Total Graduates	44	48	63	68	74	82	95	+116%
Technicians								
Arkansas	0	0	0	4	5	8	11	—
Idaho	1	1	1	6	10	10	10	+900%
Minnesota	6	6	6	6	7	7	8	+33%
Subtotal	7	7	7	16	22	25	29	+314%
Total								
Arkansas	12	13	15	22	24	29	33	+175%
Idaho	22	26	38	44	52	60	71	+223%
Minnesota	17	16	17	18	20	18	20	+18%
Three State Total	51	55	70	84	96	107	124	+143%

Western Forest Environment Discussion Group Meeting, Tacoma, WA 1978 Co-Chair Mike McCloskey, Executive Director of the Sierra Club and author (r.).
I wrote Mike July 1996 and asked him if he would consider giving a sort of positive-negative endorsement of the book since he seemed to think I was a relatively good citizen despite having forest management objectives that differed from his. He begged off due to having to read the whole book and principally because of too much other work. He did say " Jay, I do respect your sincerity and integrity, as well as experience".

233

Hunting

Note To The Anti-Hunting Folks

Some of my best friends are antihunting. I can readily understand why. Even some people who will go to heaven are against hunting. However, they should recognize that there are nice people who hunt. And, hopefully, some hunters probably also get to heaven.

If I had not been a hunter before going into the service I would have had a greater chance of ending up under a white cross on Luzon. Other service vets have told me the same thing about themselves.

My Early Introduction To Firearms

As I mentioned previously, when I was eight years old my Dad, who was normally sane, gave me a .22 rifle. He also gave me explicit, but brief, instructions on firearm safety that went something like this.

1. A .22 can easily kill a person and is dangerous up to a mile.

2. Don't ever point a firearm at a human. To an eight-year-old, in 1932, he didn't think it necessary to exclude enemy soldiers or a human threatening someone's life.

3. The first time you pick up a gun, check to see if it's loaded.

4. Assume every firearm is loaded, until you KNOW it isn't.

5. Remember that bullets skip on water (We lived almost-on the Fox River in northern Illinois at that time).

Thanks to Dad's advice plus caution, luck, and the Grace of God, I have never accidentally injured a person with a firearm. For 63 years of firearm use, that should be an OK performance.

The only animal I killed accidentally, that I know of, was a house wren when fooling around with a beebee gun in my pre .22 era. I tried to atone for this senseless act by giving the wren a decent burial with a lot of tears.

My hunting, until World War II, was mostly for squirrels and rabbits. Since I didn't have a hunting dog, pheasants were few and hard to find, but we occasionally got one. Once I enrolled at the University of Illinois, further south in the state, bobwhite quail were part of the bag. Ducks were common, but I never used a blind or decoys, so most of those I bagged jumped up from a creek or pond.

M1 Carbine Stopping Power

During the war, while training in New Zealand, I shot cottontail rabbits with a .30 caliber M1 carbine borrowed from our platoon leader. An experience with the stopping power of a carbine convinced me that I didn't want to carry one in actual combat, even though it was really a pretty good weapon.

Rabbits would come out of the brush and nibble grass in the pastures (called paddocks in NZ). One was in the paddock about 15 feet from the brush and 50 yards away. I sat down and squeezed off a shot that went "splat" hitting him in the center of the body. As he dragged himself toward the brush, I shot again. Hit him in about the same spot and still he dragged himself toward cover squealing. By then I was desperate and ran down and hit him with the rifle butt as a finisher. After that, I tried to never shoot a rabbit behind the shoulder and vowed I'd never carry a carbine in combat if the M1 Garand was an option.

After being battlefield commissioned, though I was supposed to carry a carbine, I kept my M1 (serial number 1 051 653). I'd pay a lot to have it hanging on my wall. It only jammed once in hundreds of rounds of combat firing, and that was my fault. I didn't clean it after firing 50 or 60 rounds my next to the last day of combat.

235

It would be easy to write a big-game hunting tome, since I started hunting deer in 1946 in Colorado and elk in 1951 in Washington — that would put most readers to sleep. Instead, here are a couple of true hunting stories that will hopefully be interesting, and maybe make you laugh. I'll start with one from the 1950's and end with our 1995 elk hunt in Idaho's River of No Return Wilderness Area (Also called The Frank Church Wilderness).

Lake Blanco For Goats

Washington state mountain-goat hunts in the middle 1950's (like today) were on a permit basis. One year, about 1958, there were 300 permits given and 1,200 applicants.

After applying four times, I was finally drawn. The first year I made a four-day hunt near Mt. Pilchuck, in the Cascade Range, but never saw a goat. On my next goat hunt, my "scout" and friend Neill Bowman, Monroe, Washington urged me to try the Lake Blanco country. The lake is up the North Fork of the Skykomish River in the North Cascades. Neill knew that my first criterion for a place to hunt was that it be beautiful, rugged country. Blanco was that and it had some goats.

The three-day hunt started off badly. My partner couldn't make it, so it was hunt alone or don't go. That was an easy decision. The next mistake was made when I carefully chose what would go in my pack. The hike into the ridge saddle, above and east of the lake where I would make my base camp, wasn't very far, about 3½ miles, but it was steep and all uphill. Even though I was only going to be out three nights I decided to take an air mattress. However, to lighten my load I decided to not take the air mattress repair kit — weight about two ounces or less — believe it? I hiked in at night. Of course, the mattress sprang a leak as soon as I blew it up by lung power. A good education doesn't make you smart.

The first day's hunt was in spectacular alpine beauty but without goats. It was September and the late wildflowers were out in full glory. Columbia Glacier lies just above Lake Blanco. Of the hundreds of photos my Mother saw, which I had taken in the high country, the photo I took that day was her favorite. I took it into the sun from the edge of the glacier with the lake and it's rugged outlet canyon as the subject. (See photo.)

I had left camp just before daylight going north and immediately ran into a rocky notch in the ridgeline that couldn't be crossed safely in the dark, even with a flashlight. So I waited for first light.

For the second day's hunt I decided to go back to the same place. But I wanted to be in the best spot at daylight and was worried about getting through the notch in the dark. Finally, I decided to take just the sleeping bag, with minimum supplies and camp to the north of the notch. What helped make the decision was the possibility that other hunters might chance the notch in the dark and beat me to the best spot. Only two other hunters were in the area, and they were in a camp a quarter mile south of my camp.

So I left my flat mattress and "yarded" (carried, in logging jargon) pack and rifle up the ridge. The darn ridge, where I wanted to sleep, was very steep on both sides and so sharp on top that the only place I could find to spread my mummy bag was in a goat bed. The bed was only big enough for a goat, and I'm longer than a goat. If I had rolled a few feet either way I would have tumbled. It was a long night — but I woke to a great sunrise.

After eating a piece of bread, an apple and some cheese (sharp cheddar, my favorite) I started to hunt. After a couple of hours, I had some luck. As I glassed a sheer cliff, about 150 yards away a big billy showed up, strolling a narrow ledge. His off-white color contrasted with the dark cliff and made him look even bigger than he was. What a sight. With my faithful old 30/40 Krag (made in 1898) and Redfield peep sight, with 180 grain soft point bullets, with a sling in a sitting position, it would be an easy shot. In fact I could have shot five or six times before he was out of sight. There was one major problem. After I shot him he would fall at least 400 feet before landing in a rock pile. Chances are his horns would have been broken. With some regret, but not as much as you might think, I let him go. He just stood there and watched as I left. They aren't the high IQ'ers of the animal world, but they are a joy to watch. In a steep spot they will actually stand on their hind legs, reach up with their front hooves, get a hoofhold and muscle themselves up, like a man. They go places where a mountain sheep can't.

Later, I saw a blue grouse sitting on a rock below me, looking downhill and about 40 feet away. Normally I might have tried to head shoot him (I used 220 grain Army ammo for grouse since it was cheap), but I wanted to bring at least a grouse home. The three kids loved baked grouse. So I held far forward on his backbone and shot. The heavy bullet hit a little lower than planned. He was easy to clean. Mostly all that was left was the untouched breast and the legs. I wouldn't be writing about this hunt if I had taken the usual head shot.

Another Mistake

It was getting late in the day so I hurried on the ridgetop through alpine meadows thick with sweet huckleberries. I was worried about getting through the notch before it got too dark. As often happened, I hadn't left quite enough time and spent too much of it enjoying the scenery. I even ran part of the way. Within a few hundred yards of the notch, I looked over the hill and below me, on a limb, sat another grouse. This was a spruce grouse or foolhen, a little smaller than a blue. And this one was from that year's late hatch — and very small. It was near where I had bedded down the night before, and the ground precipitously steep. Where to shoot him was a problem. He was close enough for a head shot, but if I did that he would beat his wings rapidly, as they always did after being hit in the head, and that meant he would roll down the hill, who knows how far. But I had exploded one grouse already and that hurt my pride, and this one was so small that a shoulder shot might not leave much. So I made a mistake and shot him in the head. It took me over 10 minutes to get him. He dropped down to a ledge, fluttering his wings. I'd carefully crawl down to his level and just as I thought I had him he'd flutter some more and drop further down the hill. Finally I got him, put him in the day-pack without cleaning, and clawed my way up to the ridgetop. Now I was in trouble. It was too late to get through the notch in the daylight.

I used the flashlight, scouted carefully and decided the notch was too dangerous. If there had been a better place to sleep nearby, I might have just spent another uncomfortable night on the ridge and had a grouse dinner with no trimmings except for a couple of mushrooms picked during the day.

At last, on the lake side of the ridge I found a narrow ledge below me that looked as though it might get me past the notch. You couldn't tell for sure due to a bend in the ledge. If it didn't get me around the notch, I was on the ledge for the night due to the dangers involved with climbing around at night in cliffy terrain. It was so steep that I took a rope and lowered my rifle and pack down to the ledge. Then after looping the rope around a mountain hemlock, I slid down the doubled rope to the ledge. To my relief the ledge was long enough that I was able to get back to camp and sleep on my flat mattress.

It was a fine hunt and generated some excellent pictures but no goat.

Success

The next year, I again had to hunt alone due to my partner Jack Palmquest coming down with a bug. This time the hunt was on Mt. Persus, just south of Highway 2 in the Skykomish Valley. With some luck I was able to get a nice goat with horns nearly ten inches long. Mountain goats, no relation to domestic goats, have a rather slow metabolism which helps them survive where a misstep can be fatal. They are pretty hard to stop. Mine ran about 30 yards, toward a sheer drop-off, being hit three times in the lungs, twice while running, with 180 grain bullets from the Krag. The meat was tender but rather tasteless. After taking the head and cape off, I just touched the carcass with my foot and it bounced down the hill about a hundred yards and lost a couple of hundred feet of elevation. This worked well for a while, but I finally had to put it on a pack board and carry it out. Bouncing it down the mountain may have been the reason it was so tender.

High Deer Hunts

Like many lovers of wilderness, my favorite country is what we call "high country." The definition is not precise. Most regard the subalpine country, a couple of thousand feet below timberline, as the lower end of the high country. In the Cascades, it is characterized by lush open meadows and sparse

Mom's favorite photo taken on goat hunt Washington North Cascades: Lake Blanco, looking south down Troublesome Creek from just east of Columbia Glacier. A logger comment might be, "not much tractor ground."

Fun-duty Skykomish Tree Farm, 1956 Mt. Index (l.) and Mt. Persus (later site of a goat hunt). We were surveying a property line on a U.S. Forest Service timber sale.

timber on the south facing slopes; with more timber and fewer meadows on the north slopes, especially at lower elevations. During the late summer wildlife is abundant, the flowers are at peak beauty and the high country is the place to be.

The state of Washington has an early buck deer season for about 10 days in mid September. Hunting deer in such a gorgeous setting, with good weather, was the most enjoyable hunting I have ever had.

From about 1958 through 1968, we made a three-to-five-day annual high-deer hunt in Washington. From 1969 through 1972, the hunts were in Oregon, usually in the Three Sisters Wilderness, but also in the Mt. Jefferson and Eagle Cap Wilderness Areas (for elk). Usually we backpack in from six to ten miles and arranged for a packer to meet us with horses. If we had game, as we usually did, we walked out and the horses carried meat. One time, however, a lady packer brought in three horses for us and all we had were three grouse and a few cutthroat trout from Trap Lake, south of Stevens Pass.

Our only overhead shelter was a piece of plastic. The weather was nearly always just about perfect. Often it froze at night, but the days were pleasant. Normally our camps were at about 6,000 feet at the edge of a meadow.

Usually I went with one partner, occasionally with two or none. The trip in was nearly always uphill. Coming out hurt the most. By then we were tired, our feet hurt and the steady pounding of downhill walking was hard on the knees. My feet blistered easily and sometimes the pain from going downhill would put tears in my eyes. But we loved it. Often we would hunt the entire time without seeing another human, and sometimes wouldn't hear any shots but our own. It's that way now on the wilderness elk hunts, especially since my hearing is going.

About 1960, I started to wear tennis shoes instead of boots on the high deer hunt and this stopped the blisters, increased my hiking radius and decreased the noise. At first people thought I was nuts, but gradually the trend was to very light boots, especially on the trail. Now I sometimes wear Cabela trail shoes which give more support and traction than a tennis shoe. And the trail shoe weighs two ounces less than my Rod Laver, Adidas tennis shoe. Even with lightweight pack frames, light down sleeping bags and so forth, our packs and rifles weighed about 50 pounds.

The pack weight reminds me of something John Butkus did when sorting out equipment for the high-deer hunt. John, great guy, at the time was chief timber cruiser for Weyerhaeuser Company. To lighten the load, he was careful to take only the minimum amount of ammunition, clothing and supplies. I was impressed at his restraint until seeing the last item he put in his pack — a cast iron skillet that must have weighed five pounds. "Bacon doesn't taste right unless it's cooked in an iron skillet," was his rational.

Every year when the vine maples started to turn in early August, I'd get an eloquent letter from Rex Allison, my regular hunting partner, and we would start talking seriously about that year's high country hunt.

Rex Allison

Sure, we are ALL unique, but Rex Allison was one of the really unique — and a wonderful friend. Rex was a college graduate logging hooktender on a skyline cable logging side when I started to set chokers for him in May 1949. This was at Camp Baker on the Spirit Lake highway near Mount St. Helens. (When St. Helens blew up in 1980 it pretty well demolished Camp Baker, but it is still operating.)

Rex and I hit it off right away. I tried to do a good job, ran into and out-from the chokers and he liked that. Also we shared a love of the out-of-doors and forestry. When I came back from my year and a term at Oxford University, if I hadn't torn some ligaments in my right hand playing rugby I probably would have gone back on Rex's side in January 1951. Instead I went to work on the logging railroad section gang. It only paid $1.50 an hour while chokersetting was paying about $1.70 an hour as I recall. So my three degrees, three years in the Army and some logging experience hadn't moved me very far up the Corporate ladder at that point. I was 26.

Rex and I hunted and fished together and families visited back and forth until he died of cancer in 1982 Here is the eulogy I wrote about him which was published, anonymously, in the Washington State University forestry annual.

REX ALLISON February 2, 1918 — April 16, 1982

Logger-Forester Par Excellence

Ernest Hemingway might have been able to write a eulogy that could match the quality of life and death of Rex Allison. I can't.

The English have a saying — it's not how a man lives, but how he dies that is important — But Rex, a strong man physically, mentally and spiritually did both. He lived a brave, dedicated, productive life, and also died a strong man still totally dedicated to his family, company, friends and principles. Multiple cancer has defeated many people in spirit as well as body but not Rex.

This didn't surprise those of us who knew him well. Strength, toughness, dedication and ability have always been his characteristics.

He was born and raised around Dryad, Washington in the coast range, and hunted and fished all of his life. Last October, only two deer were taken on opening day on a well-hunted part of the Coos Bay tree farm. Despite crutches and cancer, Rex got a buck. In 1935, at age 17, he was setting chokers for the Clemons Logging Company, a Weyerhaeuser contractor. Until one week before his death, he gave helpful advice to his staff in his capacity as Woods Manager of 212,000 acres of Weyerhaeuser Company forest land in Coos County, Oregon.

College graduates seldom go into logging as a chokersetter and do all the tough jobs on the way to the top, but Rex was different. After receiving a B.S. in Forestry from Washington State University in 1947, he worked as a logging engineer for Weyerhaeuser Company in Oregon and then became a "highball" hooktender at Longview. He had already been a chokersetter and rigging slinger, so was ready for the top rigging job— running a cable logging side. He "tended hook" for high lead and skyline shows, and did some cat logging until taking his first job on salary as assistant area forester at the Raymond operation in 1953. Tree planting was one of his major responsibilities and the crews he supervised had high productivity in survived trees. Logging was his choice again and in 1956 he ran a high lead logging side as hooktender at Aberdeen, then went on salary as a logging foreman, also at Aberdeen. Now he was "really logging" and was sent to Coos Bay as area logging superintendent, 1962 to 1967, then Forest Engineer for the entire Coos Bay Operation and, finally was made woods manager in 1969, and served there until his death in April, 1982.

But this is chronology and could reflect just another good, hard working life. However, Rex grew from being a high-ball, run-run hook tender, who was pretty tough on the crew, into a skilled forest manager, who, by example and knowledge, was able to select and motivate a team that made Coos Bay one of the best run woodlands operations on the west coast. Here is an example of his success. Coos Bay, among the Weyerhaeuser tree farms, has neither the best timber nor the best ground, yet, for several years, under Allison, it had the lowest logging costs of any west coast Weyerhaeuser operation. Also, the reforestation and pre-commercial thinning programs were outstanding.

Rex served in the US Army in World War II from 1942 to 1945, rose from private to captain, and became an artillery forward observer with the 104th Infantry Division in Europe. Rex was awarded the bronze star for valor, was captured, and, typical of Rex, escaped twice. Dedication to duty and loyalty to his employer and subordinates were his hallmarks. A classic remark about WW II that illustrated his dedication was his totally serious observation about a radio man who served with him in combat in Europe. Rex commented, "He was no good. All he could think of was coming home alive."

Having "been there," including being union steward for six camps while at Longview, he appreciated the hourly worker's point of view, This helped him gain their cooperation and resulted in high productivity while setting safety records and easing union-management relations, I hope it is apparent that Rex Allison was a fine and rare professional who made a great contribution to forest management and his family and friends with a lifetime of dedicated service.

There was another side to this unique person. It almost goes without saying, he was a good family man with a quiet Christianity. But what is especially surprising to some is that the rough, tough, canny, games man and corporate manager was also a writer of poetic letters about the beauties of the forest, a devotee of high country wilderness back packing and hunting, and a kind and sensitive friend.

Productive, imaginative, loyal, kind to his family and the many friends, games man with ethics and a flair, phrasemaker, outdoorsman extraordinary, avid WSU booster, forester, logger, soldier, courageous and Christian in life and death... may God provide more Rex Allisons.

A Forester Friend
May 25, 1982

Further On The Eulogy
The eulogy was lightly edited at Washington State. They changed "gamesman" into sportsman and that eliminated a subtle point. Rex would play games with people. This included occasionally saying things that could be construed as lies. The generous, like Jack Schoening, Weyerhaeuser's Woods Manager at Longview Washington said, "Sometimes Rex had a rather different view of the truth." Naturally this drove some of the upper echelon nuts and nearly got him canned or demoted several times. Oscar Weed, the Area Manager at Coos Bay, and Rex's boss for many years, recognized his tremendous net contribution to Weyerhaeuser. Oscar understood and respected Rex and prevented his being fired at least twice. One basic of getting big things done well is having a respected leader and Rex was certainly that.

After he died, I realized he was not only one of my best friends: he was the best. In over 30 years of friendship we had only one heated argument and it was momentary.

Rex was one of the few people who loved the high country as much as Neill Bowman and I do. Eileen, his wife said that just before he died Rex remarked, "If it hadn't been for Jay I never would have known much about the land that is over 1,500 feet in elevation." It's nice to know I made a contribution to his great life.

Late summer every year, when the vine maple leaves start to turn color, Jan and I think of Rex. I'll bet there is high country where he is — and he is using it.

How To Die

The Brits have a saying, "How a man lives isn't as important as how he dies." Note: they needed this sort of rationalizing-wisdom when they lost one million men in World War I out of a total population of only 41 million in the United Kingdom.

I don't agree with the saying, but of course would like to die with some class. If I am able to die with class, that is, showing character under adversity, it will be partly because of the examples set by Rex Allison and another close friend H. Don Smith. Don died after nine years of Lou Gerhig's disease. Some people mentally deteriorate under the stress of a final illness, understandably. But Rex and Don were the same stalwart people until the very end. That's class, and luck.

Sample High-Deer Hunt, Escondido Lake, Washington

Picking one backpack high-deer hunt as an example from the 14 or 15 I've made is difficult. In their way, all were outstanding. But Rex would have to be involved for it to be truly indicative, so that eliminates five or six. So I've decided on the middle 1960's hunt where we camped for the first time at Escondido Lake, northeast of Snoqualmie Pass and a couple of miles east of the Cascade Crest trail, now officially called the Pacific Crest National Scenic Trail. This trail runs from Canada to Mexico. We tend to avoid camping within eyeshot of it on our hunts since you sometimes see a few people, even after Labor Day.

Rex and I hiked in about seven miles and camped about a hundred yards north of the creek that flows by Escondido (Spanish for Hidden) Lake, and about the same distance from the lake. The small lake itself, very shallow, was about 100 yards to the east. The creek was full of small cutthroat trout. The next year, Neill Bowman came in with us. While talking with Neill on the edge of the creek and telling how many trout there were, I said, "Don't move, and with my hand dangled my leader and number 12 coachman-bucktail fly in front of a six-inch trout and hooked him within two feet of Neill's boot in a few inches of water.

We didn't have any luck hunting north and west of the lake, so on the next to the last day I went downstream about a quarter of a mile, and took a narrow trail that went south and then west on a narrow ridge, gaining elevation. After an hour's hike, I had gained nearly a thousand feet of elevation and was in series of beautiful small alpine meadows, mostly heather and low bush blueberry. There were enough paintbrush and lupine and other flowers to provide bright spots of color. The blue berry and huckleberry were in various shades of red and pink. A few mountain hemlocks and alpine fir (actually subalpine fir) gave some height to the vegetation. It was like hunting in a well-kept, gigantic rock garden.

I eased to the top of a little ridge and looked into the next little meadow. Even though it was the middle of the day there were several does feeding in the open and a very big deer had its head down and hidden by some huckleberry. By its size I figured it was a buck. It raised its head — it was a big four-point mule deer (four points on each side. In the eastern US he would be called an eight point.) He was about a hundred yards away. I was shooting iron-sights offhand and missed him the first time, but he just stood there, and on the second shot he humped-up and I knew I had him. Where he fell had a nice background so I took a photo (with an Argus C3) — see photo). I dressed him out, covered him with some brush to keep the birds away and walked slowly back to camp, enjoying the spectacular scenery and the satisfaction of having some good venison. We ate part of the liver that night and had huckleberries and blueberries for desert.

The next morning, we left a map for the packer who was due in at noon and went up to skin out the buck. Neither of us thought that the packer would take his horses up the steep rocky side trail that had several patches of slick shelf rock that would be tricky going for steel-shod pack horses or mules. So we assumed we would have to backpack it down to the main trail. However, right after we had finished working on the deer we heard horses and sure enough here came a young cowboy, about 23, with two pack horses. What a welcome sight. Our kind of guy.

The deer weighed 207 pounds on the scale. Two years later, I got one that could have been his father, but not near Escondido Lake.

We hunted with Neill the next year. He came almost entirely to enjoy the scenery. No one got a buck. About 10 years later, Neill told me that one evening he and Rex had gone down to the creek for water and saw a two-point. They agreed, "Let's not tell Jay or he'll come down and shoot it and then we'll have to mess with it." Yes, hunting is much more than just killing something.

A Special Elk Hunt

My last backpack in high country deer hunt was into the Three Sisters Wilderness Area just west of Bend in 1972. I was 47. Since then, I've concentrated on wilderness elk hunting with some fishing. We have a packer take us in on horseback and drop us at a temporary tent camp. He checks on us every couple of days and takes out any game. This is costly, but easier on the aging body and you can get back into more remote areas. Lately we have been staying eight days, but this year it could be as long as ten. We provide the food, the packer has the camp ready with cooking gear, a propane stove, wood stove, firewood and cots. For a two-person drop-camp hunt in Idaho, you pay the packer about $1,500 per person including tax. Guided hunts (not my bag) are roughly $3,000 per hunter, if two hunters per guide. This year the hunting license is $101, and the nonresident elk tag (required whether or not you get an elk) $326. When you add in the food and other travel costs, even if you get one, the resulting elk meat isn't cheap. But the memories are priceless, to those who like it.

Sometimes we ride in 13 or 14 miles which takes six or seven hours. This can be hard on a pedestrian rider, particularly if it is a steep trail. But there is something about the moves required in playing serious tennis that makes you less vulnerable to saddle soreness. So, even my sort of bent-out-of-shape 71-year-old bod only has momentary stiffness after a long ride.

Experience With Outfitters (Packers)

There are real horror stories about outfitters who have victimized hunters. For instance there are hunters who were dropped at a camp and then didn't see a packer again for a week-and-a-half, and that was three days after they were sup-

High deer hunt about 1963 "like hunting in a beautiful gigantic rock garden", North Cascades. Mule deer buck field-dressed weighed 207 pounds.

Selway-Bitterroot Wilderness Area Elk Hunt, '74. With companioins like these every hunt was a good one, regardless. From left: Rex Allison, Glen Carlson, H. Don Smith, apparently enjoying a Rexism. Cook tent on the right and sleeping on left.

posed to be packed out. This happened even though he had promised to check every two or three days and take out meat. Or sometimes the horses they are supposed to ride aren't really broken and buck them off, or try to scrape them off on a tree. In our case, we have always been very satisfied with packer performance.

I've been on at least a dozen wilderness elk hunts with six different packers and have had at least good service from all of them. With some the stock is a little better or they may be a little more punctual. But overall it has been a fine experience, and the cowboys and cowgirls are fun to be around. The high-deer-hunt packers were also very satisfactory. Part of the reason we had such good luck is that we nearly always checked on the reputation of the outfitter before hiring him or her.

The Hunt

I've hunted elk at least two of every three years since 1951, so it's difficult to give a representative sample with one hunt. But I'll tell in some detail about a late 1970's hunt in Idaho, and then briefly describe last year's hunt.

Rugged Creek, Salmon River, Idaho

As close as I come to being snobbish is when it comes to choosing elk-hunt partners. Bad partners can mean a bad hunt. With good partners the hunt is nearly always good, regardless of whether you get any game. At least that's the way most of my hunting friends feel. The three I went with on the Rugged Creek (Idaho) hunt were all great people, close friends of mine and liked to laugh; Rex Allison, whom you already know, Glen Carlson, Lewiston, Idaho an exceptionally good rifle shot, and the best dentist I know, and Dave Price, then the Chief Forester for Potlatch Corporation, also Lewiston, a very savvy hunter.

We drove to where highway 95 crossed the famous River of No Return — the Salmon. Then took a gravel road about 20 miles upstream on the south side of the river. A jet boat met us there and we went upstream another 25 or so miles to the James Creek Ranch. The next morning we rode horseback for about three or four hours to a drop-camp on Rugged

250

Creek, which is a tributary of the South Fork of the Salmon. This is in the River of No Return Wilderness Area.

Since I tend to come in after dark, especially in new country, I hung a six-foot-long orange ribbon where the little trail to our camp joined the main trail. After hunting hard all the first day I ended up a little too far from camp to make it in by dark. But since I had a flashlight and was on the main trail, I didn't expect any trouble, particularly since I had carefully marked the trail junction. About two hours after dark I knew I was in trouble. I hadn't seen the huge ribbon, but thought I had passed the trail junction. So I reluctantly fired a shot — no answer. I fired again, and finally heard a faint answer. I was way below the camp, assuming it was my partners doing the answering. That question always adds spice to coming in after dark. I hiked fast for a half an hour and here was the tent, lit up like a circus, just a hundred yards or so off the main trail. My "friends" had assumed I would be out all night so hadn't bothered to leave the lantern on and had gone to bed early, hence the need for my second shot. We had a big laugh about it and I vowed for the umpteenth time to never come in after dark again. In the morning I saw that my ribbon was very prominent IF you were on the uphill one of two parallel trails. Live and learn, slowly in my case.

As I walked down the trail by flashlight a big-sounding bull elk had bugled at me from less than a hundred yards away. When I gave him an answer in my best elk-talk, I got dead silence, as usual. But we knew about where he was. And sure enough, we bagged two near there the next day.

That particular area showed on the map as Republican Flats. Someone wondered out loud about the derivation of the name. Rex said, "Probably because there is so much deadwood around here."

A Mushroom Mistake

That night we were all feeling lighthearted and happy, especially after opening the celebratory champagne, and the meal was going to be pretty fancy; breast of grouse, wild mushrooms, baked potatoes, the works. We all liked wild mushrooms and I had picked several pounds of a new one that we had keyed out, in the book, as being edible. But being old

251

hands at this sort of thing, we had a strict rule. With a new mushroom, on the first eating, only the person who found it would eat it. Then if it was bad we, at the worst, would only lose one person. But Rex, the cook that night, had cooked up a huge batch of the new mushrooms and I kept exclaiming how good they were. We finished the champagne and started on the Cabernet Sauvignon. Pretty soon we were all eating the new mushroom. It turned out it wasn't the one we thought it was, but fortunately it was edible.

Wilderness Grouse

That year the woods were thick with grouse. To make a gross understatement, "Wilderness grouse often aren't very bright." At this particular eight-grouse dinner, all but two of the grouse had been killed with rocks or sticks. On the first day of the hunt, just after daylight, I came up on a big cock blue grouse, feeding on the ground. It was so alarmed it flew up in a ponderosa pine tree about 10 feet from me and seven feet off the ground. The fifth rock I threw knocked the limb out from under him and he had to fly away. And the Fool Hen (spruce grouse) are REALLY dumb. Later that day I reached around the trunk of a small grand fir with a stick and bagged a Fool Hen. This is the only one I've gotten without throwing the stick. Sticks work best when thrown so they are whirling parallel to the ground.

Grouse populations are cyclical. The past two years I have taken only three grouse, on the two elk hunts, with a .22 pistol.

The Argument

I still remember the delicious dinner vividly, because it was the only time in over 30 years of friendship that Rex and I exchanged a few heated words. He liked pepper and had the grouse so peppered-up they looked like black rocks in the frying pan. As I unobtrusively tried to rake off a couple of layers of pepper with a paper towel I was told in no uncertain terms, "Sonny, when I'm cooking, you eat what I cook!" I barked back, but then realized I was in the wrong and poured us both more wine. Incidentally, none of us drank too much.

It was an extra good hunt, but the next year we went into another Wilderness Area and got skunked. We were always looking for the perfect place. My criteria are so high that I will never find a perfect elk hunting place, but I'm close, and this year will return to last year's campsite —barring a catastrophe.

The October 1995 Hunt

These are my criteria for an ideal elk hunting spot, in decreasing importance.

1.   Gorgeous subalpine country in a Wilderness Area; must have rocks and crags.
2.   No chance of encountering a legal mechanical vehicle,
3.   Very little chance of encountering other hunters,
4.   A reliable packer with good horses and mules,
5.   Accessible, good trout fishing,
6.   A reasonable chance to see bull elk.

In recent years, my elk-hunting success has been such that Jan has said a couple of times, "Look, if you are going to go and not get an elk, why don't you go and not get one closer to home, rather than Idaho." My rationalizations aren't worthy of being repeated. In the interest of further accuracy (read, pride) I must reveal that I have not missed any elk during this soon-to-end drought.

However, since working for the US Forest Service on the Magee Ranger District of the Coeur d'Alene National Forest in northern Idaho, the summer of 1942, Idaho is for me the US equivalent of my overseas special-place, New Zealand. Incidentally, the extremist right wing minority in northern Idaho keeps Idaho from being relatively perfect, for me — despite beautiful country, great people, good friends.

We camp at 8,300 feet in the Frank Church, River of No Return Wilderness, north-northeast of the Sawtooth Mountains which are about 60 miles northwest of Sun Valley. The outfitters are Jeff and Deb Bitton, Mystic Saddle Ranch, Stanley, Idaho, 83278, phone (208) 774 3591.

Usual And Unusual Luck

My first-time partner, Dave Woodall, had never hunted elk before. He is a good deer hunter and tough former marine rifle platoon leader who survived the Iwo Jima campaign. He lives at Friday Harbor in the San Juan Islands, Washington.

On the third full day of hunting, he was hunting in new snow and recounts, "I was following fresh tracks of two elk when I spotted a big one, not one I was following, lying down under a fir tree, not moving a muscle. He was only 40 feet away and I had made a lot of noise, so I thought he might be dead. But I looked with the binoculars and I could see his throat move as he chewed his cud. So I shot him high in the neck, to protect the meat." It was a nice four point. My half of the cut and wrapped meat weighed 95 pounds.

A Statistical Improbability

This is the appropriate time to tell an elk story that is so mathematically improbable that I'm sure many people who hear this and don't know me, will think it's a fib. It isn't.

In my elk-hunting career, which began in 1951, during elk season while hunting, I've seen somewhere between 1,200 and 1,400 elk. The number is high because I hunted the Twin Harbors country (Willipa and Grays Harbors counties) of western Washington in the 1950s, when the elk population was at the all-time high. This was mainly due to clear cuts in the old-growth timber providing just what the deer and elk wanted for feed in the regenerating areas, plus low hunting pressure during the war.

For example in 1955, the year of the Big Freeze, when the temperature dropped 70 degrees in 24 hours (and killed the tops in millions of trees), I hunted three days and saw over 200 elk. Every one was a cow.

I've taken about 15 bulls and two cows. YET DURING ALL THIS TIME I HAVE NEVER SEEN A BULL ELK THAT WASN'T A SPIKE (a single point on each side) — so help me. This is so much fun to tell that in a way, a very minor way, I hope I never do. Statistically, this is virtually impossible, yet it has happened. And I have a reputation of being a pretty fair hunter and I still hunt hard. We don't have the advantage of hunting during the bugling season.

In my imagination, I have shot big bull elk from every conceivable angle, under every weather and cover condition and know where I'll aim at any range with him traveling at any speed. Since I have never had buck-fever while shooting either man or beast my odds will be pretty good, if I can only see one within range long enough to get off a shot. Such is life.

Incidentally, as with about everything else, I don't feel a bit sorry for myself. Just surviving World War II and meeting Jan was enough luck for a lifetime.

Bird Hunting

In total pleasure received, I suspect my upland bird hunting outranks elk hunting. This is because of my Labrador retrievers. If you really love hunting dogs there isn't a whole lot of difference between getting a few birds and limiting; as long as you can watch a good dog work and have it as a companion.

Hunting chukars (chuck' ers), until recently, has been my favorite upland bird sport. The chukar is a partridge native to the Himalayas that has done spectacularly well in the dry, rocky, cheat grass regions of the western US, below about 3,000 feet elevation. Often you flush them from the edge of a rimrock and they rocket off downhill. Tough shooting. They are a pretty bird, mostly blue-gray with a tinge of orange on the tail, pink bill and feet, with a blackbarred whitish breast. The meat is white and tasty. In recent years, there have been very few chukars. That, plus the steep rocky ground in chukar habitat being so hard on Buddy's feet and my knees, have moved pheasant hunting to the top of the list.

I've weighed dozens of chukars and pheasants. The first year I was in Idaho, I brought in a monster chukar that weighed 1 pound 14 ounces. So I was sure I'd eventually get a two pounder. Wrong again; the second largest was only 1 pound 10 ounces. The largest ringneck I weighed was four and three-quarter pounds and 37 inches long.

Until moving to Lewiston, Idaho in 1973, I had little chukar-hunting experience. Jan gave me a Lab puppy that year and Potlatch Rip was a winner from the very first. He finally weighed about 105 pounds and had a massive head — hard-head by the way. He'd occasionally get out of the kennel and run downtown, which was a couple of blocks downhill from our great old 1898 home. Soon after, Jan would get a call from a tavern and the bartender would say, "Ripper is down here drinking beer, again. What should I do with him?" Jan would apologize and go down and pick him up.

New Zealand Chukar Story

In 1979, we flew into Queenstown, New Zealand, a beautiful little town on Lake Wakatipu. There were rimrocks around the town and it looked like it could have chukars. But when I asked the pilot he said, "Nope." A little while later he came back and said, in a strong Kiwi drawl, "You know, we do have some 'chew-cars'" — but no chuck'-ers. English IS a tough language.

Ripper didn't have a mean bone in his body, but he had the bad habit of jumping up on you and trying to lick your face (remember, I, trained him). He was so darn tall he licked a lot of faces. One day a policeman came to our home and gave Jan a citation. He said Rip had jumped up on a little old lady and dirtied her coat. She had to go to court and this bothered her since I was the new corporate Vice President of Lands and Forestry, and Potlatch wanted their people to be good citizens. I was in Washington, D.C.

Concerned, she went down to the crowded courtroom. Finally the clerk called her to the bench and read the charge. She explained to the judge that Rip was in a kennel 99 percent of the time, wouldn't hurt a flea, this would never happen again. The judge leaned over and whispered to her, "What kind of a dog is he, Mrs. Gruenfeld?" Jan said, "A black Lab."

"I have one too. They can be a handful, can't they. Case dismissed." Our kind of judge in our kind of town.

Like anyone who hunted ten years with a good dog, I could write a book full of stories about Rip and his performance. But here I'll only tell two.

Glenn Carlson and I agreed on about everything regarding hunting but choice of bird dogs. He liked Brittany Spaniels, his was named Mita. Of course I was totally sold on Labs, though I had had only one real hunting Lab. My first one, Skookum, was a loser — any duck he could retrieve, I could retrieve. One time a greenhead mallard jumped up from an ice-covered pond and I folded him. The darn dog wouldn't budge, so I waded out in hip boots, in water over chest deep, broke the ice and retrieved the duck. As I staggered up out of the pond I slipped on the muddy bank, fell down, and Skookum came up and licked my face. I darn near shot him —nah, not really.

One Saturday it was 11 a.m. and for the first time in years of hunting birds, it looked like Glen and I were going home empty-handed. Hadn't even fired a shot. Then a small covey of chukars ran across the road in front of the Blazer. Fortunately for this story, Mita was left in the truck and only Ripper came out. Rip put up four birds and we collected them and he did a nice job of retrieving. Another single went up, I dropped it and Rip was bringing him in when another bird went up and Glen knocked it down. Rip went over and scooped up the second bird into his gigantic mouth and of course brought them both to me. And these were mature birds. "Now you show me a Brittany that can do that," I said to Glen.

Actually, a couple of years later I did see, Mandy Miles' Brittany, Brandy, do the same thing, but the birds were from that year's hatch.

Ripper's Last Night

Jan likes both cats and dogs. As with many men, I prefer dogs. After the following episode, however, cats rose in my estimation.

We had a wild-eyed, wild black Persian cat named Sammy, that lived outside much of the time. As he did with anything else, Rip wanted to make friends with the cat, but Sammy would have nothing to do with him. Wouldn't let him get within five yards.

At age 10, big old Rip got really sick, was taking medicine, but we weren't sure how sick he was. I took him for a walk on a leash at 1:15 a.m. Good ole Sammy came out from under a bush and for 15 minutes walked at my right side with Rip on my left. I went in and told Jan what had happened, and that I didn't think Rip was going to make it. I put him in his kennel. At 3:30 a.m. he was lying on his side and breathing rather heavily. At 8 a.m. he was gone. Cats do have extra sensory perception.

I made it through a lot of tough stuff during the war and yet only had a few tears in my eyes and never cried. When Rip died, I cried like a baby. It's too bad humans aren't a little more like dogs in loyalty, dependability and giving.

Jay's Seahurst Buddy

As I've said, I'm very partial to black Labrador retrievers. Sudden thought, if I ever have a real world-beater Lab it would be fun to name him after my favorite athlete and call him either Michael or Jordan.

Speaking of Michael Jordan, a reporter (can't remember his name, it started with a D.) wrote one of the most profound and complimentary sport sentences about Michael I've ever heard. It was approximately this, "If you want to see integrity in sports, watch the greatest offensive player in the history of the game play defense." Wish I could write like that. Come to think of it, I'd like to hunt elk as well as Michael plays basketball — and he's a good role model too.

Buddy, the current Lab, was 10 last January, but still has the vitality of an adolescent. His Dad was Zip Code, a National Amateur Field Trial Champion, and the mother Kettle River Kate was a field trial champion, so the bloodline is good. But he was the last of the litter to be sold, and I think the trainer knew he would never be a field trial dog. Too much vitality and a short memory. But what a great dog for us. He loves to hunt even more than I do, especially pheasants. Buddy has a fine nose and keen hearing.

Jan and her ex-husband field-trialed Labs. This is her seventeenth Lab. She said that, until I trained him she thought that this dog had the highest puppy-IQ of the seventeen. Since he is just another good, not excellent bird dog, that doesn't say much for my training ability, does it? To give an example of his awareness; when he was just a pup, Jan changed the arrangement of some plates on the wall near his basket. The next time he came into the room he saw something was different, hackled-up and barked and barked.

He may be a little hard-mouthed, but his joyful affection, enthusiasm and spirit are going to be missed a ton when he goes to the place where Ripper is.

We are in the group of believers who think that, if at all possible, there should be a big dog in the family, to help raise the kids in addition to being a companion.

Fishing

Prior to 1969 when I became a serious tennis player, I was an avid fly fisherman and fished for steelhead with lures. Now, most of my fishing is an occasional trip with the grandkids and as a supplement to the wilderness elk hunting.

The Best Salmon Trip

My Dad really liked to fish, but never had a chance at trout and salmon, so he came out from McHenry Illinois in 1952 eager to give it a try. We drove from Monroe, Washington over to Sekiu on the north end of the Olympic Peninsula. We fished whole herring just off the bottom, raising and lowering the pole tip. Locals call this "mooching." In 45 minutes, he caught 45 pounds of king salmon, 30 and 15 pounders. Happy as a clam.

On another trip he was with Hank and Teresa Henry. Dad had a nice king on when Teresa said in fright, "Jule, there's a whale." The whale was a monster Gray, about 40 feet long and only 25 yards away. Dad looked up nonchalantly and said, "Yeah, it's a whale all right," and kept playing the fish and then boated it — a 25 pound king. He loved to fish.

Now It Can Be Told

In 1950, while in western France on an Oxford University forestry field trip in the Jura Mountains, we fly fished for brown trout. I've never seen tougher conditions. It was the middle of the day on a forty-foot wide, gin-clear slow moving stream, just a half mile from its source, a big limestone cave. No one caught anything until I lucked out and caught a 10-inch fish on a number 12 or 14 Rio Grande King during a gust of wind that riffled the water. About an hour later, while fishing alone, I saw an 18-inch trout go under a rock in a quiet pool. I waded in carefully, reached under the rock and caught him with my hands, totally illegal and unsportsmanlike. Despite having every intention of "fessing up," after all my friends had given me accolades for getting the only two fish, I was modestly and guiltily silent. Publishing this will remove the guilt that I have born for 46 years — lightly.

One hour until dark and three hours to camp, Idaho, near Selway Crags, Selway-Bitterroot Wilderness Area October 1975. Snow was ankle deep on the south slope and knee-thigh deep on north at this elevation, about 6,500 feet. This was the last time I had to sleep-out overnight on an elk hunt. Dinner was a couple of cups of tea. Broke ice to get the water. In the morning I hurried out before first light and reached camp, on Lottie Creek about 8 am. H. Don Smith, Tom Smrekar from Potlatch Corp. in Cloquet, Minnesota and Tom's friend, also from Minnesota were still in camp, which seemed odd. Tom, after a welcome, gave me a big glass of tomato juice. I took a sip and said, "Say, we haven't opened that vodka, I'll have a Bloody Mary." Tom looked down at the floor of the tent, Don looked at the roof, cleared his throat and said, "Jay, we waited up for you ... so we thought we'd have a party." Tomato juice and Jim Beam is a lousy drink. But this is a fun memory.

Central Idaho 1995 Elk Hunt: In Wilderness Area looking down Winnemucca Creek. Saw six elk from here. My Winchester Model 70 30/06, nice pattern in the stock. Leupold 2x7 variable scope. Am giving Leupold a plug since they did major repairs on the scope, without charge, after I fell and bashed it on a rock while on an Alaskan "moose" hunt in goat country. (Got neither, but partners got goats.) Did shoot my only ptarmigan with the '06 and saved the meat.

Chukar hunting 1991 in extreme southeast Washington: Buddy in cheat grass with frozen Grande Ronde River, Idaho in background. Walking stick in foreground.

261

Consulting
Late 1979 to March 1997

Forest Resource Consulting, Plus

After Leaving Potlatch

We quickly decided to relocate to Seattle on the salt-water. Teaching at the University of Washington College of Forest Resources was a possible option, but the combination of shaky funding for such a position and the thought of getting into an academic bureaucracy eliminated it.

Consulting was a natural career capstone for me. Twenty nine years with Weyerhaeuser, Brooks-Scanlon and Potlatch and my Army combat service had given me an unusual breadth and depth of experience, a good reputation, confidence, financial strength, and many contacts. In addition, the log export business was booming and there was a strong demand for consulting expertise. The non-business reasons for my choosing a consulting career included having more time to devote to helping people retain at least equality with non-humans in the Wars over management of our forests. This shouldn't be necessary, but Congress in forest legislation has been kinder and gentler to the non-human parts of the ecosystem. Forest-wise, over the past 25 years, Congress has been mostly critter-kind and people-cruel.

Alston Chase Excerpts

From his book *In A Dark Wood*, page 418, Alston Chase makes the following comments:

"A truly ecological perspective recognizes that humans and their activities are part of nature, and that enhancing all aspects of their lives — including their surroundings — begins with cooperation between individuals, based on mutual trust. This means that rather than following one strategy, we should mimic the Indians and encourage a multiplicity of regimes. Rather than halting or reversing disturbances, we should embrace change. Rather than excluding man from the garden, we should welcome his cultivation of it.

Rather than feeling compelled by metaphysical imperatives to save pseudoscientific *ecosystems*, we should seek to sustain a variety of landscapes simply because they please us. And rather than impose draconian environmental laws that divide society, we should encourage cooperation which builds trust and seeks to heal the social wounds that thirty years of philosophical conflict have caused.

This demystification and democratization of preservation would ensure the diversity of life that many environmentalists desire, and would redefine the role of ecologist from guru to guide. Instead of helping to shape policy objectives, as they often do today, these scientists would merely evaluate and implement mandates. They would address means, not define the ends."

About Consulting

A principal advantage of a consulting career, providing you are successful and/or otherwise financially comfortable, is the freedom that you have between projects to do whatever you wish. Also, you only have to go after or take on the projects you want to do. Once a consultant has located and/or developed capable associates (subcontractors), your personal-time flexibility increases. You are your own boss despite having clients who must be satisfied. You have the power to do things your way, if you wish — at least ONCE with each client. Usually, you are hired to do things your way since you are being paid for being an outside expert.

It isn't any secret that a wise consultant listens carefully to what is said by in-house personnel. Often managers hear what the outside "prophet" says even though someone on their staff had been saying the same thing, but wasn't able to communicate effectively. Sometimes this indicates the boss doesn't listen as carefully to his staff as he does to a highly paid outsider.

Two principal reasons we have been able to make a comfortable living at consulting are associates Robert Flynn and Jack Gates. Both are personal friends and capable consultants with their own businesses.

Where we live geographically is especially important to Jan and me. We are home, family and view-oriented. As a consultant, you have great freedom to choose where you live. You may starve to death, but no one other than your spouse is saying where you should live. I have an intense dislike for long commutes. As a result my home-to-office commuting time as a consultant has, for 95 percent of the time, ranged from zero (office in the home) to a tops of the current 10 minutes.

A Word to Those Who Wish to Be Consultants,
Especially the Young

I was fortunate in being able to earn a good living consulting while having many fringe benefits including living where we wanted to, setting my work hours and having a short commute. It isn't easy to do — especially for recent graduates. So be warned that it may be difficult to get started in the consulting business.

Who-you-know is especially important, both for obtaining work but especially for obtaining information. Young people normally don't know as many people as someone with more experience so this is often a roadblock. Working with a consulting firm is an ideal way to lengthen the who-you-know list. If you are going to gain experience in non-consulting work, you may be better off in a smaller company where you are more likely to rapidly get a good view of the whole picture. Needless to say, this depends somewhat on your specialty.

I urge young people who want to consult to obtain a specialty. Know enough of the big picture so that you know how your specialty fits — but by all means have a specialty of some sort. Choose your specialty with some care. There isn't much demand for buggy whip experts.

A primary reason I say this that I have been repeatedly surprised at how relatively easy it is to become an expert in a narrow field or new field — and there is a market for many kinds of specialized knowledge. Correlatively, it is possible to manage with only superficial knowledge of factors that have a big impact on profits, if you have help. Good managers recognize that sometimes it costs less and is more profitable to get some specialty help from third parties. Examples are taxation, marketing and personnel recruitment.

In my case, log exporting was a specialty. Over time this led to an above- average knowledge of Japan's wood market. Now, I'm regarded by some as a useful consultant on marketing Russian forest products. This is not because of my knowledge and experience inside Russia, but because Japan is the primary export market for Russian wood.

Conference Series and a Publication

By 1982, it appeared that there was need for a marketing publication that focused primarily on export log prices. Alaska is a favorite place for me and partly because of that I began doing consulting work that required knowledge of the market for Alaskan logs. Alaskan natives in the mid '70s had been given some of the best timber in Alaska as part of the Alaska Native Claims Settlement Act. They and others needed better communications about log prices so we, (Jay Gruenfeld Associates Inc., with Jan being very involved) started *The Alaska Forest Market Report*, a quarterly, usually 36 pages in 1982.

We combined the market feasibility study for such a publication with a pre-publication discounted subscription fee. When we started to publish there was enough cash from the pre-publication subscriptions to assure no out-of-pocket loss for over a year.

I made about 40 trips to Alaska and several to Japan from '79 through '89, but I still traveled away from home less than half the time than had been required at Potlatch.

The Alaska Forest Market Report (AFMR) was a trial balloon to test the market for a publication with a broader audience. The AFMR was a success, so, in 1985, we began publishing the *Pacific Rim Wood Market Report* (PRWMR), at first bimonthly and then monthly, 16 pages. The PRWMR was sold to Linda Keller Barr in 1994. She has made some improvements and seems to be doing very well. I am a contributing editor.

The Conference Series
There appeared to be forest products marketing communications need that could be filled by conferences. Our first conference titled Marketing Forest Products of the Pacific Rim was held in Juneau, Alaska in 1983 at the Baranof Hotel. It was a success.

Our 31st conference was in May of '96 in Santiago, Chile (jointly with Fundacion Chile), our 3rd in Chile. The 32nd and 33rd will be December 2, 3, and 4, 1996 in Seattle. The 34th, our sixth overseas, is planned for Vladivostok, Russian Far East for next May 13 and 14, but may be canceled.

The Vlad conference would be held within a 100 miles or so of the range of the Siberian tiger, an endangered species. Hopefully, I can use some of the profit from the conference and spend a couple of days trying to see a tiger. (Wilderness recreation does cost money.)

The conferences offer a chance to visit informally and there is time for discussion of each presentation. So we do act as though we really believe in two-way communication. The proceedings we publish are of marginal economic benefit to us, but make us feel good since they are a tangible contribution to knowledge.

Consulting Overview
Our first major consulting project set a standard for fun-income that I have never equaled despite having many enjoyable assignments. An entrepreneur based in Phoenix needed a forester to prepare a major report for utilizing Caribbean pine (P. caribea var. hondurensis) plantations in Fiji. I made several trips there and was impressed with the people the scenery and the pine trees. Until visiting Fiji, my greatest sports thrills had come from body surfing near Aitape, New Guinea during World War II. (You can imagine how a kid from northern Illinois, who was a competitive swimmer and had never been in saltwater, would take to those big warm-water waves.) But those thrills had to take second place to snorkeling around (I mean 360 degrees) little Treasure Island, off the west coast of the main island, Vite Levu, Fiji. The vivid colors of the fish and the underwater coral and vegetation made

it an underwater paradise. Just writing about it makes me want to go back.

We did forest business work for individuals and a wide variety of corporations. For our small company, the largest contracts were in the $50,000 range and usually related to some phase of wood supply. One project was on the supply of wood for chopsticks, another on high-grade spruce for musical instruments. I marketed several cargoes of Alaskan logs to Japanese and Chinese companies.

Chili

Another especially enjoyable assignment and perhaps the most flattering testimony to my consulting work, came from Joe Henri, an attorney, the president of South Central Timber Development Co., Anchorage, Alaska. We had several assignments from Joe in the '80s. A couple of years after those assignments, in '90, Joe asked me to accompany him on a trip to Chile to look for forest investment opportunities — at my normal fee. I disclaimed any real expertise on Chile, but gladly accepted the assignment. With his daughter, Carolyn and son, Stephen, we spent over a week in Chile, looking, from Santiago to Punta Arenas, about 1,500 miles to the south, near Tierra del Fuego. Radiata pine, eucalyptus, coique (coy' way) and lenga were the species of particular interest. Later, Carolyn worked several years in Chile. Now she is now married and completing her dissertation on forest plantation management for a Ph.D. from North Carolina State U. Joe Henri is now a regent of the University of Alaska. I've made four business trips to Chile.

Foresters often get to work in spectacular country. Icy Bay, Alaska 1986: At South Central Timber Development Co. (owner Joe Henri) logging camp with John Schulz forester-timber cruiser (l.). You couldn't drive to this camp. All the roads started in camp. There were many brown bears, so I carried a Ruger .44 Magnum revolver (Dirty Harry's was a Smith & Wesson) — never was even close to using it. Camp is about 100 feet above sea-level. Timber above 400 feet elevation was reserved for mountain goat habitat. The logged timber was mostly Sitka spruce with some hemlock, white fir and Alaska Yellow Cedar.

Valdevia, Chile, May 1996: Unfortunately our forest product marketing conferences are serious affairs with no time for fun. Everyone in this photo was on the conference field trip, except the bartender. Represented are the U.S., Canada, Philippines, South Africa, Brazil and Chile. The star must remain anonymous but knows a lot about giraffes. Author photo.

Chile: May 1996 on our conference field trip, near Valdevia. Norm Brocard, forester, Renton, WA. Eucalyptus nitens, 3 year old plantation; tallest trees about 30 feet. Norm, a personal friend, ran the Pioneer/Starma timber operation in Russian Far East for over two years.

272

Tennis

In the foreword to the 1995 book *Tennis and the Meaning of Life*, George Vecsey says, "This anthology confirms my belief that tennis is the perfect sporting metaphor for life." This may or may not be true, but I'll personally give vouch for tennis as being a fun sport in which old guys like me have a chance to stay in reasonable physical condition and have fun doing it.

Starting in the late 1950's, I began playing tennis to help stay in shape for my backpacking and hunting trips. Now, it is still a conditioner but much more. The senior Pacific Northwest (Washington, Oregon and British Columbia) tournaments are enjoyable social and competitive events. The rankings aren't a very big deal, but I always seem to know where I'm ranked — not very high (11th) in 70s singles (my favorite), and fairly high in doubles (with partners, Frank Gaylord, Gene Simard and currently 3rd with Gil Anthony). My tennis career has had one noteworthy event that I'll recount. The names are fictional.

A Gentlemen's Game?

Soon after we came to Seattle from Idaho in late 1979, I was warned to stay clear of the Slow family. They had no visible means of support and played tennis about eight hours every day on the Lincoln Park public courts —monopolizing at least one court. The father, Dan Sr., was a foulmouthed person who had three adult sons. He was a despotic cult-type family boss. You couldn't play tennis or even warm-up with one of the boys without getting his permission. Rumor had it that they had been involved in some assaults.

Despite the warnings, I played the boys occasionally since they were good players and all could beat me most of the time — and I felt sorry for them. Dan Sr. was about eight years younger than I, but I could beat him easily.

One morning I went to the courts. The four Slows were the only ones there, so I told Dan that if one of the boys wanted to play singles, I was available. Later, Dan Sr. came over and we started to play.

At the end of two games, he had given me four blatantly bad calls, and mouthed-off every time I called one of his shots "out." I was up 2 - 0. Early in the third game he hit a deep lob, and I smashed it for a winner that was in by a foot. He called it "out." I said "Dan, life is too short to take calls like that, I quit."

He went berserk. Tried to hit me by serving a ball from ten feet — missed; he was swearing a torrent and practically foaming at the mouth. Finally he grabbed me in a headlock and tried to wrestle me down to the court. I couldn't believe it and just stood there like an old ox with him reefing on my neck. Pretty soon all the boys were standing around watching, but not doing anything. By this time I was having trouble breathing and had to do something. So, I locked legs with him, lucked out, and thumped him down on the court with me on top.

The boys (ages about 28, 21 and 19) then started to beat me with their fists from the back of my neck down to the big scars from the war on my lower back. I grabbed Dan Jr.'s arm, and his pulling lifted me up off of Senior and the fight was over. I had a broken rib and a bunch of fist-size bruises. They had pounded hard on my most sensitive war-scar and I was hurting.

The Ultimate Epithet

Dan Sr. was purple with rage, hadn't said anything and was getting all revved up for a super string of swear words. Despite my army and logging time, and 57 years of living, I figured I might learn a new swear word or three. Finally he blurted out, "You, you, you ... old fart." I think I smiled.

Jan's Reaction

I called my wife Jan from the hospital emergency room. She is one of the sweetest, kindest people I have ever known, and is "afraid" of mice and petrified by any kind or size of snake. But, when she heard what the Slows had done to her sweetheart, she was furious.

If we had taken some of our guns and done what she wanted to do, we would both probably still be in prison.

I had a long-standing dinner date that night at Bonaparts (a nice French restaurant) to interview a candidate Pat Joensuu for a big forestry job in Alaska. Over her objections we kept the date. After a couple of Manhattans I only hurt when I moved anything but my eyes.

Courage

My immediate reaction was to prosecute the assailants, but I was concerned about what the Slows might do to Jan, and my daughter and son, who both lived in the Seattle area. Unanimously, and with feeling they said, "Go get 'em Dad, don't worry about us." So we started proceedings.

We discovered the Slows had made three other attacks, two on tennis coaches, in the three prior years. No one had prosecuted.

During the war I saw some great examples of courage, but no one showed any more courage than a little lady of oriental ancestry, who was severely crippled and taught tennis from a wheelchair. Her friend, and co-tournament director, had been threatened with death by Slow Sr. over the scheduling of a match. One of the Slow boys was in the tournament they were running. When I told her we were going to take the Slows to court, she said, "Jay, I'll testify against them at any time or any place, you want." Talk about courage.

After Slow Sr. and Jr. had twice failed to show in court for an arraignment, the judge issued a bench warrant for their arrest. It is still in effect. The Slows left the state.

Aftermath

About a year later, I was called by an excited high school tennis coach, Dennis Neilson, Bend, Oregon. He said, "Your Slow family has changed their name and they are up to their old tennis tricks in Oregon."

The US Tennis Association (USTA) gave us good support as they had from the first. Dan Sr. and Dan Jr. were banned from any USTA sponsored tournaments. Apparently because of this, they left Oregon and we have heard nothing since.

A Recent Unique Happening (Hopefully)

Last month, a USTA sanctioned tournament was held at the Lakewood Racquet and Sports Club my new club — a nice bunch of people. My first match was on Thursday.

The last thing I remember telling Jan was I wished the tournament was a day later because I felt a little crummy and it was very hot. I returned to normal in the hospital about 3 p.m. with zero recollection of what had happened during the prior six hours. After playing my singles match (against Spencer Kern from California) I kept asking Gil, my doubles partner, "Did I get hit in the head?" He kept saying no, as far as he knew. About the sixth time I asked he figured maybe something was wrong and called Jan. Dr. Vern Larsen, a tennis friend, then walked me into a cold shower suspecting I had had too much heat. Since I still wasn't making any sense, he took me to the hospital emergency room.

They cat-scanned me and found nothing wrong. Finally, I came out of what was later called Global Transient Amnesia. Jan said the first six or seven times we went through the following dialogue it was kind of funny and sweet —

"What happened?"

"I don't know," Jan said.

"What was the score?"

"I don't know."

"Guess I didn't win then. Ha, ha, ha. Are You okay, hon?"

However, by the thirtieth time this same conversation was repeated, she was ready to scream. I was okay before she had to hear it the fiftieth time.

Guess Global Transient Amnesia isn't all that unusual and isn't related to a stroke. Heat can bring it on. I played in another tournament three weeks later and felt fine.

Tennis is a life sport and I love it. Pete Sampras is my favorite player and Rod Laver was. Laver is Pete's favorite. Both have class in addition to great tennis games.

A Tennis Racquet Opens Foreign Doors

I've carried a tennis racquet on many overseas assignments and always seem to find a game, regardless of the language barrier.

In Tokyo in the 80's, I used my best Japanese phrases to get into a doubles match. When it was over, one of the players said in English, "Your Japanese is okay, we're Korean."

A Tennis Fringe Benefit

Years ago someone told me that tennis playing did something to your legs that greatly eased the aches and pains that usually follow long horseback rides by non-riders. I can vouch for that. My horseback riding is usually limited to one elk hunting trip per year of riding four to six hours, each way, on a wilderness trail that is sometimes steep and rocky. This can be a real workout. But my post-ride stiffness is over in a few minutes while my non-tennis playing partners are sometimes sore for a couple of days.

Russian Forests

My Consulting Today Is Russia Oriented

Now at age 72, my consulting work continues but on a part-time basis. Most of it relates directly or indirectly to the Russian forest resource. Though the Russian old-growth trees are small by Pacific Northwest standards, they are usually fine-grained (slow grown) and will produce high quality products. My professional hope is that we foresters (Russians, Americans, Finns et al) can help the Russian people benefit from their immense forest wealth on a sustainable basis. One of the failures of USSR Communism was in not adequately reforesting the land that was harvested. Reforesting the land is not just good stewardship it is good long-term business. Most forests in the United States are being regenerated (often by planting seedlings) within a year of logging or soon after. It should be the same in Russia and the other Confederated Independent States. Fortunately much of Russia's softwood timber has never been harvested so there is an opportunity to reforest adequately.

Russia Is Not A Happy Place — But Log Exports Continue

The consensus of Americans I have talked with who have worked in various businesses in Russian is that "Russia is not a happy place." Now, more specifically, six years after the overthrow of communism — despite Russia's having about one-half the softwood sawtimber of the world — Russia is not a happy place to do forest business.

Some of the reasons "Russia is not a happy place" are obvious. Here I'll focus on the background and magnitude for one of these obvious reasons whose impact is probably underestimated. This reason was shockingly stated to me personally in 1993 by a Russian man. Later, it was repeated virtually word-for-word by a Russian woman to a small group. In both cases, the discussions involved major factors that would influence the speed with which Russia would be able to secure the benefits of democratic capitalism. Both Russians said, "Remember, our best people are dead."

Think, if you will of the impact of World War II on the populations of America's young men and the nation as a whole. (I lost two cousins to the war and a couple of friends.) Now, imagine what the impact of World War II would have been if we had lost twenty times that number. And Russia's loss was 50 times greater than ours, proportionately. (WW II US/Russia populations 132/190 million; we had 290,000 die; they lost about 22 million. Their losses included a significant number of women).

In addition, if you mention their WW II losses, the Russians will sometimes say, "Stalin killed more than that." And Stalin can be credited with "killings" that continued long after his death in 1953. Make your own evaluation of the relative quality of those who died. Wouldn't those who died have been above average in idealism (e.g., opposing Stalin)?

Vast Russian Forests

Russia has about 50 percent of the world's commercial softwood timber. Though rich in forests, Russia is capital poor. Lack of capital is one of the reasons total wood production has been dropping since the 1990 revolution. However, log exports have been increasing since they are a source of capital.

Russian Log Exports

Japan is by far the major market for Russian logs. Despite a drop in total Russian harvest, log exports to Japan have continued to increase.

Table 1. Japan Imports of Russian Logs (all species all grades) million cubic meters JAS (Japan Agricultural Standard)

Year	Volume	% inc. fr. prior year
1995	5.4	12.5
1994	4.8	6.8
1993	4.5	25.0
1992	3.6	N/A

Source: JAWIC (Japan Wood Products Information Center)

Note: Russian log exports to Japan peaked at nearly 9 million cubic meters in 1988, but then declined until 1992.

Through May 96, Japan received 2,296,000 cubic meters in the first six months — down 3 percent from 1995 (Japan Lumber Reports).

Note: Japan housing starts in 1996 through May are up 8.9 percent over 1995 so there should continue to be an excellent demand for Russian logs. Total starts in 1996 will be about 1.6 million.

Larch Prices Have Risen Dramatically

Larch (principally Larix dahurica) is the dominant Russian softwood species, especially in the Russian Far East where larch is about 60 percent of the total volume.

In 1987, larch log prices CIF Japan were 40 percent less that spruce logs of similar quality. In June 1994, larch prices were only 10 percent below spruce. In July, larch prices were higher than spruce. (See below.) Now in November 1996, spruce is higher. The increased use of larch in making plywood in Japan accounts for much of the increase in price. Also, virtually no larch is exported from North America while significant volumes of spruce are exported, primarily from Alaska. In addition Scandinavian countries exported over 500,000 cubic meters of logs, principally spruce to Japan in 1995.

1996 July And May Prices CIF Japan In GOST Cubic Meters

	July	May
Spruce (ezomatsu in Japanese)	$102	95
Larch (karamatsu) primarily	$102	102.50
Red pine (akamatsu, mostly Scots pine primarily)		
	$120	122

Source: Mokuzai Shinbun

Russian Log Export Potential Is Massive

In very approximate numbers, the total wood consumption of Japan is about one cubic meter of wood per person annually, or just over 100 million cubic meters. This is about the same as the calculated-allowable cut of Russian Far East that is presently only harvesting, totally, about 11 million cubic meters. However I would not put much faith in the calculated-allowable cut figure, since my experience is that in undeveloped areas, such as Siberia-Russian Far East, the calculated cuts tend to be high. Also, the actual harvest will be reduced by economic feasibility and the necessity to protect the environment while providing more wood for domestic consumption. Nevertheless, there is great potential for increasing exports.

Forecast of Russian Log Exports to Japan in 2000 and 2005

I'm sticking with my 1993 guesstimate that Russian log exports to Japan in 2000 will be approximately seven million cubic meters, and in 2005 will be 10 million cubic meters. Hope I'm around to see if I am right.

Personal Note

I had planned to do consulting work in Siberia (red pine, P. sylvestris) for a short time next month. Like the name of the airline destination near Lake Baikal, Ulan Ude (uoo lahn' uoo day'). This is a couple of hundred miles north of Mongolia. It was possible that we would even have seen the Russian cousins of our North American elk.

On the return trip, I had planned to visit Vladivostok to check on arrangements for our May 13-14, 1997 wood marketing conference. However, the trip was canceled at the last minute. Perhaps this is too typical.

Russians Like This Joke

Even good jokes often don't go over well when translated into a foreign language. For example, after a few failures I gave up trying to tell jokes through an interpreter to the Japanese. However, here is a joke that wowed a small group of Russians one evening in Komsomolsk-on-Amur. Before telling it, I asked the lady interpreter if the Russians would understand one of the joke's key words and she assured me that they would.

Story — One time a young Russian forester was hunting grizzly bears in a Siberian Ancient Forest far from any roads. He saw a huge bear and shot, but only wounded the bear which then charged. Then the young hunter's rifle jammed and wouldn't fire. He knew he was as good as dead, and being a Christian, dropped to his knees, folded his hands, bowed his head and began his last prayer while waiting for the bear to strike. After a few seconds, nothing had happened so he looked up and saw the bear on its knees with its paws folded in the same prayerful attitude. The hunter exclaimed, "Thank heavens, a Christian bear." But the bear said, "I don't know about you, brother, but I'm saying grace."

The interpreter had difficulty translating the punch line because she was laughing so hard. In 45 years of my telling, this story has never failed to get a satisfactory laugh. Maybe I'll try it on my next trip to Japan.

Russian Far East: Pioneer/Starma's new logging camp on Siziman Bay, Sea of Okhotsk, just west of Sakhalin Island, only two sailing days to Japan for the barges and ships load here. There are grizzly bears and salmon. The timber is mostly small high grade, old growth spruce (Picea obavata) maximum DBH (diameter at breast height) about 36 inches with maximum height 80 feet, Norman Brocard managed this operation in '94 and '95. We had looked at it together in '93 prior to any logging.

283

More Communications

Self-Communications

Soon after starting my own business, I was making an unusual number of mistakes especially in office procedure. Too many things were being done the way they had been done before. Things had changed, but I hadn't changed my actions accordingly. In a nutshell, I was doing too many things the way I had done them when I had a full-time secretary and was part of a fairly large corporate staff. After starting a consulting business, it was just Jan, part-time, and me to do routine office work. For example, I realized that I was sometimes writing letters when I should have been phoning. I hadn't changed with the change in staffing.

This forced me to stumble into semi-formalizing a communications technique that readers might find useful. We all do it, but most of us don't do it enough. I call it self-communications. It consists of asking yourself relevant questions, listening to your answers and then acting accordingly. It has helped improve my decision making.

Here is an example. Someone phones and asks you to call back. Rather than make a knee-jerk decision to call back it helps to ask yourself, "Is it possible that a hand-scribbled FAX would be better for both of us?" (Not if he doesn't have a fax.) For example, there are times when you are pretty sure the caller would be out and the best action is to FAX, "Am in now, or will call you tomorrow a.m. if that's okay."

We all do this to some extent. For instance, an efficient hostess giving a dinner party will usually ask herself, "What is the best seating arrangement?" She will listen to her answers and act accordingly. To allow people to sit wherever they wish is seldom optimum.

Self-Communicate Ahead Of Time

Tragedies can be avoided by deciding ahead of time on a course of action so that a person's reaction is instantaneous. In a war combat situation, survivors have learned to plan ahead using self-communications. For example, you decide that when mortar fire hits (or you hear the explosion at the tube) it's usually best to get-down, fast. If you are in the open and get rifle or machine gun fire, its usually best to find cover of some sort, not just get-down.

A common failing of some is that they freeze when an enemy (or game) shows up close and unexpectedly. These people might have avoided a sometimes fatal delay by mentally rehearsing what they would do in various situations enabling them to act instantaneously without thought. But most of us don't think ahead enough and waste time at the time of an emergency trying to figure out what to do. Deciding ahead of time what you are going to do in an emergency is also necessary in civilian life.

Learning From Experience

In using self-communications, it is often helpful the remember that experience is the best teacher. However, what is often better is learning from the experience of <u>others</u>. The lack of action by others has caused me to think ahead. Two examples stand out.

One night in Glacier National Park, a woman in a crowded campground was repeatedly mauled over a long period of time and finally killed by a grizzly bear. No one tried to help her despite her cries. If I had been there I might not have done anything either. Now, however, I've vowed that in a similar situation I *will* help. (Planning to have a can of mace at-the-ready could prevent a tragedy.) But whether I have mace or not I will do something.

The second example deals with mass killings. In a supermarket, a single killer shot several people as they stood frozen with fear. I have vowed if this ever happens where I am, I will yell, "Throw things!" and begin throwing jars or cans. No sense going down without a fight.

After the Slow family attacked me on the tennis courts, Jan and I obtained concealed weapons permits and each of us self-communicated. After asking myself questions on likely encounters with the Slows, I had a simple plan on how I should act in the most likely situations, including use of the .38 Special (Smith and Wesson) revolver that I carried in my tennis bag for a year after the attack.

I continued to use the public courts, sometimes alone, hitting on the backboard. Being a basically kind and forgiving sort, if a miracle had happened and Dan Sr. had come up to me with an apology I probably would have accepted it, though continuing with the assault lawsuit. There was no apology to say the least.

Five or six weeks after the assault, the first time I was able to play tennis, the Slows showed up. The dialogue went something like this.

Dan Sr. — "Next time we're going to break your f—— head."

Later, Jay — "You'd better bring some help; you don't fight any better than you play tennis and that's damn poor." This was said where the three sons could hear it. That was our last encounter. The bench warrant for the arrest of Sr. and Jr. is still in effect.

Sequencing

In doing anything that involves more than one action, it is useful to use self-communications. There is always a "best" way to sequence actions, so you should often start by asking yourself, "what is the best sequence for the action steps?"

Communicating Forest Truths

There seemed to be a propitious time in '90 to expand the industry communications program. So I wrote some hgih-level forest industry leaders.

July 1, 1990

Messrs. Weyerhaeuser, Hollern, Madden, Pope, Andrews, Vitulli, Folquet, Fery, Leland, Heist, Hampton, Swindells Jr., Hayes Jr., Stewart, Spences, Waltz Jr., Ingham, del Valle, Taniguchi, Nutter

Subject: Expanding Timber Supply and Forest Management Communications — The Time Is Right

Dear George, Mike, Dick, Peter, Dolph, Marco, George, John, Dave, Whitey, John, Bill, Ed, Stub, Chuck and Bob, Bob, Tom, Juan, Steve, Lee:

This first-of-a-kind letter to you special people recommends action that I sincerely believe will benefit the country, the people and the forest industry short-term and long-term — it's not a JGA sales pitch.

My Plea to You

Please get the industry to spend more money communicating on the timber supply/forest management issue — and do it fast. The time is right.

Sorry, but this letter is not written primarily to help the industry. It's written to help the country and its people get a greater sustained stream of material benefits from public forests and private forests (and to make an old forester feel like he is trying to make a contribution).

All of you know me well enough that I can legitimately first-name you, so you also know that for a long time I have been heart and soul in the effort to expand communications with the public — including the other side and the legislators.

Many legislators know that the Endangered Species Act is sloppy, people-cruel, wasteful legislation that needs amending. Also, the National Forest Management Act needs amending to give some stability to families and communities while providing forest products and other benefits of wood-producing forests.

This is a war. Truth is on our side, but the other side is outspending us massively, has more bodies and also has the worldwide environmental roll with them.

This is a strategic time to get a higher ROI on spending additional money to communicate forest truth. The other side has been a little greedy and is vulnerable. We need to generate more grassroots support by telling, in an emotional but credible way, about the need to use public lands to provide employment, community stability, and other material benefits. And we need to present a "people" approach instead of an environmentalist "critter or "nature" approach.

Obligation

A major justification of our business system is that it helps allocate wealth wisely. But the forest industry, in total, has done an anemic job of conveying truth and its side of values debate. Partly because of this lack of communications effort, sustainable tree harvest is banned in huge areas. People suffer because industry has failed to communicate adequately. The industry so far has failed to meet its communication obligation — so, the country and the industry suffer. This is my opinion based on 40 years of business experience, and I suspect it's an opinion shared by most industry professionals.

Favorable Signs

There are favorable signs. You know them. More and more people are questioning whether it's wise to trade-off employment for 28,000 people, and all the other benefits of sustainable harvest, to aid an owl and appease those who don't want to cut over mature trees.

But the current battles and the war require a lot more money than has been provided. Sure, you and your organizations have all given a lot — but it hasn't been enough — or, in total, as much as it should have been. Industry focus, generally, has been too much on the short-term bottom line, rather than the long term. So we must play catch-up and change some things.

We should supply grassroots organizations with videotapes and other support. If our story is told often and told well, the common citizens, media and legislators would believe more strongly that things are heavily off balance in favor of the preservationists and against the interests of the people and the country. The anti-industry bias of the media sometimes shows in the form of pro-nature stances that are really anti-people on impact.

Nationalize the Forks, Washington Hurt

Forks, Washington is 90 percent dependent on timber harvest for its employment. Forks makes good media copy. With the right communications program, the rest of the nation would start to get the picture that the Forks thing could happen in their communities. After all, the owl is only one of hundreds of critters that are threatened, endangered or are indicator-species; the potential people impacts are catastrophic. Amendments are needed for the Endangered Species Act and the National Forest Management Act, but it won't happen without more communications by industries — a lot of industries.

Another Plea

In the present battle, with the enemy vulnerable and visible, now is the time for masses of firepower, not precision. What we have now is a target of opportunity. Avoid delay. Truth is mostly ours, but it must be communicated. Please help.
Thanks for reading.   (END OF LETTER)
Note: There has been some improvement but not nearly enough.

Forestry Statesmen Needed

The last forester in the West that I would call an industry forestry-statesman was W. D. Hagenstein, Bill is in his eighties now and retired from the Industrial Forestry Association about 20 years ago and lives in Portland, Oregon. He had been mentored by Col. W. B. Greeley and E. T. Allen a couple of forestry giants residing in the Pacific Northwest. Articulate Bill and 6'5" frame was a respected presence on Capital Hill in D. C. and in other legislative areas. Bill had intellectual courage in addition to credibility and communications skills.

Perhaps we lack statesmen because we lack mentors.

289

Quick Communication

Walt Schiesl was the custodian in the old Weyerhaeuser Building on 11th and A St. in Tacoma. I often worked late and we would chat occasionally. One fall after I hadn't talked with Walt for about four months, I saw him in the hallway.

Without preamble I said, "Walt where are you going to go?"

"You know Jay, I thought I'd go up Slippery Creek. When I was fishing I saw a big buck up there," he quickly replied.

Guess what we talked about a lot.

The Far Side Communicates

Gary Larson's *Far Side* cartoons are a favorite of ours. The name Gruenfeld is unusual (despite being little different from greenfield in German), so I wrote Gary about how he happened to use Gruenfeld in a couple of his cartoons. And, was it possibly because he had briefly known my twins Kimberly and Wendy at Curtis High School in Tacoma? He said, "Very possibly," and sent this reprint of an episode in the life of "Mr. Gruenfeld."

THE FAR SIDE   By GARY LARSON

With the surgical team passed out, and with help from the observation deck, hospital custodian Leonard Knudson suddenly became responsible for bringing Mr. Gruenfeld "home."

The Media

Media Bias Against Industry and Favoritism for Preservation Rather Than Use

The media generally favors preservation of forests rather than use of forests. Also, they are usually biased against industry and for environmentalists. My media friends agree the bias exists. Some of the bias comes from a feeling that profit, the primary goal of industry, is just another name for greed. (Some of this anti-profit bias could be overcome with an expanded two-way communications program by industry.)

Some of the media bias is from lack of knowledge. The lack of knowledge results partly from the failure of industry and professional foresters to communicate. One reason for the media's lack of knowledge is that reporters (and editors) have a relatively low capacity for absorbing new information/knowledge, especially when they are emotionally biased against that information.

A friend of mine who is a retired journalist described it this way, "Jay, you must remember that reporters, due to the pressure of deadlines and exposure to masses of constantly changing information — pressures relative to new information, and so forth are usually much more like funnels than sponges. Not much sticks with them, so the task of keeping them adequately informed is a real challenge, much more difficult than you would first think."

My personal experience over the past 45 years and my logic both confirm his observation. Political actions are based principally on perceptions, not facts, so the media is tremendously important.

James Carville, a master strategist in the election campaign of President Clinton said some very interesting things about the media and reporters in the book *All's Fair* (pg. 186) which he co-authored with his wife Mary Matalin. There may be overstatement in the following, but he isn't the only one who has said essentially the same thing, and there is truth in it.

"They like to think of themselves as learned and insightful and thoughtful and considered. They claim the mantle of truth. Hell, truth is they make instant snap judgments and after that all of their time, all of their energy, all of their creativity is spent on nothing but validating their original judgment. Something happens and three minutes after the event they all talk to each other and decide 'This is the story,' and the story must remain thus in perpetuity. They claim the moral high ground; their job is to report facts and tell people the truth. But information is secondary to them, self-justification is primary. Once the collective media mind is made up, it will not change. Until you understand that, you can never understand the media. (Emphasis added.) Their original take is the one that is going to last....

"...Once they've got their story they stick to it. At some point they stop thinking about an issue and just pursue it. There's no one who has dealt with the national media who has not gotten any number of phone calls saying, "I'm writing a story and I want to say this. Can you say it for me?" Reporters try to get you to say what they want you to say, not what you've got to say. If you say what *you* want to say, they keep coming back to try and get you to say what *they* want you to say.

"...If an undeniable fact runs counter to the story they want to write, they will ignore the fact.

"They try to be honest people, a lot of them I like, but they're so into self-justification that they have turned journalism into the one institution in America with the least capacity for self-examination and self-criticism. The ultimate arrogance is that they view any criticism as some sort of censorship or media-bashing. But the media, they never criticize each other. Thou shalt speak no evil of another reporter." (End of quotes.)

The media is hugely powerful, therefore when you combine bias, a fixed opinion, and self-justification with slow learning with inadequate communication of the facts, it isn't any wonder that the industry which clearcuts trees is in trouble with the media.

The media thrives on conflict and can label the contestants. Often they will identify an industry-environmentalist conflict. Seldom is it labeled a preservationist/worker conflict though that is what it is.

Clearcutting

Most of the media appears to have decided that clearcutting forest is usually bad, even though clearcutting corn or wheat is acceptable. It doesn't seem to matter that practically all foresters recognize cutting all trees on a specific selected area of, for instance Douglas fir, is often the best way to regenerate (reproduce) a stand. Most births are unpleasant to watch. Regardless of its acceptability, few foresters deny clearcutting looks ugly.

Like the ugly part of the birth of a baby, clearcutting is a small part of the total life of a forest, just as the birth is a small part of a total human life. Unfortunately, clearcutting can be viewed by the public, and can be a shocking sight that makes some people so emotional that they fail to consider: this in the long run is the best way to get the species back which will produce the most benefits for humankind. For example, this is the only way to gain the full benefit from breeding genetically-improved seedlings.

The forest industry continues to make too many oversized clearcuts in scenically sensitive areas -- but they are improving.

Repetition Tends to Make Untruths Believable

Repeated untruths tend to be believed. So, when the media, using information given them by preservationists because of either bias or ignorance, keep repeating an untruth, it tends to be believed. This is the case with the idea that "clearcutting is bad."

Another example in recent use regarding the Tongass National Forest in Alaska is that the Tongass is "the last rain forest" — it isn't, although the statement is made repeatedly. When I wrote *Newsweek*'s editors and complained that an article in the October 2, 1995 issue was stating a falsehood, "and in addition used a blatantly biased photo to damn clearcutting, I received a "brush-off" letter from a staffer that didn't mention my clearcutting propaganda reference, misspelled forest twice (though correctly at least once) and admitted that they should have said, "complete rain forest." This is also incorrect, but *Newsweek* appears to learn slowly (more like a funnel than a sponge) since the September 2, 1996 issue used clearcutting as a slur and repeated the error of calling the Tongass "the last rain forest." I considered canceling our subscription. But, since, as Carville might say, the media has collectively decided that clearcutting is bad, so other news magazines might be the same. Also, another publication wouldn't have Col. David Hackworth's military column, which I usually agree with and always enjoy.

Summary Comment:

The media plus a vocal minority often equals legislative victory.

October 4, 1995

Newsweek, Letter to Editor

The Oct. 2 article "The Alaska Assault" by Martha Brant is well-written and only normally "anti" using forests to produce job, newsprint and homes, etc. Except that she refers to the Tongass National Forest in Alaska as "...the nation's last rain forest." This is grossly untrue and shows ignorance about the facts or willingness to lie. For one example, come to Washington and see preserved rain forests by the hundreds of thousands of acres on the Olympic Peninsula.

The photo, of an exceptionally ugly clearcut, is about as relevant to the life cycle of a forest, as a picture of the ugliest part of childbirth is to a useful human life.

The histrionic caption repeats the untrue phrase, "the last rain forest."
Let's have more balance in your forest management coverage, please! (End of letter.)

Forestry Reflections

My bumper sticker reads "For a forester, every day is Earth Day." We do care about forest practices. If foresters had controlled more of the cutting practices in the pre-1970's, the forest industry's public relations would be better.

Today most of the cutting is controlled by professional foresters and the practices assure that the land will continue to be productive and more care is taken about the size and pattern of clear cuts. Clear-cutting is an ugly but necessary part of much good forestry.

Two Small but Memorable Personal Forestry Happenings

Out of the hundreds of forest management memories from a professional career of over 45 years there are two minor but memorable events that stand out. Both relate to silviculture (the art and science of growing trees).

The Ernie Mann Plantation

Early in 1955 Ernie Mann one of our Skykomish Tree Farm logging contractors removed a few scattered trees from a 4.5 acre bush patch northeast of Sultan, Washington (Section 15, Township 28 North, Range 8 East). His contract included planting the logged area with two year old (2-0) Douglas fir seedlings. He was paid 2.5 cents per tree so, the planting cost was about $20. per acre. We knew the trees would be planted well because Ernie was totally reliable.

Most of his life he had been a timber faller but after falling timber for about 25 years he bought a small John Deer tractor and started his own 2-man logging company.

The trees were planted in early May 1955 the year of the Big Freeze when after a balmy fall the temperature dropped from 70 degrees (F) to zero in 24 hours. Some small trees were killed outright but millions had their tops killed.

I examined the plantation, in December right after the freeze. Seedling after seedling had been completely defoliated by the frost or had every needle killed. But the buds looked healthy. We feared that the plantation might be a failure, especially since this was highly productive land that would produce fast growing underbrush that could choke out the planted trees. The productivity class was high Site II, Site Index 180, meaning that the average height of the dominant and codominant trees at age 100 would be 180 feet. Today, height at age 50 is the index used, since age 50 is often the most economic age to harvest Douglas fir on good sites.

The Ernie Mann plantation proved again that the land in the Pacific Northwest "wants to grow trees." The little plantation flourished and the trees jumped-out of the ground, survival was about 85 percent despite the Big Freeze and the brush.

After six growing seasons the tallest trees were 12 to 16 feet, which is unusually good early height growth for Douglas fir which is a slow-starter compared with, say, the Southern pines. (See photo.)

The Pre-commercial Thinning Slash Mystery

My other silvicultural mini-forestry remembrance absolutely dumbfounded me when it occurred in 1971 near Bend, Oregon on Brooks-Scanlon land.

Ponderosa pine that regenerates naturally often comes in in thick dog-hair patches that must be thinned to produce an ideal spacing. The trees cut in the thinning operation are too small to be sold for a profit, so this type of operation is called pre-commercial thinning. After the unwanted trees are cut, usually with a small power saw, the resulting slash (debris) is dense and is a great fire hazard. Central Oregon where this occurred is on the edge of the Oregon desert and the fire

February 1961 forester Neill Bowman, Skykomish Tree Farm, Weyerhaeuser Co. in the Ernie Mann plantation. Neill is 6'4". At age 20, some of these trees were 14 inches in diameter and 50-60 feet tall.

danger is often high. In fact as I write this, August 1996 there is a 95,000 acre fire raging in Central Oregon.

This was in the early days of pre-commercial thinning on private land in Oregon. We were trying various methods of treating the slash so that the fire hazard was reduced.

One method was to use a small tractor that had mounted on its front a rotating drum with short pieces of heavy chain attached. This chain-flail would beat the slash into small pieces and spread it evenly over the forest floor.

After this test area had been pre-commercially thinned the slash in some places was thigh deep and very dry. The leave trees were 2"-4" in diameter, and 150 or so per acre, about 14'x14' spacing. Ted Young, a forester the Raw Material Supervisor for Brooks waited until the slash was nearly bone dry and then had it chain-flailed.

We went out together to look at the results. The slash had disappeared. Ponderosa pine needles are 4 to 6 inches long and it was as though they had been taken away with a giant vacuum cleaner.

"Ted, where is the slash?" I asked, "Did you bury it?"

He assured me that nothing had been buried but said the tractor operator had done a fine job and the slash was in perfect condition for flailing. It was amazing. The fire hazard created by the thinning operation had been virtually eliminated.

This was a little thing that has stayed in my memory because the results had been so perfect. Pre-commercial thinning is now standard practice on many forest holdings. Chain flailing is sometimes used to treat the slash.

Suggestions to Improve Management of Federal Forests

My hope is that federal forests in the future will provide and sustain greater human happiness. As a professional forester with over 45 years of diverse ongoing forestry experience, more than most, I know both the dollar and non-dollar values involved in making forest management choices. For example, my working life has required that I be a relative expert in the dollar value of trees as a source of wood to serve people's needs, including jobs, homes and profit. In addition I have managed two large tracts of private forest land and watched the ecosystem respond to various harvest systems. In contrast, my 71 years of living show that I value highly the non-dollar aspects of life, such as preserving Wilderness Areas, the source of my favorite outdoor recreation. Also, I have been a bird watcher since I was five years old. This broad value spectrum and experience gives a solid foundation for knowing what the tradeoffs are in making forest management decisions.

In addition I am a relative idealist who believes that two-communications will ultimately lead to more trust between people who have diverse views on what benefits should provide to people and other parts of the ecosystem.

Increasing the level of tree harvest in the federal forests of the Pacific Northwest is necessary and desirable. Here are some of the reasons.

World Tree Values Are High and Will Get Higher

The federal forests of the Pacific Northwest are a great source of potential wealth in both dollar and non-dollar terms. For our federal forests, my concern is that people are not benefiting enough from the potential wealth of these forests. The forest industry is an important part of having a happy life for many of us. Industry provides work; it is a means of obtaining jobs. Industry provides the tax base for good schools, strong law enforcement agencies, environmental protection, the gamut. But industry is a means not an end.

The tree values have gone up in real terms and when compared to the cost of logging and the value of the products produced by the tree. Here are some examples.

Examples of Wood Value

Today, second-growth trees (not old-growth Ancient trees) are so valuable that in 1995 over 500,000 cubic meters of good sawlogs (mostly spruce) were shipped from northwestern Europe (principally Scandinavia) down through the Suez Canal to Japan. Stockholm, Sweden to Japan via the Suez Canal is 12,000 miles and 39 sailing days (at 13 knots). The alternative route via the Panama Canal is 13,300 miles and about 42 sailing days. If the ships were loaded entirely with logs, this volume would have required 20 very large ships.

New Zealand radiata pine logs (coarse grained logs cut from plantation trees most less than 30 years old) are now shipped regularly to California. They are then milled into lumber to build California homes.

Russian logs, primarily 100 to 150-years-old are trucked to a railhead and are then frequently railed over a thousand miles to a port where they are loaded on a ship that delivers them to Japan. Radiata pine comes over 7,000 miles to replace the trees preserved for the spotted northern owl.

Second-growth Douglas fir sawlogs in the Pacific Northwest of average sawlog quality are sold today for an alongside ship price of $1,000 per M (Scribner scale) for export to Japan.

Here in the state of Washington, some second-growth hemlock sawlogs are being logged on the northwest part of the Olympic Peninsula, trucked about 75 miles to Port Angeles where they are loaded on barges, towed to Oregon, unloaded, loaded on trucks and shipped to an Oregon sawmill.

Low quality logs for pulp are shipped from South America to Europe.

Wood moves these vast distances because it is valuable. And remember that normally the older a tree is the more valuable it is, other things being equal.

At the beginning of this century, here in the Northwest, it wasn't uncommon for the value of an accessible standing tree (called stumpage value or stumpage, for short) to be only 20 percent of the cost of making it into logs and transporting it to a market. If the cost of logging was $8 per thousand (M) board feet (BF) you might have paid $1.60 for the right to cut the tree. That is, logging costs were five times the value of the tree. Note: An excellent source of information on the early Pacific Northwest forest industry is the book *George S. Long, Timber Statesman*, by Charles E. Twining and his later work *Phil Weyerhaeuser, Lumberman*.

Today, on a large private timber sale, other than for salvage timber, the price paid for the tree (stumpage) is frequently double the cost of logging or even triple or more.

Logging Methods Have Improved

In the early years of this century Pacific Northwest logging was usually done by oxen. Today various types of mechanical harvesting are used on the more level ground with portable tower cable systems used for the steep ground. Helicopter logging is expensive, but can often be justified when the objective is preservation of scenic value or the necessity for special protection of soil, water and other ecosystem values. Sometimes helicoptering is the least expensive way to log due to high-road building costs.

This combination of high value for logs (and of the ultimate product) is especially important when managing federal lands. Trees can be harvested selectively and despite the high logging costs still have a high stumpage value (value standing.) On many areas, clearcutting is no longer necessary for a profitable operation.

Selective logging is usually more labor intensive so provides more jobs.

The following Forestry Reflection was special enough to deserve a short chapter.

302

A Special Forest Day

August 15, 1996 was a special day for someone who loves forests and sunsets. I attended a Makah Forestry Enterprise meeting at Neah Bay the most northwesterly town in Washington state, at the tip of the Olympic Peninsula. The meeting was over about 4 P.M. and as usual had been productive and interesting. I bought two sockeye salmon, caught that day, at the fish processing center on the dock (only $2.10 per pound). Sockeyes are a premium eating fish with bright red meat. Each fish weighted 5 pounds, dressed but with head. I then headed east alone.

It was a beautiful day and I enjoyed the trip along the water through Sekiu and Clallam Bay and then took the longer route to Port Angeles via Sappho and the Olympic National Park. This is one of the most productive forest areas in the world and the hillsides were covered with evergreen trees, mostly spruce and hemlock, along the water, with more and more Douglas fir as you gain elevation. There were only a few logging trucks. The Olympic National Forest, once a high-volume producer of timber on a sustainable basis has nearly stopped harvesting timber due to the impact of the Endangered Species Act and related legislation and regulations.

Sunset is my favorite time of the day. Though I'm only a moderate drinker, cocktail time is a nice part of each day. And I wanted to have my ritual Manhattan in a place with a sunset view. Incidentally a Manhattan with the color combination of the marichino cherry, bourbon and sweet vermouth (six to one for me) looks like a sunset.

After turning left onto U.S. 101 at the little town of Sappho I drove about five miles and turned left of a Forest Service blacktopped road, one-lane with frequent turnouts. Most of the drive was through big second growth timber, some of it was probably 21-blow timber. These are evenaged stands that came in after a big windstorm in 1921 -- a clearcut by nature. Some of the trees are two and three feet in diameter. After a few miles the road was blocked by a locked gate. Since I wanted a scenic outlook I backtracked and turned south on a spur road. Soon I was in thick 10 year old reproduction but in about a mile had gained enough elevation to have a view-scape. There was a turnout on the top of a ridge where I parked the Pathfinder.

As I slowly mixed my drink, several band-tailed pigeons flew over headed east, a Stellars Jay with its black head and crest and bright blue body flew west. The sun made all of the colors rich. Looking east, it was easy to see the boundary of Olympic National Park. Much of the Park is flat-topped old growth timber which contrasts with the sharp crowned second growth trees and reproduction on the cutover lands outside of the park. Below me on gentle ground was a fully stocked Douglas fir plantation , about 10 years old with some trees 20 feet tall and taller. There was a red topped tree or all-red tree, or so on many of the acres. Red foliage in an evergreen nearly always means that the red part is dead. I suspected that the all-red trees had been girdled by bears in the spring. Bears strip the bark off the trees to chew on the cambium layer under the bark. The dead tops were probably from porcupines who feed on the bark or from insects.

It was a beautiful scenic spot and made me appreciate being in a profession where you spend so much time on the job or traveling to and from work in scenic outdoor habitat. Most foresters enjoy viewing logged-over areas on the Olympic Peninsula because they are mostly very well stocked with desirable species. This is true whether the ownership is private, state or federal. Usually seedlings are planted immediately after logging and there is always some natural fill-in. Quite a change from the pre-World War II days when relying on natural regeneration was usual and results were spotty.

National Parks are National Treasures

Olympic National Park is one of the treasures in our National Park System that is managed by the Department of the Interior. No trees are cut to produce forest products. Emphasis is on preserving scenic beauty. Trees are cut only when required for road building and other park maintenance activity. It takes money to maintain these treasures. Admission fees don't come even close to covering costs. Encircling Olympic National Park is the Olympic National Forest administered by the U. S. Forest Service, part of the Department of Agriculture.

National Forests of the Pacific Northwest were once National Treasures

National Forests of Western Washington and Oregon (often called the Douglas Fir Region) contain some of the most valuable publicly owned softwood timber in the world. Until the Endangered Species Act was used to virtually stop logging, ostensibly to protect the Northern Spotted Owl, these forests could have been call National Banks that provided big revenues to help run federal and county government and also provided sustainable jobs and other economic forest benefits. Now these national forests no longer produce bounteous flows economic benefits that can be used to meet the costs, for example, of maintaining the National Park System. The Olympic National Forest can be used as an example of what has happened to the revenue production from our national forests.

The Olympic National Forest Federal Forest Management Gone Wrong

In the 1980's the Olympic National Forest produced many millions of dollars of revenue. The peak year was 1987 when 253 million board feet was harvested. This generated $28.9 million of revenue. The county share at 25 percent was $6.3 million. Now there is very little revenue and few jobs and other economic benefits from the forest.

Makah Forestry Enterprise, A Contrast in Forest Management

The Makah Tribe's reservation is the 27, 000 acre block of mostly forest land at the northwest tip of the Olympic Peninsula, also the northwest tip of Washington State. I've been one of the non-Native American Directors since the Makah Forestry Enterprise (MFE) was formed in 1985 to sell and market timber for the tribe on a sustained yield basis. This has been highly successful though neither the land nor the timber is nearly the quality of the nearby Olympic National Forest that is run by the U. S. Forest Service. In a rough comparison, on a scale of one to ten, with ten being the best I'd say the Olympic National Forest land and timber would get a nine and the Makah land and timber a six. And remember that much more than sustained timber revenue is considered in the management of Makah lands. Here is our Mission Statement:

The Mission of Makah Forestry Enterprise

To efficiently and sensitively protect and enhance the forest resources and other resources of the Makah Tribe so as to provide a high level stable flow of dollar and non-dollar benefits to the Makah people. This will be done while preserving the unique culture and heritage of the Tribe.

Economic benefits will come primarily from sensitively developing profitable market-oriented businesses that utilize the forest and subsurface resources of the Makah Tribe. Timber will be carefully harvested at a sustainable rate.

Profitable business diversification is a long term goal.

Some of the major non-dollar values to be protected are water and fisheries, soil, scenery wilderness and species diversity.

Principles that will guide MFE activities include: employment and training of tribal members when feasible, emphasis on good public relations (off Reservation, too), open two way communications, sustainable development, and a high level of stewardship in the management of human and natural resources. (End of Mission Statement)

A comparison of the material benefits to society from the management of the Makah Tribal land with the Olympic

National Forest is shocking. In 1995 (the latest year for which figures are available) the 632,000 acre (988 square miles) Olympic National Forest, that includes some of the most productive forest land and best softwood timber in the world harvested only 4.8 million board feet of timber generating a gross stumpage revenue of $1.3 million dollars. The Makah Tribe, with 96 percent less land and an even lower percentage of timber, harvested 6.7 million board feet (much less than their sustainable allowable cut of 12 MMBF) and generated a revenue of $2.5 million.

To say it another way the Makah forest provided 39 percent more wood and 92 percent revenue to society than the Olympic National Forest did on 25 times as much higher quality land with far more than 25 times as much timber (maybe over 100 times). In addition the Makah operation generated a big profit while the U.S. Forest Service suffered a net loss on its timber sales, due to being a bureaucracy strangled by bad legislation and poor regulations.

The Message

The revenues cannot be compared directly, but the message is crystal clear. Some of the finest wood growing land in the world is doing virtually nothing to meet the wood, jobs, revenue, and the economic needs of the country.

Congress is principally to blame because it passed bad legislation. The Endangered Species Act and parts of the National Forest Management Act are two acts of Congress that are the most flawed. It's no wonder the country operates with a huge deficit. And the people suffer, especially the poor throughout the country and the blue collar workers.

Those who have suffered the most are people in the small communities of the Pacific Northwest and the communities themselves. These small communities that are heavily dependent on loggers and mill workers of the forest industry for their economic and social well being.

Dr. Robert G. Lee, a professor at the University of Washington, in his must-read book on the subject, *Broken Trust, Broken Land* (1994, Book Partners) has this to say about the Pacific Northwest federal timber harvest drop.

"Government Ownership As A Cause For Suffering

Environmental disruption and social and economic suffering also results from uncertainty about rights to use public
lands. Advocates for revolutionary change blame private property owners, technological change, and "the industry" for creating economic chaos. Past mill closures, timber liquidations
and gains in labor productivity, no matter how disruptive to a
local area, were relatively small disturbances compared to the
massive social and economic disruption being created by federal government decisions to suddenly terminate timber harvesting over a vast three-state region -- if not all federal lands.
The conclusion is clear for all to see: government ownership,
not private ownership, has been the most destabilizing influence on social and economic life in the Northwest."

Relation to Olympic National Park

It's especially ironic that the Olympic National Park
of over 900,000 acres (over 1,400 square miles) where zero
commercial timber harvest is allowed, actually touches the
Olympic National Forest on most of its boundary. (The park
is the big hole in the national forest donut.) In 1938 when the
magnificent park was established it was understood that the
adjoining national forest would provide the jobs, wood products, and revenues that people need. Now, for the time being,
only I hope, we have another "park" nearly as large where
timber harvest is minute compared to its sustainable level.
What a waste of sustainable wealth. This land management
folly is too idiotic to last, but it is tragic that it happened at all.

For those of you who mistakenly believe that the public supports what is happening; please remember that people,
in a 1993 national poll, rejected by a vote of 5 to 1 sacrificing
10,000 jobs to help the Spotted Owl survive. (Yet the
President's Forest Plan eliminated over 30,000 jobs.) Ultimately the politics of federal forest management will swing
from people-cruel, critter-kind toward people-kind, critter-kind
--providing the truth is communicated.

This will happen faster if the forest industry and the
forestry profession greatly improve their communications with
the public and the media becomes much more even-handed in
dispensing information. I'll be dead before the latter occurs.

Opinions and Suggestions on the Management of Federal Forests, the Forest Industry and the Country

If this book does any appreciable good for the country it will be because of what is said on the following pages.

I am striving to be both truthful and believable; truthful, because that's the way I am, and believable so that my suggestions on how to improve forest management on public forest lands will encourage wise actions.

People are being unnecessarily hurt by bad forest management legislation passed with best intentions. The Endangered Species Act is a prime example.

Summary Of Author's Qualifications On Forest Land Use Issues And Some Forest Management Opinions

I am a professional forester with over 45 years experience and three academic degrees. Like many foresters, I entered the profession partly to improve land stewardship. Mostly I became a forester because I wanted to make a living in a profession that enabled me to do something beneficial to society while spending some time out-of-doors in beautiful country, on-the-job. My formal and informal education expanded my belief in the importance of balancing dollar and non-dollar values when choosing between alternatives in forest management and life.

My system of values places great emphasis on the importance of non-dollar values. If I placed a high value on a big dollar income, it is unlikely I would be a forester. Similarly, it is unlikely I would be a forester if I didn't place a high value on preserving the productivity of the land, on sustainable harvest, and the importance of humans and non-humans in the ecosystem.

Personal Philosophy And Beliefs

I now describe myself as a realistic-idealist while believing for most of my life that I was an idealistic realist. (Some things I learned late.)

Beneficial idealism is rare at the upper levels of business, government, politics and other human activity. Citizens, when you find it, cherish, protect and nurture it.

My personal outdoor recreation is oriented toward wilderness. I go into the Wilderness areas to enjoy the solitude, beauty, challenge and serenity of these gorgeous places. Yes, I hunt in Wilderness, but I haven't shot at an elk for ten years and yet my enthusiasm for this year's Wilderness elk hunt to Idaho is as great as it was when I took elk regularly.

My understanding of how the US political, social and economic system works is above average, principally because of my experience and training. Intense infantry combat, (five wounds, three Purple Hearts) and other parts of nearly 72 years of living have resulted in a life philosophy that recognizes the power of emotion and communications to influence decision making.

Changing Business

To change what business does, it's important to recognize that business managers, CEO's in particular, respond strongly to the rewards-system by which they are measured and rewarded.

To change the actions of managers, change how they are rewarded. Example: Corporate managers, especially top corporate managers, tend to do things that maximize their income. If they are highly rewarded for short-term results, their actions will be oriented to the short-term. If they receive big bonuses for improved long-term communications with the other side and the public, long-term communications will improve. Boards of Directors please note. My personal experience as a Director supports this conclusion. Industry on average fails to communicate effectively with its publics, including its employees.

310

Tradeoffs

We each have our own set of values that we put on such nebulous non-material things as scenic beauty, opportunity for solitude, protection of ecosystem integrity and ecological diversity. But often when choosing between alternatives involving material and non-material values, what is lacking is knowledge of what you are giving up in material benefits such as —jobs, tax revenues, school income, tax base value, lower housing costs, lower product prices, and profit (which is required to keep people employed, in a capitalistic democracy).

To summarize: Because of having 45 years of varied forest business and management experience, and a broad education — more than most, I know what the public gives up in dollar values for what it gets in non-dollar values.

Some of those who oppose the harvesting of Ancient Trees (even before the Clinton Forest Plan, in Washington and Oregon we had 7,000 square miles permanently preserved from cutting) think they know the facts when they don't. Others have a value system that says preserving Ancient Trees is such a good act (even a "Godly act") that any price is worth paying. This to most foresters is an extremist position that is in the not-much-weight category, along with "cut all Ancient Trees because they are over-mature and will die anyway." Usually, in a democracy ,the best course of action lies between the extremes but not always.

Compromise, a keystone for getting something done politically is an important tool, but is not always applicable. To say that wise action ALWAYS lies between opposing is overly simplistic and therefore wrong. Whether compromise is applicable or not depends on the situation. Too often this fact is ignored. Many of us (politicians especially) court compromise too much because it provides an easy cop-out when it's too painful to stick to a principle.

Bureaucracy

Beware of bureaucracy, anywhere. Government is necessary, but is inherently bureaucratic, hence rarely efficient. If the private sector can do it, you can bet the cost will be less for the same end result and it will take less time. Bureaucracy is the curse of government worldwide, but also of any organization that is big, private or public.

Trust

I want for our forests what was adopted unanimously by acclamation as part of the Vision at the recent 7th American Forestry Congress (February 1996, Washington, D.C.) by the 1,500 attendees.

"In the future our forests will benefit from strong trust between diverse stakeholders." Note: Bureaucracy, (which includes orientation toward "process" rather than "results") prevented the trust-goal from being included in the proceedings of the 7th American Forestry Congress.

We certainly don't have much trust now. The media is partly to blame. All sides are partly to blame. We need more dialogue, more listening and telling between our diverse citizens who have diverse value systems. Dialogue usually develops trust. New electronic communications will help.

My Politics

I've voted for both Democrats and Republicans and consider myself a moderate and independent voter. Usually I vote Republican. Here is a personal happening that illustrates where I am relative to the conservative/liberal stereo-typing.

With US Representative Steve Symms, Idaho

After a year or so with Potlatch Company in Lewiston, Idaho as corporate Vice President of Lands and Forestry in the mid 70's, I was in Washington, D.C.. One of the stops was at the office of Idaho Representative (later Senator) Steve Symms. By then I knew him pretty well since he was one of only two representatives from our sparsely populated state. The senators then were Frank Church and Jim McClure.

Steve was pretty far right in his economic and social beliefs, but despite that I liked him and he knew it. We were walking over to the steps of the capitol building so I could have my picture taken with him, and were having a good visit and joking around when I said, "Steve, seriously now, I don't want to mislead you. I'm kind of a fiscal conservative, but I'm also a moderate social liberal."

He grinned widely, pounded me on the back, gave me a hug and said, "Why, Jay ... I am too!"

I think he meant it. We all define things a little differently.

Fiscal Conservative/ Moderate Social Liberal — Defined

Utilizing (not very much) my study of politics, philosophy and economics at Oxford, 71 years of living and much thought, I have developed the following core definition:

"An American fiscal conservative/moderate social liberal is — someone who wants a sustainable bigger national 'pie' that is shared a little more equitably, with welfare-equity to be based more on effort by the receiver than it has been."

The man I hope to eventually see as the Republican President of the United States in his recent biography refers to himself as "a fiscal conservative and social liberal." That is one of the reasons I wrote him the following letter:

February 28, 1996

General Powell (USA ret.)
S 767, 909 N. Washington St.
Alexandria VA 22314

Dear General,

It is two hours since I sent Mrs. Powell and you a FAX saying among other things — some blacks don't think the country is ready for a black president, but our white friends, many very conservative otherwise, think it is.

You have a chance to be one of the greatest presidents.

The country needs a sustainable bigger economic pie that is more equitably distributed (hindsight comment: get a better word, like shared) and a moderate Republican President can do this best, in our opinion.

313

By just being yourselves you two would do more to improve race relations than Mr. King would have thought possible.

We are not wealthy but would donate $1,000 to your campaign initially, and would knock on doors for you. Thank you both for what you have already done for the country.

Since sending the first FAX, a couple of us have decided to have a Draft Powell organization meeting, either in small but wealthy Gig Harbor or in Tacoma.

Please give us some statement to sustain our hope e.g.,"If drafted at the Republican Convention I will serve," or "If a ground-swell develops I will reconsider."

Summary Comment: I'm 71, studied politics and philosophy at Oxford University though a forester (didn't smoke m. and got a diploma). After talking with over 200 people of diverse backgrounds in the past 15 days, I'm convinced there is plenty of time and you will win with a massive margin, if you run.

May God guide the choice you and Mrs. Powell make. And this is from two infrequent church attendees.

Signed,
Jan and Jay Gruenfeld

Note: We never received any encouragement and never held the meeting, but have hopes for 2000.

Sierra Club
The following is written especially for those who have an interest in Sierra Club actions.

Sierra Club Logging Ban Proposal Destroyed Trust
Despite the diverse value values of its 1,500 attendees, the 7th American Forestry Congress in February, 1996 adopted, by acclamation, the following primary goal as part of its Vision Statement —

"In the future ... Our forests will benefit from strong trust between diverse stakeholders."

Trust is the key to good relationships — and now, by its selfish action (wanting to stop all timber harvest on federal lands), the Sierra Club has destroyed much of the trust it

314

had with those who believe federal forests should have as a primary purpose — provide wood to meet the needs of people.

The Seventh American Forestry Conference attendees represented virtually the full range of opinions on how our forests should be managed. On the last day of the conference, the "trust" statement was introduced and supported by Brock Evans, Vice President of the Audubon Society, after it had been formulated by a professional forester (me) and given enthusiastic approval by the Chief of the U.S. Forest Service, small private landowners, forest industry executives, academic leaders, leaders of the Society of American Foresters —everyone. This, despite not having been developed in the well constructed conference process.

Ironically, considering the Sierra Club recent vote of 2 to 1, to ban logging on all federal lands; the next highest level of agreement by the Congress was rejection of a proposal to — ban all logging on public lands. The logging ban was rejected by a resounding 91% "no," 4 % voting "Yes" and 5 % "uneasy" (total votes 1,087). Note: The published conference proceedings are in error on the total voting on this issue, though right on percentages.

Sierra Club Harvest Ban Is More Than Selfish

In the Pacific Northwest, the federal government owns some of the most valuable forests in the world. Unbelievably, in the state of Washington today, only one acre in five (20%) of federal commercial forest land OUTSIDE national parks and Wilderness areas is available to produce timber. Oregon's similar figure is about one in three (33%). So far, preservationists have triumphed.

Yet the Sierra Club voters, a club which boasts of the high income and education level of its membership, want to stop ALL timber harvesting on federal lands. Not harvesting would eliminate many tens of thousands of jobs and increase all forest product prices somewhat. Not cutting will eliminate big federal revenues from Pacific northwest timber harvest and will probably result in increased taxes.

To totally deny people the jobs, school revenues, building products, community stability and other benefits coming from perpetual harvest of renewable federal forests is not just cruel, selfish and thoughtless, it is ... (I needed a strong, accurate additional word and found one) — defined in the dictionary as:

"Causing an undesirable condition, as ruin, injury, or pain .... Morally bad or wrong; wicked, ...sometimes CAPITAL. That which is destructive, corruptive or fallible, whether from natural circumstances, or by human ignorance, error or design."

So I used this word and the completed sentence reads—

"To deny people the jobs, school revenues, building products, community stability and other benefits from perpetual harvest of renewable federal forests...is not just cruel, selfish and dumb — it is Evil."

Note: If the reader would like to describe with another word what the Sierra Club voters propose, they should remember — Evil, unnamed, is still Evil.

Comment: I doubt that a majority of the Sierra Club's total membership wants to stop all logging on federal forests. I predict the Sierra Club will have another vote on the logging ban within a year. But damage has been done. Trust between diverse stakeholders has been destroyed. The Sierra Club has hurt its image by letting its extremism show.

Even the ultra-liberal Seattle Post Intelligencer had an editorial this year condemning the Sierra Club vote as "being extremist."

A Political Paradox

Isn't it amazing that the Democrats, "the working man's party," are primarily responsible for legislation that allowed an Owl to eliminate 30,000 plus big jobs based on sustainable harvest of trees, a renewable resource? Part of the reason for this is the basic distrust that unions and industry have for each other. A union president said to me at the height of the spotted owl controversy in 1993 after it had been going on for several years — "It's only in the past few months that our union sees the Endangered Species Act and the owl as anything but a

problem of management. Now we know it's our problem too."
Shocking, but it's worse than that. At the last February ('96)
7th Forestry Congress, a union vice-president told me his union
still didn't act like it saw the Owl et al as a workingman's
problem. Where have they been. Where have the communications failed?

Yet the Republicans, with the notable exception of a
few leaders like Washington Senator Slade Gorton are more
silent than you would expect them to be about people-hurts
inflicted in the name of the Owl and Ancient Trees. I know
some of the reasons for the less than expected outcry about
people-cruel actions that also hurt some industries.

Industry Leaders Are not United

One reason is that forest industry companies and individuals who own their own trees, know a simple fact. When
federal timber harvest drops, the value of their timber rises.
It's easy to imagine a big political giver of either party saying
to a President (and other legislators), "Don't worry, Bill (or
George or Ronnie) we can grow the wood on privte land, go
ahead and trade off dropping the federal allowable-cut for
something that will help us big-givers." At least it's naive to
think that more than a few companies are going to give a very
high priority to opposing an action that raises the value of
their timber while hurting competitors.

Society of American Foresters Characterized

The silent majority of people whose interests are negatively affected by an artificial decrease in wood supply, wood
users for example, have little organized help. The Society of
American Foresters (SAF), 21,000 strong that is the professional voice of foresters, is quiet on the issue. This is because
a significant minority of its membership opposes anything "so
unprofessional" as strongly voicing a majority opinion and
taking effective political action when society needs help.

Though there is an overwhelming majority wanting the
SAF to take action on amending the Endangered Species Act
and other hurtful forest management legislation so that it gives
more consideration to people impacts, *it is like asking a clam*

to sprint up the beach. It isn't built for it. So long as there is a vocal minority, especially in academia and public forest administration opposing action the SAF remains relatively mute. The SAF does not take strong direct action "to benefit society" unless there is close to unanimity, hence doesn't take on the toughest issues. As a result many action oriented members have left the Society. Others like me remain members and work for change and and endure intense frustration.

The current president and president elect oppose the drift toward bicentrism and its relative disregard of people-hurts. This is wrong and unprofessional.

In my opinion, if the Society of American Foresters does not change in response to the leadership of these two people there is a good chance a new organization will be established, either within the SAF or outside it. The new organization would strive to take effective action when a heavy majority of the membership believe such action is beneficial to society.

Leadership from the Council and the Executive Director are necessary to overcome the drifting inertia within the SAF. The drift is toward a blind worship of undefineable questionable concepts such as biodiversity and the protection of ecosystem integrity with little regard for people-interests.

A Key Forest Fact

In a September 16, 1992 letter that was published in the Seattle Times, I highlighted a key economic and people-impact fact that should be given top priority notice by federal legislators and others who determine how much federal timber should be harvested (on a sustainable basis). Please remember that the amount you can harvest is related directly to the size of the area available for harvesting.

"That fact is that the number of forest jobs and products is most directly related to the volume that can be harvested. If you have six million acres (9,400 square miles) of over-mature forest that's not harvested because of the owl (this is roughly the present plan), then you lose the harvest-related jobs and products from that land. Automation and log exports are irrelevant to that particular loss. If you don't harvest, you don't get the massive harvest benefits that are available forever under careful forestry. After the decision is made not to cut. All you can do is reduce the hurts caused by that decision. If someone's personal value system says the over 30,000 jobs lost and the other negatives are offset by retaining ecological integrity and tree preservation, OK, but they should admit to the loss of jobs."

People Said They Wanted More Forest Jobs Than Clinton Plan Gave

President Clinton, when he spoke at the Forest Summit in Portland, Oregon in 1993, sounded so sincere about not causing unnecessary unemployment among forest workers, that I was surprised a little at the devastating option chosen in his plan. I thought he might go with majority opinion rather than the loud and articulate preservationist minority. He disregarded advice and information in the following letter and will probably continue to do so. His plan unnecessarily eliminated a minimum of 30,000 - 40,000 PROVIDING you share with me mainstream values that include believing that people are fully as important as owls and old trees.

June 18, 1993

The President Bill Clinton
The White House

Dear Mr. President,

Since you were elected partly because you and your advisors heard the people, therefore used the campaign slogan, "It's the economy, stupid," perhaps you will hear the message in a recent poll results on the spotted owl.

The May 1993 national poll by Opinion Research Corporation showed that the 1,039 adults responding gave the following answers.

Question: Whether you would or would not be willing to see the following levels of job losses to protect the spotted owl.

5,000 jobs lost Would 31%
Would not 59% Would-not to Would, 1.9 to 1
Don't know 10%

10,000 jobs lost Would 15%
Would not 75% Would-not to Would, 5 to 1
Don't know 10%

50,000 jobs lost Would 7%
Would not 84% Would-not to Would, 12 to 1
Don't know 9%

Please remember this was a national poll. The Pacific Northwest results are even more heavily in favor of jobs rather than owl protection.

So, by a ratio of 5 to 1 people would oppose losing 10,000 jobs to protect the owl. And by a ratio of 12 to 1 they would oppose losing 50,000 jobs to the owl.

About 40,000 jobs would be lost under the owl protection plan that called for preserving roughly 6 million acres of old growth timber for owl protection. So the people questioned are saying, indirectly, by a 5 to 1 majority that they are opposed to setting aside even 1.5 million acres (25 percent of the plan, so 10,000 jobs) of federal timber for owl protection, because the job loss is too big a price to pay.

I think the Endangered Species Act (and other legislation) must be amended if the timber supply deadlock and the resulting unemployment and other hurts are to cease. I'm in the majority.

The Washington State Society of American Foresters voted 2.2 to 1 to approve their video that carried the clear message, "The Endangered Species Act must be amended to give more consideration to negative impacts on people."

On the Pacific Northwest timber gridlock — please hear the people; don't yield to the professional lobbyists in the major environmental organizations.

Sincerely,
Jay Gruenfeld

Puzzled Comment Relative to Statistics in the Letter to President Clinton

To this day, I can't understand why the results of this national poll weren't communicated more. The timing was excellent. The poll was taken just before the Forest Summit and was done by a corporation used by President Clinton. Why wasn't it given top communications priority by the National Forest Products Association, The National Association of Homebuilders and the hundreds of other industry associations, union, grassroots organization, the Society of America Foresters, even the NAACP, and others who knew that more-timber-amend-the-ESA was in their best interest and the public interest?

Too little communication money was doubtless part of it. We sent out about 30 letters to legislators and mentioned it in our Pacific Rim Wood Market Report. About a year after the poll, at one of our conferences, I asked for a show-of-hands from an audience of about 140 on the question "Have you heard these poll results before." Of the five or six hands that went up, two were communications specialists. Sickening.

First Politics

My earliest political recollection is being told by Dad, when I was about eight, "There isn't anything wrong with the people of the world, they could get along together, it's just the damn-governments." At age eight, I only had a vague idea of what he was talking about. At age 14, I thought it was a gross over-simplificaiton and not too useful. At age 24, while studying politics at Oxford University,, I figured the old guy was right on and I still do.

Democracy at its best requires adequately informed voters and first-class leaders and we don't have either. Here are a couple of quick thoughts and suggestions regarding informing the voters.

ADVICE TO THE BUSINESS SECTOR

1. Perform well, because "good public relations is good performance publicly appreciated." (So far as I know, this gem was by a Weyerhaeuser PR person Roderick Olzendam in the 1940s.)

2. Recognize the importance of the media and dedicate about triple your present budgets for education of the media. Remember when educating them you must listen carefully and remember that in absorbing information (when its favorable to you especially) they are much more like funnels than sponges. This is an on-going task since there are new people to educate every year and masses of new relevant information.

3. To Corporate Directors: The long-term interest of your corporations are in your hands. Currently your focus (hence the focus of your CEO's) is entirely too much on short term bottom-line results. Increase the rewards to your CEO's for improving long term public relations and improvement will follow like night-follows-day. Conversely, cut the CEO's bonus when short and long-term public relations programs are unsatisfactory. As a Director in three businesses, I have seen this happen.

4. Spend more on field trips and less on ads, especially when the media is showing its anti-industry anti-forest worker, anti-working forest biases.

5. Clear-cut smaller areas, use partial cuts more. Remember that clear cutting a scenically sensitive area is often perceived as the equivalent of spitting-in-someones-face, and generates corresponding political action.

To the Media

1. Prove that Jim Carville's criticism of the media is not justified by establishing Press Councils that point out bias and otherwise act as a sounding board and then correct the bias. Press Councils have been around a long time. They started in England and are used about as much as common-sense during a nightclub fire.

2. Stop publishing unsupported environmental extremist dogma unless you give the other side a chance to counter at the same time. An example would be the Sierra Club President's major piece saying and titled "Federal Timber Harvest Ban is Not Radical."

3. View the 13 minute video by the Washington State Society of American Foresters, "The endangered Species Act Spotted Owls and People" and then urge the Congress to amend the act so that it is much less people-cruel while still being critter-kind. The video can be purchased for $11. from:

Video, P. O. Box 2087, Gig Harbor, WA 98335

More Foresty Reflections

Washington State Federal Timber Harvest

Why has the timber harvest on the federal lands of Washington dropped to such a pitifully low level?

Answer: Existing laws, plus effective and legal pressure from those environmentalists who desire preservation of species and ecosystems at the cost of sustainable jobs, lumber and other people-products of the forest.

What are some of the principal reasons these people have such great political strength?

1. The worldwide desire for an improved environment and effective communications by preservation oriented groups.

2. Clearcutting, which offends people visually and reduces biodiversity.

3. Ineffective communications from industry and the Society of American Foresters. This is one of the reasons that organized labor is not more active in trying to increase the jobs, and other benefits available from federal forests through increased harvest.

4. The media distrusts industry. Media favors preservation-oriented groups and preservation alternatives as opposed to a reasonable sustainable harvest level

5. Voters and other citizens lack factual information and credible emotional communications that explain the costs and benefits of various alternatives.

Author's Major Forest Management Concern

People are not benefiting enough from our Pacific Northwest federal forests. These valuable over-mature forests can be harvested at many times the present rate on a sustainable basis. Here are three key economic facts,

Fact 1. The number of jobs and volume of forest products for homes and other people-needs produced from a forest is most directly related to the amount that can be harvested. The more you harvest (on a sustainable basis) the greater the people benefits such as jobs, lower building material costs, lower paper costs, increased revenues from timber sales and taxes. The more you harvest the greater the benefits, so long as it us done properly.

If the harvest is less than what could be harvested the total benefits are reduced, they cannot be replaced except at greater cost.

Fact 2. There is a huge economic difference between a well-paying primary job, based on a renewable resource like trees that PRODUCES tax revenues and other revenues, and a make-work job or retraining program that USES tax revenues.

Fact 3. The federal forests of Washington state are some of the most productive and valuable in the world. But, less than one fifth of the commercial forest land is available to produce the primary forest products and jobs that people need.

The rest is locked up. Much of the locking up is caused by flawed legislation.

Fact 4. The state of Washington has over 2,300 square miles (472,000 acres of Ancient Trees) already.

Concluding Thoughts

"In most lives, usually it's best to be kind and successful
rather than truthful and right." Author

The Power of Emotion

As I've aged, my recognition of the power of emotion
in determining the actions of people has increased. There are
many examples. Warfare quickly teaches that emotion regularly overcomes logical self-interest. Survival, a logical objective, frequently becomes secondary to performing at a level
acceptable to your buddies, or commanding officer or conscience.

Observing national elections gives many examples of
emotion as a determinant of action. People often vote from
gut-feelings rather than logic. The success of preservationists
in public land management is largely based on emotional appeal. Industry too often tries to counter red-hot emotion with
cold hard facts and usually loses.

Although I've recognized the power of emotion since
my service days, and even before, the older I get the more I
act as though I really believe it.

Here is an example relating to my early 1994 planning
for a return to the Philippines for the 50th Anniversary of the
Luzon beachhead in 1995.

I made six calls to Washington, D.C. to try and learn
what the Filipinos were planning. None of the officers and
enlisted people had heard of any plans for a celebration. These
were all relatively young people — forty and younger. A couple
volunteered that the political problems between the US and
the Philippines might prevent any joint celebration by the na-
tions. Had I been thirty and discussing a possible 10th anniversary celebration, I might have thought, "well maybe you're

right." But being in my 70th year, I tried to very positively but gently say, "Regardless of the international politics, the Filipinos love us for liberating them from the Japanese and they practically worship General McArthur. There will be a big celebration. All we have to do is find out when and where." I could have added that the president of the Philippines was an astute politician and politicians know it would be unwise to not grant the emotion-based wish of their people.

I thought of this initial lack of information as I watched a stupendous 50th Anniversary reenactment of the beachhead before 25,000 or more people at the small town of Lingayen; and again when I saw the colorful and accurate commemorative stamp and envelope shown below. The stamp is over three inches (eight centimeters) wide and shows the insignias of the four infantry divisions that made the beachhead. They are from the left the 6th, 37th, 40th and the 43rd. I apparently purchased number 26, which will soon be framed.

Military Cemetery Thoughts

My first thoughts in a military cemetery are often of mothers. Women bear much more than 50 percent of the pain in the world, and a mass of white crosses helps prove the point. When a woman's child dies, she has gone from pain to pain — she has completed the cycle from birth to death. I hope that women's great capacity for understanding includes adequate recognition that many of the troops died in the act of doing what they wanted to do and unafraid. Many of these service men "...had glared unawed at the gates of death" as Kipling said in his poem "The Ballad of Boh Da Thone."

This in no way means that I believe war is anything but a stupid, beastly and wasteful event — in which some good things do happen. (During a war people often down their lives for their friends.) Unfortunately war is part of the human condition and we had better act as though we believe that fact and be prepared.

We have made progress since one of the Duke of Marlborough's vets wrote in the 18th Century, "God and the soldier we adore in time of danger not before. The danger past and all things righted, God is forgotten and the soldier slighted."

Speaking of slighting soldiers, some of the me-generation lives with the memory of having spat on a returning Viet Nam service man. If I had witnessed someone spitting on a combat soldier, I'm afraid my clean police record would have been in jeopardy. I certainly would have become emotional and might have been jailed for assaulting the spitter — at least verbally or with fists. Freedom is a virtuous generality but its excess is a vice.

Speaking of dumb inaction. Why wasn't every planeload of returning Viet Nam vets met with a small band (good experience for high school bands) and someone to express gratitude? Nam for the US was a bad war fought by good people with inadequate political leadership.

Another thought that many veterans share is one of joint thankfulness and obligation. We survivors lucked out and are thankful and feel an obligation to both try and make it a better world and country (a common objective in wars of the United States) and enjoy the life we have been granted. Most of us do better on the enjoyment side, but that does make it a happier world.

Bill Mauldin with his great cartoons and writing made World War II a happier event. To get an insightful glimpse of the big war, read his book *Up Front*, printed in 1945. This was written when he was 23 and had about five years of Army experience. Combat veterans occasionally refer to themselves as "a fugitive from the law of averages." That was the key phrase in a Mauldin cartoon. Audie Murphy, our most deco-rated WW II soldier, referred to himself as "a fugitive from the law of averages" in his biography *To Hell And Back*.

A New Zealander told me that for the Brits the classic World War I cartoon showed the old veteran and the raw re-cruit, who has just asked a question, sitting in a small town that had been completely devastated by shellfire. There are huge holes in the partial walls that remain. The caption is one word — "Mice."

The World

I'm not cynical about the state of the world. Mankind has made some progress in nonmaterial things, too. Note: Once we elect Colin Powell president we will have underlined great progress toward racial equality. I've been amazed at how ac-ceptable he is to my conservative friends.

A keystone of my personal beliefs is that "The excess of any virtue is a vice." Like most of "my" better thoughts someone else had them a couple of thousand years ago. The Bible advises "moderation in all things". I understand the Chinese say, "Do everything a little bit," which also relates to my belief in "The importance in life of recognizing the in-finite difference between zero and one (which is also a math-ematical truism)."

Instant Closeness to a Small Group

A few times in my life I have had a vivid, instanta-neous feeling of mutual acceptance, understanding and friend-ship on first meeting with an individual or small group. This has happened during the war with a few soldiers and later with loggers, foresters and fishermen. Despite my admiration and appreciation for women, this kind of rapport has only hap-pened with men. About 1970, I read *Green Hills of Africa* written in 1935 by Ernest Hemingway, who commented on this bonding in a similar vein. He tells about a couple of Masai warriors he had just met in Kenya who ran easily alongside his jeep.

"I had never seen such quick disinterested friendliness. Nor such fine looking people.Only Garrick seemed impressed in a different way. For all his khaki clothes and his letter from B'wana Simba, I believe these Masai frightened him in a very old place. They were our friends, not his. They certainly were our friends though. <u>They had that attitude that makes brothers, that unexpressed but instant and complete acceptance that you must be Masai wherever it is you come from."</u>

This passage impressed me so much that I wanted to include it in this book though it required some library work. To me, Hemingway does much better with his man-to-man writing than woman-man, man-woman. Nevertheless, how great it is that America produced a writer like Ernest Hemingway.

Political Courage By Politicians

Too few politicians vote their conscience and principles when it requires courage. Senator Scoop Jackson (D) Washington is one who did, but Scoop has been gone a long time. Here are a couple of examples from the careers of two Senators who are still serving. First, Senator Mark Hatfield (R.) Oregon.

It took me too long to decide that we should get out of Viet Nam. But Senator Mark Hatfield of Oregon was against it very early on and said so at a time when it was not in his political best interest. Thank you, Senator Hatfield. I introduced the Senator to a Oregon-wide meeting of the Society of American Foresters about 1971 when most of us had decided that Nam was a bad war and we should cut our losses and get out. In the introduction, I mentioned the honesty, wisdom, and courage he had always shown on the Viet Nam issue. Even before he spoke, the foresters gave him a standing ovation.

At one time in the 1960's, Senator Hatfield thought that lack of adequate low-cost housing was the number one social problem in the United States. Drugs and crime have doubtless moved the need for affordable housing down the priorities list, but the need is still there.

Excerpt From Paper Delivered At Annual Meeting Of Society Of American Foresters, 1991, San Francisco, CA.

The most sensible statement by a legislator that I have heard regarding the Endangered Species Act and the northern spotted owl was made June 25, 1991 by Senator Slade Gorton of Washington. Quote:

"Mr. President, our productive citizens and their families and communities deserve our consideration in at least a measure equal to that lavished on the spotted owl. If that is not possible under the law as it is written today — and our courts have told us that it is not — then we in this Congress must change the law. We cannot — we must not — avoid our responsibility." Hang in there Slade.

To Foresters

I've been in this magnificent but relatively mute forestry profession for over 40 years. I have come to a conclusion regarding communications that may be helpful to foresters, workers and managers who would like to see a sensible sustainable level of employment and products from our public forests. The struggle with the other side is a communications battle, it's like a baseball game. To win the game we must get up to the plate and swing the bat. We as a profession have under-communicated on land use issues, partly because we have been afraid of failing, of striking out. Let's remember that Babe Ruth, the greatest homerun hitter of all time, struck out 1330 times about double his home run total. Without some strikeouts it's almost impossible to win a ball game — especially a hard ball game. And that's what we are in.

A final comment to you professional foresters. If we, as professionals, want to abide by the first canon of our profession, quote "to use the knowledge and skills of the profession to benefit society" we must get further into the national debate, further into the process. We must listen and hear, but we must also speak out. We are professionals, but we are also citizens and have responsibilities in both sectors. Our obligation is to be part of the decision making process . . . Let's do it!

To those Considering Forestry As A Profession

Being a forester can be an enjoyable way to make a living while being of special benefit to society. If you believe that people are, at the least, an important part of the ecosystem I invite you into the forestry profession. If you don't, I wish you luck in any other profession except politics or law.

A Political Comment Regarding the Federal Timber Harvest

For the life of me I can't understand why the Republicans don't make more of an issue out of the unbelievably low harvest on the federal lands in the Pacific Northwest. Here is a chance to do something that is directly good for people in the hourly working class. It is a chance to show the inconsistency and inequity within the Democratic party where it is the highly educated, salaried Democrats, such as the many Sierra Club members who eliminate blue-collared jobs for people who usually vote Democrat. Much of it must be another aspect of communications failure by forest businesses, the Society of American Foresters and the affected workers and communities.

Republicans seem to be listening too much to radical elements of their party. An example is the attempt to essentially gut the emotionally supported Endangered Species Act instead of merely strongly amending it. I suspect few House and Senate members know that in a national vote (the only one I know of) people voted five-to-one against sacrificing 10,000 jobs for the spotted owl (later the Clinton Plan eliminated over 30,000 jobs).

One of the many under-used, emotionally appealing arguments for harvesting trees is to make homes more affordable and paper less expensive. Sure, you must also make a profit. When the annual timber sale level drops six billion board feet as it did in the owl-inspired Clinton Forest Plan, the cost of forest products inevitably goes up and usually hurts poor people the most. Black are disproportionately poor and especially in need of housing. In addition, blacks make almost no use of Wilderness Areas and have the highest unemployment levels. They would like trees to produce jobs and lower-cost housing. Michael Jordan, we need you on our side.

protected permanently in wilderness, parks, and other no-cut areas.

Philosophy

My life has been largely happy. My happiness is due partly to luck. Examples are surviving World War II and meeting Jan. Luck is not transferable, but the following thoughts on what has contributed to my happiness may be of some use to the reader.

Avoiding mistakes contributes to happiness.

The older I've become the more I have been able to avoid mistakes by benefiting from the wisdom of a judge named Rentoul, (I know nothing more about the judge. I suspect the judge was male since the original of the following included a gender bias.) I've underlined the one that seemed most helpful to me when I put them up on the office wall about 1960.

The five great mistakes people make in life, Judge Rentoul:

1. To measure the enjoyment of others by our own.
2. To expect uniformity of opinion.
3. <u>To fail to yield to unimportant trifles.</u>
4. To refuse to make allowances for the weaknesses of people.
5. To estimate the worth of strangers by their looks, their clothing, their mannerisms.

Personal

For me it was also helpful to remember —

"To all of us, but especially the young — there are times when one should be kind rather than truthful or successful rather than right." True story: This was on my wall for 20 years next to the Rentoul list, but, during a move, disappeared for about ten years, and was rediscovered recently. I thought when I found it, "By golly that's right, I wonder who wrote it?" I had.

Virtue

When I went into the Army infantry at age 18 I had a pretty standard set of things I admired, including a list of virtues. These had been shaped by my family background, interface with others, the church, and formal and informal education. Sincerity, dedication, efficiency and strength were on the short-list.

Now at 72 I'm more aware that without a subject, sincerity, dedication and efficiency could simply magnify a vice, rather than being a virtue. Two examples follow.

The Germans who participated in the Holocaust demonstrated, sincerity, dedication, efficiency and strength.

The on-the-ground-tree-huggers demonstrate sincerity, dedication, efficiency (sometimes), media-political strength, and courage; as they destroy livelihoods, hence families and futures -- to preserve Ancient Trees, for awhile.

My war experience made me to value toughness over strength.

Now, unsurprisingly at the top of my virtue short-list is love one another. Truth is a dangerous virtue, as many have said. Truth must be tempered with kindness to make the short-list.

Managing People

A common failing in managers is in not delegating authority. Theodore Roosevelt had this to say on the subject —

"The best executives are those who have sense enough to pick good people to do what they want done, and self-restraint enough to keep from meddling with them while they do it." (for more effective communication "men" was changed to "people.")

Conservation

I also found it helpful to have on the wall an Aldo Leopold quote that is relevant for most of us dealing with land:

"A conservationist is one who is humbly aware that with each stroke he is writing his signature on the face of the land. Signatures of course differ, whether written with ax or pen, and this is as it should be."

Today Leopold is most often quoted as an ecologist. It's comforting to some of us to know that Aldo Leopold was also a hunter.

Parenting

Jan, my wife, is the best parent I know. Somehow, with a little help from me and an unknown amount of help from the ex-husband, she has raised three children who have become well-adjusted, productive, kind and generous good citizens. One of her secrets is that except on a few super-important things like kind-honesty she doesn't expect perfection. My words for part of her philosophy would be, "Anyone who has perfection as a goal in human activity is probably going to produce unhappiness for themselves and anyone else involved." A story illustrates the point.

Buddy, our present Labrador retriever is Jan's 17th. She and the ex-husband field trialed them. She knows dogs and people. The story involved Rip (a.k.a. Jay's Potlatch Rip) Buddy's predecessor.

One night at dinner, after we had been talking about various aspects of raising kids and dogs, Rip left his mat and moved about eight feet to under the table by our feet. Jan said, "Rip, get on your mat." Rip got up and slowly and reluctantly walked over and flopped down about six inches short of his mat. I was watching this exhibition in dog handling out of the corner of my eye. Jan knew I was watching and after a pause said, "See, that's how I raised my kids, close is good enough." Guess it works with children, if not field trialing.

The Power of a Person

Books have been written on the power of positive thinking and other ways to more fully utilize the mental strength that most of us have been given. It helps to know that we have it and to be encouraged to use it. The worst parts of warfare have provided examples of strength that inspired Siegfried Sassoon to write (as mentioned before):

"I was rewarded by an intense memory of men whose courage had shown me the power of the human spirit... that spirit which could withstand the utmost assault... against the background of the war [with] its brutal stupidity those men had stood glorified by the thing which sought to destroy them."

A more recent and more famous writer is said to have given the following as his total speech to a group of girls at their graduation ceremony.

"Never give up! Never give up! Never give up! —Winston Churchill.

One of the great calls for citizen action is attributed to Edmund Burke who advised in the 18th Century —

"The only thing necessary for the triumph of Evil is for good people to do nothing."

Final Communication

To everyone who strives for good in the world, but especially to my children, grandchildren and foresters. Believe in God, believe in yourself, including recognizing the incredible strength of the human spirit. Laugh a lot. Learn to find happiness in love, friends, sunsets, weather and other things money can't buy. Communicate well, be honest but kind -- and never give up on the big things.

Finally, remember, "The only thing necessary for the triumph of Evil is for good people to do nothing."

Gig Harbor, Washington
March 1997

Appendix

Suggested Reading

<u>War</u>
"Wartime" Paul Fussell, 1989 (excellent on the difference between how combat-was and how it was reported)

"The Face of Battle", 1976 John Keegan (and anything else by him)

"About Face," 1989 and " Hazardous Duty", 1996 Col. David H. Hackworth, U.S. Army, ret. (About Face is the best I've read on Korea and Viet Nam warfare.)

"We Were Once Soldiers and Young", Gen. Harold G. Moore, 1982, (the second best on Nam that I've read)

"U.S. Army in World War II" 1963, U.S. Army (for Luzon, Philippines campaign the volume "Triumph in the Philippines")

"The Pacific War 1941-1945", 1982, John Costello (a useful one volume overview)

"Upfront", 1945, Bill Mauldin (great cartoons and wise prose about WWII.)

"To Hell and Back", Audie Murphy (fascinating combat autobio by our most decorated veteran of World War II. His 3rd Infantry Division had the highest casualties of any U.S. division.)

"The Last Convertible" (the best overall novel-view of the WWII era I've read), "Once and Eagle" (a fine novel on soldiering from WWI-Viet Nam) by Anton Myrer, an infantryman who died in '95. I treasure my correspondence with him.)

"Memoirs of an Infantry Soldier", 1931, Siegfried Sassoon, poet and author.

"With the Old Breed at Peleliu and Okinawa", 1981, Eugene B. Sledge (a must-read for anyone who wants to know what Pacific Theater infantry warfare was like. He was with the 1st Marine Division. He details the horrors of the worst parts of intense and prolonged infantry combat where I am often horror-general.)

The war poetry of Rudyard Kipling, Robert Graves and Siegfried Sassoon

Forestry, Wilderness, Environmental Forest Wars

Note: I'm fortunate that three of the top academic leaders in the forest management debate over our public and private lands live in Seattle WA. I know and respect Messrs. Franklin, Lee and Oliver.

Dr. Jerry Franklin, D. R. Berg, D. A. Thornburgh and J.C. Tappeiner, 1996. Alternative silvicultural approaches to timber harvesting: variable retention harvest systems. In K.Kohm and J.F. Franklin. Creating a forestry for the 21 st Century, Island Press, Washington DC. (Jerry Franklin is the leading expert on "New Forestry")

Dr. Robert G. Lee, "Broken Trust Broken Land — Freeing ourselves from the war over the environment." 1994 (Bob Lee is both forester and sociologist and deplores the hurts caused to Pacific Northwest people and communities by the unnecessarily sharp drop in Federal timber harvest.)

Dr. Chadwick Oliver, "Achieving and Maintaining Biodiversity and Economic Productivity" *Journal of Forestry* 90 (90): 20-25.

Dr. Alston Chase, "In a Dark Wood — The fight over the rising tyranny of ecology", 1995 (This book is a must-read for anyone who wants a scholarly and relatively objective examination of the philosophical background of "biocentrism".)

Richard N. Jordan, "Trees and People, Forest and ecosystems and our future", 1994 (outstanding source book and for a conventional forester's view of ideal forest management. He recognizes people as having a primary role in the ecosystem.)

Allan May, "A Voice in the Wilderness" 1978, Nelson Hall, Chicago (an insightful look at conflict over Wilderness; an experienced reporter, who lives in Everett, WA)

Charles E.Twining, "Phil Weyerhaeuser, Lumberman", George S. Long, Timber Statesman" (excellent for Pacific Northwest forest industry history prior to 1957).

Roderick F. Nash, "The Rights of Nature- A History of Environmental Ethics", and "Wilderness and the American Mind" (both are classics)"

Jay Gruenfeld, "Forests Communicate But Can't Talk", keynote talk at 1977 Annual Meeting of Puget Sound Section, Society of American Foresters. (Clearly one of the best of my many papers.) Mike McCloskey, then the Executive Director of the Sierra Club said this in a July 6, 1977 letter about the paper.

> "I think it is an absolutely splendid address, and I want to to congratulate you on it. It is one of the most statesmanlike presentation on the subject I have ever heard, and it makes me proud to have a chance to work closely with you."

I appreciated his praise then and still do. In my opinion the basic thoughts have stood the test of time. I included the basics of "Forests Communicate But Can't Talk" and more in a 1991 presentation at the Annual Meeting of the Society of American Foresters, "Pacific Rim Forest Resources: Sustainable? for Whom? Kinder Gentler?; see Proceedings.

Jay Gruenfeld   March, 1997

- MY ORIGINAL COPY-
HEADQUARTERS SIXTH ARMY
APO 442

AG 210.1 - Gruenfeld, Julius J.   15 February 1945
                                                          (date)

SUBJECT: Temporary Appointment.

TO   : S/Sgt Julius J. Gruenfeld 16120422,
          103d Inf Regt, APO 45.

THRU   : Commanding General, 43d Inf Div, APO 45.

          (Temp. Appointed 2d Lt. AUS Assigned to Inf)

1. By direction of the President you are temporarily appointed and commissioned in the Army of the United States, effective this date, in the grade and section shown in the address above. Your serial number will be furnished at a later date by the Commanding General, USAFFE.

2. This commission will continue in force during the pleasure of the President of the United States for the time being, and for the duration of the war and six months thereafter unless sooner terminated.

3. There is inclosed herewith a form for oath of office which you are requested to execute and return promptly to this headquarters. The execution and return of the required oath of office constitute an acceptance of your appointment. No other evidence of acceptance is required.

4. This letter should be retained by you as evidence of your appointment as no commission will be issued during the war.

5. This letter of appointment and paragraph 1, SO 58, Headquarters Sixth Army (copy inclosed), is authority for discharge from present status and entry on active duty in commissioned grade.

                              By command of Lieutenant General KRUEGER:

                                                  JOHN B. COOLEY,
2 Incls: Colonel, A.G.D.,
  Form for oath of office.   Adjutant General.
  SO 38, Hq 6th Army.

Oath of Office completed on 15 February 1945.

  1997 NOTE: I HAVE BEEN JAY   ROBERT O. BLAKE,
  MY ENTIRE LIFE; BUT TOLD THE   WOJG   USA,
  ARMY I WAS BAPTIZED JULIUS JAY   Asst. Adjutant.

(GO# 57, 20 Dec 45, Hospital Center, Cp Carson, Colo, cont'd)

Pfc Robert M Karnahan Jr Det of Pnts, USA GH	37237484		(SWPTO)	21 Apr 45
Pfc Edward C Perlman Det of Pnts, USA GH	37595048		(ETO)	6 May 45
Pfc Clifford M Skeeters Det of Pnts, Cp CarsonConv Hosp	37635918		(SWPTO)	11 May 45
Pfc John P Strachan Det of Pnts, USA GH	36645115		(ETO)	19 Jul 45
Pfc Sylvester C Wendler Det of Pnts, Cp Carson Conv Hosp	37724263		(ETO)	15 Apr 45
Pfc James P Wentworth Det of Pnts, USA GH	36983856		(ETO)	28 Mar 45
Pfc Chester B Wood Det of Pnts, USA GH	37498017		(ETO)	15 Aug 44

SECTION II

AWARD OF THE OAK LEAF CLUSTER TO THE PURPLE HEART: Under the provisions of AR 600-45, 22 September 1943, a Oak Leaf Cluster to the Purple Heart for injuries received in action against the enemy theatre of operations on dates as indicated, is awarded the following named Officers and Enlisted Men:

1ST LT HAROLD W BUSHACHER Det of Pnts, USA GH	01312515 Inf	(ETO)	15 Mar 45
2D LT JULIUS J GRUENFELD Det of Pnts, Cp Carson Conv Hosp	02007488 Inf	(SWPTO)	13 Feb 45
2D LT JULIUS J GRUENFELD Det of Pnts, Cp Carson Conv Hosp	02007488 Inf	(SWPTO)	13 Mar 45
1 Sgt John R Morton Det of Pnts, Cp Carson Conv Hosp	20746654	(ETO)	4 Dec 45
Sgt George E Landis Det of Pnts, USA GH	37529622	(ETO)	25 Jun 45
Pfc Morris Kjono Det of Pnts, Cp Carson Conv Hosp	37774399	(SWPTO)	24 Jul 45
Pfc Clifford W Skeeters Det of Pnts, Cp Carson Conv Hosp	37635918	(SWPTO)	24 Jun 45
Pfc John P Strachan Det of Pnts, USA GH	36645115	(ETO)	29 Jul 45
Pfc Sylvester C Wendler Det of Pnts, Cp Carson Conv Hosp	37724263	(SWPTO)	28 Apr 45
Pvt Bernard J Matuszewski Det of Pnts, USA GH	32131708 (2)	(ETO)	19 Dec 45 SO# 57

1945 Clipping, New York City Newspaper
sent to me by Brammer in 1946

This clipping is reprinted to add credibility to the war stories in the book and as an example of wartime reporting (especially) being weak factually. Bram is very truthful and says he gave the reporter all the facts. The article is correct only in identifying Luzon the Infantry Division, Bram, his state and the number of enemy. It is incorrect in describing how it happened, Bram's rank, statement and weapon, calling him a smoker, and saying we "scattered the rest" (all died). Also, we didn't return to the command post and I had the saber. Like many error filled pieces it still reads OK to the uninformed.

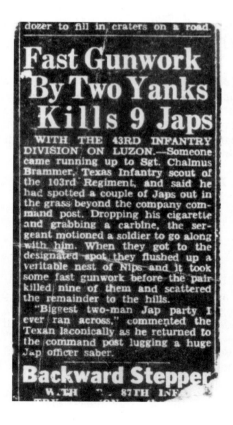

dozer to fill in craters on a road.

Fast Gunwork By Two Yanks Kills 9 Japs

WITH THE 43RD INFANTRY DIVISION ON LUZON.—Someone came running up to Sgt. Chalmus Brammer, Texas Infantry scout of the 103rd Regiment, and said he had spotted a couple of Japs out in the grass beyond the company command post. Dropping his cigarette and grabbing a carbine, the sergeant motioned a soldier to go along with him. When they got to the designated spot they flushed up a veritable nest of Nips and it took some fast gunwork before the pair killed nine of them and scattered the remainder to the hills.

"Biggest two-man Jap party I ever ran across," commented the Texan laconically as he returned to the command post lugging a huge Jap officer saber.

Backward Stepper

WITH THE 87TH INF.

30 January 1445 Philippines (sic) (excerpt)
Dearest Mom,

... Things have been pretty rugged but we can take it all, and then some. Remember that my greatest worry is you. I myself really don't need to worry about myself because the Lord will take care of my future ... We have sharpened senses of humor and it really helps. In New Zealand a NZ sailor was eyeing Fecser's 12-1/2 EE feet. Fecser said, "Well?" and the sailor said, "Oh, nothing, I just wondered where (sic) the upperdeck was." Heh. Heh.
All my love, Jay

10 February LUZON (excerpt)
Dear Dad,

... P. P. S. Eleven of us got ten Japs the other day,
Love, Jay

12 February 1944 (sic) (continuous excerpt, written while Mom was in California with her ill brother.) It had been confirmed that my cousin J., J. Oliver Buslee, Park Ridge, Illinois, was KIA while piloting a Bl 7 over Germany. He had been MIA since August.)

Dearest Mom,
Received letters 8 & 1 0 today, and sure am sorry to hear about J When I heard he was missing I had a hunch it was for good, but hoped and prayed. Just hope that Aunt 01 can be a good soldier and take it to God in prayer. I know J. would say the same thing - in fact we used to talk about war, and agreed that death itself could be accepted, but it was the suffering of our parent (sic) which worried us...

Your Loving Son, Jay

21 February (1945) (continuous excerpt, written six days after being commissioned)

Dearest Mom,

... Eventually I will be assigned to my new outfit and only hope that it is as good an outfit as L Company. I will appreciate the position of the enlisted man having been one myself for so long. I pray that I will never forget the men under me as they are the ones whom I will be relying on when the show down (sic) comes. And like in everything else I will only get from the men what I give them. My prayers are still that I may have strength to do my duty and thus far with God's help I have I believe done my duty.., Lots of Love, Jay

1997: My prayer sounds more self serving here than it usually was. Usually the troops came first in my prayers and actions because they were the troops and my job was to take care of them.

29 March 1945 (continuous excerpt)
Dear Folks,

I'm still doing great. My outfit is strictly a bunch of real soldiers and we get along fine. My Jap total keeps growing, and the experiences keep piling up. If responsibility (sic) builds character Mom I should be some character. I'll give you an indication of how busy I am. I have received 2 large mail deliveries in 1 0 days and each time it was a couple of days before I had the time (sic) to read my mail. Our life has been fairly rugged. I have washed once (a bath it was) in a week. (H 20 is too precious), not shaved in about two. But, we have plenty to eat and there is no monotony so we are in good spirits. To top it off they had a carrying party bring our beer ration out, and I guess the Nips thought we were nuts, singing and laughing (during the day only of course) even though they were close. The mail has been really coming in and I sure enjoyed all of your letters.

Lots of Love, Jay
P.S. Know nothing about Giff except that he lived. Might be back in the states by now. Love.

1997 Note: We had been on wilderness hilltop objective Lively Lady (see book for more on it). Had drunk water from Nip canteens we were so dry when Lt. Verl Shufelt, Company Executive Officer, despite our being in a fire-fight, led in a foot party of mostly Filipinos carrying water, ammo, food, and beer (the only time we ever got it while in action). The Army priority is as listed but we could have put beer first (though it was the first time I didn't trade my beer for fruit bars). One of my indelible war memories is of Verl coolly and carefully checking off his list of incoming supplies as we were fighting a serious skirmish with the Nips, 100 yards, or so, away. In our fight we had run out of grenades and instead of delegating the task (as I should have) I ran down to get grenades, had seen the party coming up the trail, and then ran back.

The reader may recall that Giff, veteran L Company Staff Sergeant, Gifford, great squad leader and friend was later killed by friendly 155 artillery fire. War sucks!

BIO

Jay Gruenfeld is president and owner of Jay Gruenfeld Associates Inc. (JGA), Gig Harbor, Washington. JGA, founded in 1979, does forest resource consulting and has given 33 conferences on Marketing Forest Products of the Pacific Rim. The first conference, 1983, was given in Juneau, Alaska, and the 31st was held in Santiago, Chile. The 34th and 35th will be held December 1-3, 1997, in Seattle and the 36th in Santiago, spring 1998.

From 1982-94 JGA published the monthly Pacific Rim Wood Market Report (and its predecessor the Alaska Forest Market Report) until its sale in 1994 to Wood Note Publishing (Linda Keller Barr).

Over 45 years experience growing, protecting, logging, buying, selling, and marketing forest trees and other forest products. For Weyerhaeuser Company: After setting chokers in cable logging operations and gaining other basic experience, became Manager of Timber and Log Sales, Director of New Business Development, Timberlands; and Manager of the 70,000 acre Skykomish Tree Farm in northern Washington. For Brooks-Scanlon Inc.: Resource Manager, including a 200,000 acre central Oregon forest. For Potlatch Corporation: Vice-President, Lands and Forestry, with corporate staff responsibility for 1.3 million acres of forest in Arkansas, Idaho, and Minnesota.

Since starting a consulting practice in 1979 Jay's experience has included work in Russia, Japan, Taiwan, Korea, Fiji, New Zealand, Chile, British Columbia, Alaska, and much of the contiguous U.S.

He is currently a Director of the Makah Forestry Enterprise (Native American) and retired Director of Pope Resources.

Special Communications Activity: Started the Western Forest Environment Discussion Group in 1977 jointly with the Executive Director of the Sierra Club, Mike McCloskey. Served on the Old Growth Commission, State of Washington, 1988-89. Held Pre-Forest Summit Symposium 1993. Initiated and chaired preparation of video by Washington State Society of American Foresters, "The Endangered Species Act, Spotted Owl and People," that urges amending the act to give more consideration to people impacts.

Society of American Foresters: Served on National Council, chaired Puget Sound Section, chaired National Meeting 1980; served on National Accreditation Committee, elected Fellow 1982.

Education: BS (Science & Arts), MF (Forest Management, Colorado State U., then A&M); Diploma in Forestry (and Humanities), Oxford University as a Fulbright Scholar. World War II, 1943-46 rifle squad and rifle platoon leader, 43rd Division, Pacific Theater (battlefield commissioned and three Purple Hearts). Other Honors: Phi Kappa Phi, Xi Sigma Pi; honor alumnus CSU; honor alumnus CSU College of Forestry and Natural Resources.

His auto-bio book, "PURPLE HEARTS AND ANCIENT TREES, A Forester's Life Adventures in Business, Wilderness, and War" was published, 1997 by PB Publishing, Seattle, WA.

The following individuals are mentioned in the book. Some are also mentioned in the index.

Adachi, Gen. Hatazo
Alinski, Sol
Allison, Rex
Andrus, Gov. Cecil
Anthony, Gil
Bannister, Sir Roger
Barker, Ed
Barr, Linda
Barron, Lt. Col. Lloyd
Bate, Ed
Bauzon, Romeo
Bingham, Charles
Bowman, Neill;
Brakenrig, Elra
Bramlett, General David A.
Brammer, Chalmus
Briones, Joe
Brocard, Norm
Broderick, Dan
Brookhart, Don
Brumfield, Virgil
Burdick, Eugene
Burgoise, Pfc.
Burke, Edmund
Cant, Gilbert
Carlson, Glenn
Carville, James
Chadwick, Chase
Chase, Alston
Chase, Capt.
Choate, Harris
Church, Sen. Frank
Churchill, Winston
Clapp, Norton
Cleland, Maj. Gen. Joe
Clinton, Pres. Bill
Cook, James E. Pfc.
Costello, John
Craven, Dick
Daley, Larry
Dimke, Vernon and Shirley
Dooley, Lt.
Dukes, Mike
Dvorak, Bob
Evans, Brock
Fecser, Frank
Fernandez, Virgilio & Elvie
Flynn, Robert

Fraley, Jack
Franklin, Jerry
Friddles
Fussell, Paul
Galt, Tom
Galyea, Capt.
Garey, Carl
Garmany, Robert Jack
Gates, Bill
Gates, Jack
Gaylord, Frank
Gervais, Dick
Giffen, Craig
Gifford, Sgt. Giff
Gilbert, Ted W.
Gorton, Sen. Slade;
Graves, Robert
Greeley, Col. W.B.
Hackworth, David H.
Hagenstein, Bill
Harlow, Sgt.
Harrison, Bob
Hatfield, Sen. Mark
Heacox, Ed
Hemingway, Ernest
Henri, Joe
Henry, Hank
Herrick, Johnny
Hitt, Francis
Hoe, Ed
Hollem, Mike
Horne, Harry
Hopper, Leo
Ingram, Charley
Jewett, George F. "Fritz" and Lucy
Joensuu, Pat
Johnson, Medic Bert
Johnson, W. J. Bill
Jones, Alden
Jones, Ken
Jordan, Michael
Jordan, Richard N.
Karboski, John
Karl, Jeff
Keller, Judy
Ketcham, Pete and Bill
Kipling, Rudyard
Kneale, W.C.

Knutz, Amual
Labbe, Howard (?)
Larson, Gary (The Far Side)
Larson, Vern
Lee, Robert G.
Leopold, Aldo
Long, George S.
Lucas, Dick
Magrames, Louis
Mailer, Norman
Marsh, Mrs. Shirley
Matalin, Mary
Mann Ernie
Mauldin, Bill
May, Allan
May, Marvin
McAllister, Loren
McArthur, Gen. Douglas
McCloskey, Mike
McClure, Sen. Jim
McMahon, John F.
McNutt, Jim
Meyers, Paul
Milius, Hans
Minor, Pfc.
Mitchell, Bill
Moore, Gen. Harold G.
Morang, Hollis
Morgan, H. E. Jr.
Mullins, Lt.
Murphy, Audie
Myrer, Anton
Nash, Harry
Nash, Roderick
Neilson, Dennis
Nelson, Ted
Oliver, Chad
Olmstead, Lew
Orell, Bernie
Owen, Bill
Palmquest, Jack
Perez, Eugelio
Powell, Gen. Colin
Price, Dave
Pickett, Highclimber
Reeves, Bill
Redford, Robert
Remington, Jack
Renton, Jim
Rice, Bob
Rice, Delbert and Danny
Robinson, Allen

Roosevelt, Theodore
Rush, Don
Sangster, Ernest
Sassoon, Siegfried
Schaeffer, Prof. Walt
Schiesl, Walt
Schoening, Jack;
Schulz, John;
Shakespeare, William
Shaw, Bud
Shaw, Don
Shufelt, Verl
Simard, Gene
Sledge, Eugene
Smith William L.
Smith, H. Don;
Staebler, George
Stansberry, Jim
Steele, Rod
Swindells, Bill Jr.
Symms; Sen. Steve
Taylor, Capt.
Taylor, Dwight D.
Thomas, Jack Ward
Thompson, Lt.
Tinker, Pfc.
Titcomb, Jon
Turner, Admiral Stansfield
Turner, Tom
Tutty, Roger
Twining, Chuck
Vilano, Lt.
Von Neuman, Bob
Wakeley, Chuck
Wayne, John
Weyerhaeuser, C. Davis
Weyerhaeuser, F. K.
Weyerhaeuser, George H.
Weyerhaeuser, Phil
Wheare, K.C.
Wheeler, Melvin
Woodall, Dave
Young, Ted
Zingg, John

Index